Heinemann **SOCIOLOGY AS** *for AQA*

D1354574

Heinemann

SOCIOLOGY AS

for AQA

Warren Kidd   David Abbott   Gerry Czerniawski

Heinemann Educational Publishers
Halley Court, Jordan Hill, Oxford OX2 8EJ
Part of Harcourt Education

Heinemann is the registered trademark of
Harcourt Education Limited

© Warren Kidd, Gerry Czerniawski, David Abbott
First published 2003

07 06 05 04 03
10 9 8 7 6 5 4 3 2 1

British Library Cataloguing in Publication Data is available
from the British Library on request.

ISBN 0 435 46710 7

Typeset by 𝍫 Tek-Art, Croydon, Surrey

Original illustrations © Harcourt Education Limited 2003

Printed in the UK by The Bath Press

Cover illustration by Matt Buckley

Picture research by Thelma Gilbert

Acknowledgements
Every effort has been made to contact copyright holders of material reproduced in this book. Any omissions will be rectified in subsequent printings if notice is given to the publishers.
p 30, Bridgeman Art Library/Southampton City Art Gallery; p 32t, Corbis; p 32b, Illustrated London News; p 34t, Topham Picturepoint; p 34c, University of Chicago; p 34b, Corbis; p 41, Topham Picturepoint; p 44, Photofusion; p 68, Roger Scruton; p 79, Trip; p 80, Science Photo Library; p 86, Photofusion; p 90, Hulton Archive; p 92, University of Chicago; p 94,Camera Press; p 98, Paul Willis; p 112t, Sally & Richard Greenhill; p 112c, Photofusion; p 112b, Photofusion; p 114, Hulton Archive; p 118, Camera Press; p 122, Hulton; p 124, Science Photo Library; p 130, S&R Greenhill; p 134, Corbis; p 136, Corbis; p 146, BBC; p 162, Illustrated London News; p 163, Granata Archive; p 164, Rex Features; p 166, Popperfoto; p 168t, Rex Features; p 168b, Popperfoto; p 172, Art Archive; p 175, Rex Features; p 179, North News; p 180, Popperfoto; p 184, Popperfoto; p 188, Source unknown; p 189, Popperfoto; p 190, Professor Cohen; p 191, Press Association; p 194, Magnum; p 196, Rex Features; p 213, Photofusion; p 215, Corbis; p 218t, John Walmsley; p 218b, John Walmsley; p 224, Photofusion; p 231, Photofusion; p 233, Peter Gould; p 236, Hulton Archive; p 241, Photofusion; p 244, Kobal Collection; p 248, Stephan Ball; p 260t, Topham Picturepoint; p 260b, Hulton Archive; p 267, Rex Features; p 268, Hulton Archive; p 270, Nigel Stead; p 277, Hulton Archive; p 281, Photofusion; p 282, Hulton Archive p 286, Gosta Esping-Anderson; p 288, Charles Murray; p 289, Rex Features; p 292, Julian Le Grand; p 299, Topham Picturepoint.

Tel: 01865 888058 www.heinemann.co.uk

Contents

Contents

Contents

Contents

Foreword

We hope that you enjoy this book. Our aim was to write a book that reflects what we think about how and why sociology should be taught at AS level. As teachers, we are trying to make things simple, make things up to date, and provide a structure for you the student that gives you a route through to the exam. We have broken down sociology into bite-sized chunks, dealing with all the ideas that you will need to know.

We have divided the book into the most popular topics in the AS exam, and have then broken each topic down into key questions or debates. By doing this we hope to show that sociology is essentially a series of debates and questions that can be answered by learning about and then applying the sorts of ideas sociologists have. We recommend that you read the introduction first as it explains what sociology is all about.

Warren Kidd
David Abbott
Gerry Czerniawski
2003.

Acknowledgements

We would like to take this opportunity to thank the following people: Sarah Mitchell, Liz Tyler, Samantha Jackman, Marcus Bell, Catherine Hurst and Claire Walker.

Dedication

Warren would like to thank his friends, family and loved ones. Thank you for your support and continued encouragement.

David would like to dedicate this book to Rosie, Christopher and Olivia.

Gerry would like to dedicate this book to Collette, Kim, Kevin, Dave, Janine and Hedge and the sociology students at Newham Sixth Form College who have continuously supplied the inspiration for much of the writing.

We would also like to thank our colleagues and students. Thank you for making teaching sociology interesting and rewarding.

Author biographies

Warren Kidd is the Senior Tutor for Social Science at Newham Sixth Form College. He is an experienced writer of sociology textbooks and vice president of The Association for the Teaching of Social Science

Foreword

(ATSS). Warren is a frequent contributor to ATSS Conferences, and is a regular provider of teacher and student conferences and lectures. He is currently a tutor in sociology at the London School of Economics and Political Science (LSE) on the Saturday School programme for A level students. Warren wrote the Introduction, Family and Methods chapters for this book and was the editor of the overall project.

David Abbott teaches at Hills Road Sixth Form College in Cambridge. He has written several text books and articles for AS/A level sociology. David wrote the chapters on Mass Media and Wealth, poverty and welfare for this book.

Gerry Czerniawski teaches sociology at Newham Sixth Form College. A former member of the executive of the Association for the Teaching of Social Science (ATSS) Gerry is an associate lecturer in social sciences for the Open University and tutors in sociology at the London School of Economics and Political Science (LSE) on the Saturday School programme for A level students. Along with producing resources for the ATSS, Gerry has provided INSET courses in sociology and is also a teacher trainer on the City and Guilds teacher training course. He is currently studying for his PhD at Kings College (University of London). Gerry wrote the Education chapter for this book.

Chapter 1

Introduction

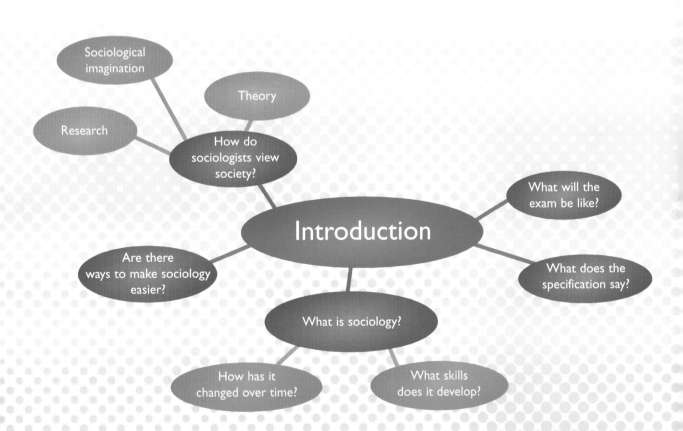

Sociological imagination

Theory

Research

How do sociologists view society?

What will the exam be like?

Introduction

Are there ways to make sociology easier?

What does the specification say?

What is sociology?

How has it changed over time?

What skills does it develop?

How to use this book

This book aims to help you be successful on your sociology course. You will find it useful in the following ways:

- It provides both classic and up-to-date sociological studies and theories.

- It focuses on what the specifications from the exam boards say about the course you are following.

- It provides a lot of knowledge, but also provides support for you for the exam. There are boxes in the margin that give you exam tips, plus sections on exams at the end of every chapter.

- It shows you what sociology is all about and what the tricks and shortcuts are to learning the subject.

- It breaks sociology down into manageable sections, focusing on the idea that there are four essential or key ingredients that you have to use in order to 'do' sociology well.

What features does this book have?

This book uses the following features:

- Margin boxes that give you tips and advice.

- Every section is a question or a key debate in sociology.

- Each section contains information to help you to think about the exam, and also to try and push your grades up as high as possible.

- Each chapter ends with some frequently asked questions that students want to know the answer to.

- CD-ROM symbols. This symbol directs you to the CD-ROM where you will find extra information such as case studies and revision exercises. Where the symbol appears, it is relevant to the whole chapter.

What do the boxes in the margin do?

There are different boxes you will come across in the margin. They each do a slightly different thing, and they are there to help you. Exam success is not simply a case of knowing the subject content, it is also a case of being able to apply what you know in the way the exam and the examiner wants you to.

- Thinking like a sociologist: this box allows you to get an idea of evaluation comments that you can make about a particular issue.

- Top exam hint: this box gives you some very quick exam tips.

- Synoptic link: this box allows you to begin to think about your sociology course as a whole, rather than as a series of separated topics or options.

- Key definition: this box contains a key term and its definition.

- Key idea: this box contains an important sociological idea explained.

- What, when and why?: this box will help you to place the ideas and people you are reading about into the historical period that they come from. This is useful for evaluation purposes.

- Who is this person?: you will find in studying sociology that you come across many different people, many different sociologists who all have different ideas. This margin box should help you to understand a bit more about the people behind the ideas.

- Coursework suggestion: this box provides a handy hint or an actual proposed idea for linking the AS topics to coursework at A2 level.

The accompanying CD-ROM with this book gives you the opportunity to be able to print off the margin boxes in specific combinations to suit your own needs. Make good use of this facility both throughout your course and at the end for revision purposes.

Key issues in sociology

What is sociology and what does it mean?

The word sociology means the study of society and it dates back to the middle 1800s. The word is most associated, originally, with the ideas of French philosopher Auguste Comte, and then later with three important founding sociologists; Karl Marx (died 1883), Emile Durkheim (died 1917) and Max Weber (died 1920). Before the word sociology was invented people studied society. Humans have always thought about, reflected upon and evaluated the conditions under which they live, be it through painting, art, philosophy, the study of history, science or literature.

Sociology is a separate subject in its own right, with a separate way of thinking about and looking at the world, and is often classified as a social science. Like other social sciences such as psychology, politics, economics, etc., sociology is concerned with explaining what is happening in the world that humans inhabit. Sociology is not a single subject. There are different sociologies, with different ways of thinking about the world we inhabit. The two main sociologies are as follows:

1 Macro sociology: this is concerned with overall patterns in society. It seeks to explain how the whole of society operates and how all the pieces work as a whole.

2 Micro sociology: this is concerned with small-scale behaviour. It aims to understand people's feelings and thoughts and how people make sense of their own lives.

Today, many sociologists combine these two sociological approaches together, looking at how the big picture relates to the small picture, how the whole of society shapes what individuals actually do, and equally, how what individuals do can shape patterns for the whole of social life.

What are the key debates in sociology?

It is possible to identify some central sociological questions, key issues or debates that all sociologists are interested in, which make the subject what it is today. The topics you study at AS and A2 level draw on these debates, and you will find many answers to these issues contained within the pages of this book.

• Is society in harmony or in conflict?

• Do people have free-will to make free choices, or are we controlled by society?

• How is power organised in society? Why are some people more powerful than others?

✓ **Top Exam Hint**

In most exam questions, a distinction between macro and micro theories will help you to make quick comparisons between sociological ideas.

- Is society fair? Why does inequality exist?
- Does society shape the individual or does the individual shape society?

The value of sociology

The value of thinking in a sociological fashion, is that the subject raises lots of questions to think about. Sociology is a critical or radical subject, it is about questioning why society is as it is. It is about digging under the surface, looking at what is really going on. In order to seek answers to the above questions and debates, sociology can be seen as being made up of two essential parts:

1   Theory: these are the ideas sociologists have; how sociologists see the world around them. These ideas shape how sociologists look at issues and determine what they see.

2   Research: this is the process of gathering evidence in order to test their ideas and theories. Sociologists gather evidence that hopefully points in the direction of what society is really like.

Sociological knowledge helps the sociologist to make sense of what goes on in society. Sociology opens up the mind, it asks people to be critical of the world they live in. Sociology asks us to question how society works, and to think again about the many untested assumptions that we might have about the world. By using the tools of sociology (theory and research) you will try to understand what the world is really like, rather than how you might have been brought up to believe it is like.

Is sociology 'hard'?

It is certainly challenging. For many it is a new subject at AS level. It also takes some time before you really feel comfortable with it – lots of unusual words and new ideas. However, the value of its 'newness' is that it is fresh, it is certainly original, and it is challenging in the sense that it explores new ways of thinking. Don't worry – do what your teachers tell you, follow the advice in this book and take it one step at a time. We are sure you will enjoy it!

● **Synoptic Link**

The questions opposite will help you to think about how all the different views in sociology relate to each other, and how they all agree or disagree.

✎ **Coursework Suggestion**

When undertaking any piece of sociological research make sure you show why sociologists would be interested in the issue you are looking at.

1.2 What do we need to know about sociology?

How does the specification treat sociology?

The specification you are following breaks sociology down into a number of topic areas (see section 15). These individual topics are all related to each other, even though you will be taught them separately. All the topics link to each other as they all deal with the same issues and themes, and they all use the same tools to think about society. The same theories and the same key words will come up in each topic, as well as some ideas that are only really relevant to each particular topic.

The whole of your sociology course is interrelated, and you must see it as a whole, rather than as a series of unrelated topics. When sociologists research social life, they often cover lots of different aspects of society at the same time. For example, a study that looks at education may also look at class, ethnicity, gender, plus it might look at the family and at deviance and sub-cultures. As you can see, there are lots of links within and between the topics you will be studying, as after all, there are lots of links in society.

Within each topic that you study, you will need to know the following:

- What the main debates and issues are.
- If there are key themes or key words that are especially important.
- What theories are relevant.
- How the different theories agree and disagree with each other.

What will you be doing on your course?

Your teachers will use a variety of teaching and learning styles for you and your class. These could include the following:

- group work
- lectures
- discussions and debates
- active learning methods, where you are asked to find things out.

No matter what style of learning you are doing, and no matter why or when in the year you are doing it, it is important to keep in mind that all sociology starts from the same point; it is all about looking at views on

Thinking like a Sociologist

In your sociological thinking, show that you understand and can see how all sociological ideas eventually fit together. This is called being synoptic and is a vital skill.

✓ Top Exam Hint

This list provides you with a very quick checklist for revision for any topic area that you study.

society and looking at how these different views try and provide evidence for what they state.

Your job throughout this course is to become a referee of all these different views. For example, no matter what topic area you are studying, you will find a number of different viewpoints or **theories**. These theories are how sociologists think and see the world around them. You will need to learn these different theories, understand what they say, and how they agree or disagree with each other.

Where does it all lead?

During your sociology course you will build up a good understanding of all the basic theoretical ideas in sociology. Along with these theories, you will also learn named examples of research and studies, and you will learn lots of key words that you will use in order to evaluate the different views on offer.

Like any subject, studying sociology ultimately leads to the exam – and then beyond into the A2 course. But, along the way you will hopefully develop some very important skills. In particular, one of the main aims of sociology is to first challenge the ideas and arguments of other people. These evaluation skills are not just important for sociology, but for many other subjects, many courses at university and many jobs. Above all else, they are important because thinking in a critical fashion allows us to really question the world we live in.

Key points to remember

- All sociology topics link to each other.
- Sociology is training you to think in a clear fashion.

❝❞ Key Definition

Theories are ideas put forward to explain something. They are supported by facts, observations and assumptions and can be tested.

1.3 What are the key features of thinking sociologically?

The basic ingredients of sociology

There are four important ingredients that make sociology what it is. All of these are important and will help you to understand how the subject works and how all the individual topics relates together as a whole:

1 Theory: all sociology has theoretical ideas or views that can be tested.

2 Key words: theories have associated concepts or key words.

3 Named examples: individual sociologists and groups of sociologists usually associate themselves with a particular theory or theories. They then undertake research that might support or attack other ideas.

4 Evaluation: you, as a sociology student, must learn how to evaluate all these ideas and studies, and try and find way to choose between them all.

✓ **Top Exam Hints**

• Use the four ingredients in your exam, especially for longer mark questions, as they will add depth to your arguments.

• Make sure that you become familiar with all the key words as soon as possible. By using these you will be able to demonstrate your knowledge and understanding.

Applying and evaluating theories

Once you learn what a theory says about society in general, it is much easier to apply the theory to a particular aspect of society, such as education, the family, the media, etc.

The sociologists you study are usually linked to a theory, and this tells you something about their values and view. Their individual ideas and studies will provide more depth on the theory that lies behind their research.

As different theories are often conflicting, and sociologists try to criticise or support each other by the research they do, you can evaluate all sociological research yourself. In any studies you read, look for comparisons and contrasts, and which sociologists agree or disagree with the findings of the research. Then think about who you agree with and why. This is when sociology starts to come alive; when you can actually use it to think about your own life.

Using the four ingredients in sociology

You should try and use the four ingredients in a number of ways:

* Every time you write a long exam answer, try and include these ingredients.

* Organise your revision notes according to the four ingredient's headings.

* Use the ingredients as a checklist. Every time you write an exam answer, think about how you might combine the ingredients together in order to get more depth in your answers.

* Every time you answer a question in class, try and use the ingredients to add detail to what you are saying.

* Make index card revision notes summarising the theories and key words.

* Make a note of which theories use which of the key terms and how they use them.

* If possible link each named example you are taught to the theory they follow.

* Link each named example to a few key words that best link to their particular study.

* For every theory you learn, memorise a list of five general evaluations and apply them as much as possible.

Thinking like a Sociologist

Evaluation, although much more important at A2 level, is important in sociology in general. It makes the subject critical and analytical. Concentrate not just on understanding sociological ideas, but think about whether you agree with them or not.

Conclusion

These 'ingredients' are an important short-cut; an easy way for you to begin to not only learn about sociology, but to be able to actually use sociological ideas in your own thinking. This is, after all, the point of the course – developing your thinking skills.

For consideration:

1 How do you think the four ingredients might help you to learn sociology easier?
2 Which ingredients do you think will be harder to learn and apply than the others? Why do you think this might be?

What is the sociological imagination?

What does this mean?

The term 'the sociological imagination' is associated with American sociologist C Wright Mills who, in 1959, wrote the book of the same name. In this book, Mills tries to describe the value of the subject of sociology; a theme that many other writers have since taken up.

In his book, Mills states that:

'The sociological imagination enables its possessor to understand the larger historical scene in terms of its meaning for the inner life and the external career of a variety of individuals … the sociological imagination enables us to grasp history and **biography** and the relations between the two within society. That is its task and its promise.'

If we analyse this statement by Mills, we can deduce that the sociological imagination:

* Allows us to see our place in the world as an individual.

* Lets us see how society is connected together.

* Lets us understand how the inter-connectedness of society relates to our own life and how we live it.

* Encourages us to think about our world, and to think about what it all means.

The sociological imagination then, is both what you have to develop in order to be able to do your subject well, but at the same time, it is the end result of actually studying it. It is the means by which to do well, but it is also what the subject promises to give you for all your hard efforts. Not just a qualification written on a piece of paper, but the thinking skills you need later in life.

How does the sociological imagination work?

The job of the sociologist, using their sociological imagination, is to think about the world in new ways. By looking at new concepts within society we open up the possibility that we might be able to describe this society better. This means that studying sociology might start to deal with things that do not seem real, but it will end up very real because you will be able to take the ideas you learn and apply them to what you see around you. You will come to know yourself better.

There will come a time when you understand how sociology works and why it works as it does. When this happens your sociological imagination will be starting to develop.

The idea is that sociology contains a number of benefits for those who study it. It not only allows you to see what society is like, but may also help shape your future. Sociology might make you more tolerant of others' views as you will have to look at many different viewpoints. It will help your evaluation skills as you are required to critique and assess the ideas you are taught. Studying sociology will improve your research skills, you will be able to find, test and gather information. This will be useful for other subjects and also for many future careers. Sociology will also make you more questioning.

Finally, sociology may change the sort of person you are, or at least how you think about who you are. Sociology is about thinking about society, and as an important member of this society, you are the subject of your own sociological imagination.

Conclusion

This new way of thinking – of being able to question what happens, why it happens, and if it does happen how we think it does – is also important for the exam. Although evaluation skills are more important for the A2 level course, the nature of sociology is such that you must become as comfortable as you can, as quickly as you can, with asking difficult questions. In other words, in taking sociological ideas, 'bouncing them off each other' and using them to contradict other ideas.

For consideration:

1   Why do sociologists think the sociological imagination is important?
2   Why do you think it is important to be able to understand your life using sociological ideas?

Thinking like a Sociologist

As you develop your sociological imagination you will become more critical and analytical of sociological research.

1.5 What is theory and why is it important?

◆ What, When and Why?

It is important that as you progress in learning about theory, you also learn the time period in which particular ideas were developed. This will help you to understand why sociologists felt the need to invent the ideas in the first place.

✓ Top Exam Hint

Evaluate theories in the exam by referring to when they were developed, and by saying that some ideas might now be out of date (make sure you also say why they are out of date).

What does this mean?

When sociologists use the word theory, they mean something very particular by it, but the word theory means a lot of different things in ordinary language. English language dictionaries tend to describe it as:

* An idea developed by facts and research.
* An opinion.
* A view of the world.
* The principles upon which a type of knowledge is based.

All these definitions will help us to understand what theories are. In sociological usage we use 'theory' to refer to the collections of abstract ideas that sociologists use in order to see what the world is like around them. Theories are hypotheses of what the world is like, and why it is like this.

Theoretical schools of thought

There are many different schools of thought (different views) that different sociologists collectively hold. In this book you will read about a large number of these different schools of thought or theories. They include the following:

* Functionalism
* Marxism
* Neo-Marxism
* Weberian sociology
* Interpretive sociology (also called interactionism and phenomenology)
* The New Right
* The New Left
* Feminisms (there are lots of different sorts)
* Postmodernism
* Pluralism
* Post-structuralism
* Structurational sociology.

There are many different theories to learn about in sociology as there are many different views on what society is like. We can use these theories as 'tools' to help us to think about society. Individual sociologists as well as schools of sociologists have two main ways of looking at the world:

1 **Epistemologies**: sociologists often ask the question 'what is knowledge' or 'what is the best way of getting true and real knowledge about the world?'
2 **Ontologies**: sociologists also ask the question 'what is the world like?' or 'what is real about the world?'

This means that sociologists have theories (to answer ontological questions) and they also do research (and in doing so, need to answer epistemological questions).

Types of theory

Sociologist Robert Merton (1957) talks of the existence of three different types or 'levels' of theory in sociology:

1 First order theory: simple hypotheses that we can try and test through research.
2 Middle-range theory: ideas about how society works that are not simple hypotheses, but are less than a whole world view. Such ideas are models; they explain how and why something works as it does.
3 Grand theory: described by Merton as 'master conceptual schemes' meaning a total world view about the whole of society and how it works.

Theories can also be sub divided into macro and micro theories:

• Macro theories: these are explanations of society that look at society as a whole.
• Micro theories: these are explanations of society that look at individuals, how they think about the world and how they relate to and interact with others.

Glaser and Strauss (1968) talk of something called **grounded theory**. This is theory that arises from research. Rather than the theory coming first, the data from research is used to formulate an idea. In this way, theories are less abstract and not totally removed from social life, but are 'grounded' in (come from) social life.

Conclusion

It would be impossible to be a sociologist without some sort of notion of what the world is like. Theories allow us to see society in different ways. As a sociology student your job is to take all the different ideas and views that sociology has and manipulate them. You can compare and contrast them; you can evaluate them; you can use them to try and think about the society you inhabit, and your place within it.

For consideration:

1 Why do you think there are so many different theoretical schools in sociology?
2 Why might the large number of theoretical schools be both a problem, and a strength of the subject?

✳ Key Idea

A test that sociologists from the micro tradition might use is to ask if the theory in question actually makes sense to those in society it is being used to describe. This means people can be critical of sociological ideas, rather than the sociologist being the expert.

❝❞ Key Definition

Grounded theory is the idea that sociological ideas and theory should be rooted or should be drawn from the data we get from real people in real life situations.

1.6 What are the problems of having theory?

What does this mean?

Many sociology students do not really see the point of theory at first. You may not understand why we have it and what we can do with it. We can summarise these concerns as the following:

- Why are there so many theories?
- Why do they disagree?
- Why do theories seem so strange and abstract?
- Why do theories use strange and difficult language and terminology?
- Why are many theories so old?

Sociology is about thinking, and thinking involves trying to see the same thing from many different views. Sociological thinking is creative and imaginative; it lets us try out and test ideas. They become the tools of our trade.

However, as there are so many theories, you may find thinking theoretically quite difficult. In this book we have tried to use theories to answer the questions in each chapter and to show how they link to each other. This means that you can start to use theory in an evaluative way; use it to think about issues, rather than simply learn it in the abstract.

What traps can we fall into with theory?

Ian Craib (1984) identifies four problems or 'traps' that theoretical, abstract thinking often leads to. He recommends that sociological thinking should try to avoid these at all costs, although it is often difficult to do so.

1 Crossword puzzle trap: some theories simply take complex social reality, and then reduce it to a simple set of ideas. To do so misses the complexity of social life in the first place. Theory simply lets us fill in the squares of a puzzle, but it does not tell us why it is patterned as it is in the first place.

2 Brainteaser trap: some theories raise interesting questions about society, but never actually try to solve them. The researcher might get bogged down by wondering what things mean, or how to define and measure something, and never actually get on with the business of explaining.

3   Logic trap: some theories contradict themselves. They try to say that lots of things are true at the same time, yet some of these things might be opposites. In this way, some theories are always right, and are unable to be proved wrong.

4   Description trap: some theories simply describe what we can already see. They do not take us beyond this, and offer no new ideas or explanations.

How can theory make society clearer?

We can break all theories down into a number of issues or questions that they are all seeking answers to:

- What is human consciousness like?
- What role do humans play in creating the society around them?
- What is power like and who has it?
- Is society in harmony or consensus?
- What causes social change?

Theory is the attempt by sociologists to try and put some distance between themselves and the world they are in. We do not simply assume that we understand how something is, but try and look at many different possibilities. At the same time, theory is also the attempt to find out about things that we do not experience; to try and understand that which does not relate to our limited experience of the world. This is an attempt to make ourselves closer to things we previously knew nothing about. Most theories also have hidden within them a political value or judgement. They may be left wing, liberal or right wing. These ideas will shape what the researcher thinks and how they express their ideas.

Conclusion

You can also use theory in your real life. Think about theories when you watch the news or read newspapers. What news items might prove or disprove particular theories? Think about your own life and ask yourself 'What would I think about this if I believed theory X'? 'What would I think if I followed theory Y'?

For consideration:

1   What do you think are the main problems with thinking theoretically?
2   Why do you think that so many non-sociologists might not see the need for theory?

✓ **Top Exam Hint**

Use the four 'traps' to help you to evaluate sociological theories.

● **Synoptic Link**

These important questions, which are behind all sociology, can be used to link ideas from different topics together.

❓ **Thinking like a Sociologist**

- Always use theory as a basis for examination answers.
- Use theory as a tool to help you organise your revision.
- Use theories in lessons; think through the eyes of theories when you answer questions.
- Use theory in your coursework; try and test theories.

✓ **Top Exam Hint**

Use theory as a way of creating links in your revision. If a person belongs to a certain theoretical school, link them to the ideas and concepts of other people from the same school of thought.

1.7 What is evaluation and why is it important?

✓ Top Exam Hint

Evaluation will give you depth and detail in any question that is not a short answer question. If you can show an awareness of why two theories or two studies disagree, then this will gain you extra marks.

✳ Key Idea

This emphasis on evaluation is central to what Mills calls the 'sociological imagination' (see section 4); the distinctive world view that sociology gives us.

What does this mean?

Evaluation is an important skill in sociology, and involves the following:

- Making criticisms.
- Pointing out that there might be problems in evidence.
- Showing that there are comparisons between ideas.
- Showing that there are contrasts between ideas.
- Saying what is good about an idea.
- Saying what is useful about an idea.
- Having an opinion which you can back-up with evidence.

Why is evaluation important?

Evaluation is very important at AS level for the following reasons:

- You need to evaluate in order to be able to put all the ideas and theories together.
- You will find some questions in the exam that focus upon evaluation, even at the AS level.
- If you can get used to evaluating quickly, you will find it easier at A2 level.
- The more evaluative you can be at AS level, the better your exam answers will sound, and therefore the better grades you will get.

How do we evaluate?

There are different types of evaluation that you can use. The following is a checklist that you can use to think about the quality of the answers you are producing:

- Use theories to criticise other theories.
- 'Think through the eyes of theories': imagine what it would be like to think in a particular way.
- Make methodological criticisms: attack a study for how it carried out its research.

- Use real life examples. An event in the contemporary world may provide you with evidence that you can use to assess what sociologists are saying.

- Use historical examples. Support or criticise a theory for saying something when history shows that something different happened.

- Some sociologists conduct research in order to prove or disprove someone else, make sure you spell out these links.

- Use synoptic tools to think about a theory or study, i.e. link an idea to class, gender, culture, identity, power, etc. (see section 8.)

- Make a note of when the idea, study or theory was invented and think about its usefulness today.

- Do not only say what is bad about an idea, but also what is good about it.

- Point out political biases and value-judgements behind theories. Some ideas might be left or right wing, and this might cloud or affect how they see society.

- Assess the contribution made to sociology by a theory; say what we would miss or lack if the idea had not been invented.

Conclusion

Evaluation, although more important for the A2 course, will allow you to gain extra marks at AS level since it is a way of demonstrating that you can use sociological ideas. You can use ideas to agree or disagree with each other. You can also use ideas to attack 'common sense' or media views. This will really help you to 'think like a sociologist.'

For consideration:

1 Why do you think that evaluation is an important skill for you to have?
2 Why do you think that evaluation is a difficult skill to develop?

🍸 Thinking like a Sociologist

Use this checklist to evaluate sources in your exam, your coursework and in class. They will take time to master, but will improve your answers when you have got to grips with them.

1.8   What is synopticity and why is it important?

What does this mean?

By being **synoptic** we mean being able to tie the whole sociology course together: being able to see how the whole six modules over the two years (at AS and A2 level) link together. It is therefore very important that you think about this right from the start, as it will be difficult to understand how AS subjects link in if you wait until A2 level to combine everything together.

You will be examined for synopticity at the end of the A2 course in either the Crime and Deviance module or the Stratification module, depending on what your school or college teaches you. This is the very last exam you will sit.

How can you be synoptic?

The idea of synopticity means that as a student you should be able to see that the different units and modules you do all link together as a whole. You will therefore need to look at the things that join the individual sections up, i.e. the connections. The whole of society is interconnected, and therefore all the different parts of the sociology course are also interconnected.

In order to be synoptic (to tie everything together) the starting point is theory. Theories let us make comparisons between topics. What a theory states about one aspect of society such as family, may then affect what it states about another different aspect of society such as education or the media. Theories let us see that society is interconnected. Theories encourage us to think about the joined up bits of the course, rather than simply see sociology as a broken-down series of unrelated topics.

Building up and breaking down

Your perception of school may be that different knowledge is taught by different teachers in different rooms. The subjects all have different names and are located in different departments. You may think there are no connections between these subjects, but there are. Learning about chemicals in Science can help you in Art. Learning about art history can help you in English Literature or in History. Schools often encourage us to break down connections because otherwise how could we learn anything? It is always easier to learn something if it is broken down into smaller parts.

This is also true for this book. We are trying to pull sociology apart to show you how it all works. However, once you have pulled it apart, you then need to re-build it again, otherwise it will not work. Being synoptic will allow us to see how sociology all links together.

What synoptic tools are there to use?

In order to see how both society and sociology are connected, we can use the following 'tools':

- Class
- Gender
- Ethnicity
- Culture
- Identity
- Location
- Globalisation
- Age.

Synopticity can also be divided into two main areas:

1 Social synopticity: this means seeing the connections between the parts of society (and hopefully using sociological theories and ideas in order to do this).
2 Sociological synopticity: this means seeing the connections between sociological ideas themselves; looking at what might link different studies, theories or debates that sociologists have.

These two types of synopticity are related. As everything in society is connected together, then everything in sociology must also be connected together. Imagine the following scenario: you leave your house and you go to school one morning. You talk to your friends on the bus about what you watched on TV last night. Even in this short extract of normal life there are numerous connections; family, education, culture (telling us we must go to school), class, ethnicity (the last two might affect where we live and also what we watch on TV). As you can see, the whole of life is one big interconnected whole. In order to 'do' good sociology, you must be aware of this.

For consideration:

1 Why do you think synopticity in included in the AS and A2 level courses?
2 What challenges do you think this might raise for students of sociology?

1.9 How has sociology changed over time?

Sociology was invented to explain the rise of early industrial society and its effects on human life and relationships.

What does this mean?

Like all subjects, sociology is constantly changing. It has its fashions and its fads, and as society itself changes so too does sociology. Equally, sociology might actually cause society to change to a certain extent. For example, the original ideas of the founders of sociology contributed to the rise of scientific thinking.

Sociology is also affected by changes in politics, as well as affecting political ideas itself. The New Right, while not a sociological view as such has been incorporated into some sociological thinking. For example, many sociologists have taken on some of the concepts and ideas of the New Right, and this view has made them think again about issues such as welfare spending. Sociology can also influence ideas in politics. Ideas on the 'Third Way' have influenced the ideas of the New Left and the New Labour government.

How did theory develop over time?

Over time we are able to chart the development of different theoretical ideas, although it is important to note that there are some problems with this. The period in which the original ideas developed, and the time they were popular or fashionable are not necessarily the same thing. For example, Marx was writing in the late 1800s, but Marxism in sociology was popular in the 1970s.

Another problem in charting the chronological development of theory is that many writers develop their ideas from other writers. To say that micro sociology was 'invented' in the 1920s in America is true, yet does not take into account that Weber was writing about these issues prior to this point.

We also have the problem that many theories have sub-branches. They can be divided into lots of different types. It is true to say that theories never really 'die out'. It is more likely that they disappear for a bit, and then reappear, maybe with a different name, or maybe combined with something new. Despite these problems, the history of sociological theorising is shown in the following table.

✳ Key Ideas

- The founders of sociology are often referred to as the 'founding fathers'. However, feminists have pointed out that by using this term we are limiting the opportunity for women sociologists to be seen to be able to make a valuable contribution.

- The 'Third Way' is the term given to the fact that New Left thinking needs to find a new third approach to thinking about society (different to the old 'right' and 'left' in politics).

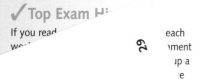

✔ Top Exam H:

If you rea~~d~~   each
w~~~~   ~~~~ment
    ~~~~p a
    ~~~~e

Introduction

Theory	Description	History
The founders: Comte, Durkheim, Marx, Weber	Now we describe this as modernism. Marx was writing before the other three founders and died in 1883. Durkheim died in 1917. Weber died in 1920.	The industrial era in Western Europe. The first published use of the term sociology was by Comte in 1843.
Early action sociology	Weber and Simmel	Early 1900s
Chicago School	Seen as the development of interactionist or micro sociology	1920s–1960s
Functionalism	Sometimes known as structural functionalism	Associated with Talcott Parsons in the 1950s and 1960s
Pluralism	Associated with American sociology, and closely linked to the ideas of functionalism	1950s and 1960s
Marxism and Neo-Marxism	Although Marx himself contributed to political and economic thought, these ideas did not become popular in sociology until the 1970s	1970s. Also led to the development of what we call various different neo-Marxisms
Feminisms. It is difficult to pinpoint when and how feminist ideas developed as there are so many different sorts. They change and rapidly develop in a short space of time and still continue to do so.	Like Marxism, this was a reaction to the dominance of the functionalist view in the 1960s.	1970s. In the 1990s some writers speak of a feminist backlash; a movement away from or against feminism.
Post-structuralism and postmodernism	Associated with the views of Foucault, Baudrillard and Lyotard	1980s, but popular in the middle 1990s
Structurational sociology	A response to the postmodern ideas of the middle 1990s	Associated with the ideas of Giddens in the late 1990s

◆ What, When and Why?

The historical pattern of the development of theories has arisen for two main reasons:

1 Theories emerge out of other theories. They either develop as a criticism of a previous idea or as a continuation of a previous idea.
2 Sociological ideas develop as a consequence of the historical context they emerge in. What this means is that sociological ideas do not exist in a cultural vacuum, but instead they are a product of the very society that they seek to explain. For example, it is no coincidence that neo-Marxism developed at a time when the UK was experiencing economic depression, as this raised issues of class in society.

Conclusion

Modern day sociological thinking has been characterised by the following changes:

- A movement from macro to micro sociologies and to theories that try and build the middle ground between these two positions.
- A change from a concern with class to the analysis of gender and ethnicity, and to a consideration of how these link together.
- A rising concern with issues of culture and identity. Although these are present in the original ideas of the founders, there is currently a re-consideration of these ideas.

For consideration:

1 Why is sociology affected by the society it studies?
2 How does sociology in turn affect the society it is a part of?

1.10 What are structural theories?

✔ Top Exam Hint

If you can show the similarities as well as the differences between structural and action theories this will help with your evaluation of studies in the exam.

What does this mean?

Structural theories look at the big picture; at how society is patterned or 'structured'. Action theories do not look at the big picture, but instead concentrate on the small-scale level of thinking about what individuals do. The relationship between structural and action theories can be seen in two different ways:

1   Structural and action theories are the opposite of each other. In this sense there are two very distinctive and different sociologies that are in conflict with each other in how they see the world around them.

2   Structural and action theories are really two sides of the same coin, and sociology needs them both. We must, in order to get the full picture, look at both how society is structured and how people live their daily lives. Modern day sociology would not be how it currently is without both ways of thinking.

What do structural theories say?

All structural theories start with the view that society is patterned or 'structured' in a particular way. They think that beyond the surface of what society might at first look like, there is an underlying structure that shapes or moulds society in a particular way.

The clearest theories that we might call structural in AS sociology are functionalist and Marxist theories.

- Functionalism: this theory sees society as being patterned like a living body, made-up of a complex inter-relationship of connecting parts. This is called the organic analogy; comparing society to a living body. Functionalism claims that there is more to society than the sum of its individual parts. In other words, society is the inter-connected whole, the big picture, rather than the individual parts. The socialisation of culture is what allows the whole pattern to function properly, with disorder being compared to sickness in the living body; something dysfunctional that will endanger the stability of the wider structured whole.

- Marxism: this theory sees society as patterned by a system of inequality that shapes everything that happens. This inequality is the fact that a narrow group of people own the 'means of production', i.e. everything that is needed to make an end product. This structure is

Emile Durkheim (1858–1917)

Karl Marx (1818–1883)

Functionalism and Marxism have had a massive impact on the structural viewpoint in sociology.

what we call class and it shapes who has power and who is powerless. Marxists refer to this **economic determinism**.

Structural sociologies see the surface variations and the hidden structure of society to be different from one another. What you see on the surface is the product of unseen, powerful forces. We need to use theories in order to understand these powerful forces, and to see how they control all social life. Structural sociologies see humans as 'puppets of society'. Humans are determined or shaped by these underlying forces that mould their identity, behaviour and the norms and values of the culture of a given society.

Marxists see social order to be based on **social control**, whereas functionalists see social order to be based on **social cement**.

Many sociological theories seek the big picture or the big pattern, and many sociologists do their research with the view that they will try and find out why something happens in relation to the unseen hidden structure moulding what goes on. Structural theories are 'macro' as they are trying to understand the whole of society and how it all links together.

Conclusion

It is probably more helpful to think of sociology (and of society itself) as being both macro and micro – as needing both 'structure' and, on a much smaller level, the 'action' of what people and groups actually do. Therefore, it is important that as students of sociology you pay attention to both structural and action theories – as discussed in the next section of this chapter.

For consideration:

1   What does it mean to see society as having a structure or a pattern?
2   To what extent do you think we are 'determined' or shaped by the society we live in?

66 99 Key Definitions

- **Economic determinism** is the idea that whoever owns and controls the economy determines (shapes) the rest of how society is patterned.

- **Social control** is where society is dominated by rules laid down by the powerful. Groups in society are made to follow the rules and are punished if they are deviant. The pattern of the structure of society is maintained over time by making people follow the same rules, even if they do not all benefit from them.

- **Social cement** is where society is maintained and the structure or pattern is continued by people being 'bonded together'. We are kept together through the learning of group norms and values that shape who we are and what we do, for the benefit of all.

✓ Top Exam Hint

If you can refer to the two concepts of social control and social cement in essays it will help you to achieve greater theoretical depth as most studies link to them in some way

1.11 What are action theories?

The work of Weber, Mead and Becker pioneered the action view in sociology.

What does this mean?

Action sociologies are those theories that try and look at the small picture. They try and understand why individuals act and interact in the ways that they do. They seek to understand how people see the world around them.

Action theories are sometimes seen as the opposite of the macro structural theories. In this sense, action theories are micro. They are called 'action' theories as they look at what people do on a day-to-day basis.

What are the ideas of action sociology?

Action sociologies start with the following ideas about society:

- Humans make society by inventing the cultural ideas that make society real.

- Humans keep society alive by interacting with each other and sharing symbols.

- Humans cannot 'act' in society without making sense of what they think society is like. In this sense they have 'meaningful action', i.e. they try to make sense of what they are doing and why they think they are doing it.

- Humans are active and creative and they have free-will. Even though the rules and ideas of a society might be laid down before they are born, they are nevertheless able to choose how to act to a certain extent within these rules.

- Humans' sense of what society is like needs to be constantly built-up and reinforced.

- Humans are constantly reflecting upon their actions, and the actions they have with others (their interactions). Humans are constantly asking why things happen; why people behave towards them as they do; what they think they should do, and how they think they should act in different situations.

Why do we need action sociology?

In one sense, we need action theories since they offer a useful 'counter' against the more structural ones, as discussed in the previous section. Whereas the structural theories allow us to see the make-up of society, general trends and historical changes, the more action theories allow us an insight into how people respond to, and work within these structural patterns. They are two sides of the same coin.

Action theories also allow us to explore more individual issues in research. They allow us to look at people's thoughts, feelings and emotions, how these are shaped by society and how they in turn affect what people do in society.

Conclusion

As we can see, this is a very different image of humans to that held by the structural theories. Structural theories are interested in what society is like, whereas action theories are interested in how and why people think as they do. Modern day theories often seek to work somewhere in between the two, looking at both the big and the small picture.

For consideration:

1 What are the main differences between structural and action theories?
2 Which approach do you think is more realistic in terms of how society is viewed (the structural approach or the action approach) and why?

☀ Key Ideas

- The action perspective in sociology sees humans as having a 'self', sometimes called a 'self-image'. This is the idea that humans are active in thinking about who they are.

- Action sociology is often associated with the idea of 'labelling', i.e. that groups or individuals with an authoritative role in society can affect how people might come to see themselves.

What skills are important for studying sociology?

What does this mean?

In sociology as with other AS and A2 examinations that you will be taking, it is not just simply a question of learning ideas, you also need to manipulate, evaluate and apply these ideas in various ways.

Sociology is marked and assessed according to certain skills, as set out by the examination boards. These skills are called assessment objectives. There are two sets of skills, and evaluation is very important for the second set:

- Assessment objective 1: knowledge and understanding.
- Assessment objective 2: identification, analysis, interpretation and evaluation.

The first set of skills are the main focus for the AS course, and the second set become more important as you move from AS to A2.

How do skills and the exam link together?

Answering exam questions is a skill in itself. It requires you to think in a particular way, and to do the particular things that the question requires you to do.

In the exam, different questions test different skills. Short mark questions test your skills of writing precisely and to the point. Longer mark questions at the end of the exam test your skills in more extended writing.

In order to pass exams, you will need to master the skill of revision (see section 18). Exams are about getting your knowledge out in an appropriate way, therefore revision should also be focused on getting knowledge out, rather than just trying to put it in.

The exams at AS and at A2 level will provide you with source items. Using these in the most beneficial way possible is also a skill; you will need to be able to draw out relevant ideas from the item in order to use these as a stimulus to think about the exam question in detail.

✓ Top Exam Hints

- Before you answer an exam question, make sure you know what the question asks you to do. Does it want you to show knowledge and understanding, or does it want you to show evaluation and other skills?

- Always look at the author and date of the source item if it is provided. This might help you to put it into context.

It is also important that the examiner is able to read your work and to understand it. This means that exams not only test your understanding of the subject, but also your presentation, spelling and grammar skills.

What other skills are needed?

- Sociology students are often required to handle simple data in the form of graphs, statistics, etc. Such sources will be used by your teachers throughout your course.

- You will need good IT skills in order to study sociology. You will need to word-process coursework and use the Internet to look up information.

- You also need to have the skill of listening. It is very important that in the sociology classroom you are able to appreciate what other people say and their different viewpoints.

- Alongside the skill of listening, you will also need to develop the skill of expressing your own opinion, especially in group discussions or debates.

- As with any other subject at this level, keeping deadlines will be a very important skill for you. It will be important that you stay on top of your work at all times.

- You will also be required to become an independent learner and to take responsibility for your own learning.

Conclusion

As you can see, there are many skills needed to learn sociology. To be able to understand sociological ideas fully, you will need to be able to put them to good use: in lessons, in debates, in homework, for revision and finally in the exam.

✓ Top Exam Hint

You should always express a preference over different views, but make sure that you provide reasons why, and that these reasons are linked to the evidence. Do not just give your own opinion and leave it at that.

For consideration:

1 Which skills do you think are the most important for sociologists to have and why?
2 Which skills do you think are the hardest to develop and why?

1.13 What do I need to do throughout my sociology course?

What does this mean?

In order to be as successful as possible in your AS sociology course there are a number of important things you should try and do throughout the course. In many respects, being successful is about getting into the right habits from the start, and making sure that you can maintain these habits over time.

Practical advice

- Keep an up-to-date sociology folder, and make sure that it is organised into topics. This will help you to look back over past work and to revise properly.

- Keep a sociology vocabulary book. This could be either in a separate little notebook, or just some blank paper at the back of your folder. This will help you concentrate on the key words that different theories use, and will be a valuable aid for revision when the time comes.

- The sociology topics you will be studying are usually divided up into smaller sub-topics. At the end of every sub-topic, when you move onto something else, make sure you re-read your notes and seek help if you need it.

- At the end of every sub-topic, summarise all the key ideas so that they all make sense for you ready for revision. One way of doing this is to make a neat and colourful brainstorm diagram (sometimes called a 'mind-map') that will summarise all the ideas, people's names, and most importantly the connections between the different thinkers.

- Make sure you have lots of coloured highlighter pens with you in lessons. These will help you to focus on key information while your teacher teaches you. It is important to make the most of all your lessons and being able to highlight things while you go along will help you to achieve this focus.

- You will find that there are lots of names to remember by the end of every topic. One way of developing good evaluation skills is to make a list of who agrees and disagrees with whom and over what. Ask your teacher to check this, and do it at the end of each topic.

- Make revision cards all the way through the course rather than leaving it until the very end. When you make your revision cards, try and divide the topics you have been taught into the four essential ingredients of theory, key words, named examples and evaluation. This will be your opportunity to learn about the topic in your own style and personalise your notes so that they work best for you.

- Try to see the connections between the topics that you are being taught. Do not see them as totally separate subjects, they are all sociology and therefore they are all connected.

- Think about synopticity all the way through your course.

Conclusion

Although this is AS level sociology, you still need to think about theory in order to do well, all the way through your course.

Technically speaking, the AS actually focuses upon knowledge of studies and sociological language more than it does on theory. However, theory is the thing that places the other bits of knowledge into context. It unites all the studies together and it allows us to think about the ideas and assumptions that lie behind what individual researchers think and do. The words that sociologists use and the things they try and investigate are often triggered by the theories that sociologists hold in the first place.

For consideration:

1 Which of the above advice do you think is the most important to do right from the start of your sociology course and why?
2 Which of the above advice do you think will be the most difficult to keep up over the course of the year and why?

1.14 What do sociologists actually 'do'?

What does this mean?

The answer to the question 'What do sociologists actually do?' might seem obvious, but it is very important in understanding what the point of sociology is and how the subject works.

Sociologists do many different things including the following:

- Localised small-scale research.

- Large-scale research trying to seek patterns or general trends.

- Conduct research in its purest sense, i.e. collect and interpret data.

- Theorise, i.e. seek to answer the bigger questions; the 'what is it like'? questions.

- Conduct research in order to develop someone else's theoretical ideas.

As you can see, there are many possibilities but they all have in common the fact that they are thinking about what society is like and are trying to offer insights into the world we live in.

The study of sociology

Sociology is both theoretical and also **empirical**:

- Theoretical: this is about coming up with ideas that say something about what society is like and how it is made-up. It is about saying what society is really like, not what we assume it might be like.

- Empirical: this is about proving evidence and data for theories.

Sociologists may look at social problems or sociological problems:

- Social problems: these are issues that are of concern to and for society. They include problems such as crime, educational underachievement, inequality, etc. These problems are the issues that governments think about and they might use sociological ideas and data to help them to think about these issues.

- Sociological problems: these are problems that sociologists have in studying society. Sociologists spend a great deal of their time thinking and researching into social problems, but underlying these are problems of theory and method: How can we gain access? What is good data? Where can we find out information? What is truth? These are all sociological problems.

In terms of their day-to-day life, most people who would refer to themselves as 'sociologists' work for a university, a research group, or conduct freelance independent research. Most of the time these people have ideas and insights and test them.

What is sociology for?

A number of criticisms of sociology include the following:

* It is all pointless, it has no real use.

* It is just a lot of long words.

* It is all common sense.

* It just complicates things.

It is certainly true to say that some sociology is quite complicated; but the point of sociology is to look into society in depth, and this is rarely going to be a simple matter. Sociologists do use long words as, like all subjects, sociology uses a technical vocabulary.

The point of sociology is to tell us things we either do not know, or to explain why things happen that we do know about. Even if it does just tell us about things we know, at least this means we are actually right. The point of sociology is to spend time thinking in the first place, not just to assume.

Conclusion

Although different sociologists do things differently, they are all still doing sociology. They are all involved in the production of knowledge for a better understanding of the world around them.

Do sociologists theorise or do they gather data?

For consideration:
1 What do you think the point of sociology is?
2 How useful do you think sociology is?

1.15 What is the specification like for AQA sociology?

It is important that you get yourself a copy of the specification you are following. Ask your teacher or use the AQA website and look up sociology. This will contain everything you need to know about the course you are doing both at AS and A2 level.

What is the difference between AS and A2 level?

The AS is a half way point between the GCSE qualification, and the A2 course. It build on skills and exam techniques developed at GCSE, and it sets the scene for the harder A2 course, and the demands on essay writing that this asks for.

The AS qualification is designed to introduce to you the basics of the subject; the key ideas and the key debates. It places more importance on knowledge and understanding, and less importance on evaluation skills, which become important at A2 level (see section 17).

What themes run through AS and A2 level?

The specifications ask you to think about a number of key themes that run throughout the whole course. These are:

* Socialisation, culture and identity.

* Social differentiation, power and stratification.

These ideas appear in every topic area, and they are some of the most important tools you will need to link all the topics together. This means that in each topic area you study, you will be asked to think about power and about inequality. You will also be asked to think about how the topic treats the idea of how people form identity and what culture does to people.

The skill of knowledge and understanding covers your awareness of what is called 'the nature of sociological thought'. This means your knowledge of the following:

* Theories.

● **Synoptic Link**

Use these themes and apply them to the different studies that you have been taught in each topic area.

- The relationship between theory and methods.
- What sociologists think about social order and social control.

This skill of knowledge and understanding also covers a theme called 'methods of sociological inquiry'. This means that you also need to know the following:

- How sociologists collect data.
- Problems in social research.
- Ethical and moral problems in research.
- How certain topics raise specific problems for research.

What topics come up at AS level?

For the AS exam, you will be studying the following:

- Methods.
- Either Family, Media or Health.
- Either Education, Wealth or Work.
- Theory.

For consideration:

1 What do you think the differences are between the AS and A2 level?
2 How do the key themes link the whole subject together?

♟ Thinking like a Sociologist

Think about the ethics of each piece of research you study. Was the sociologist justified in finding out what they did and how they did it? Often this is a good way to begin to evaluate studies.

✓ Top Exam Hint

As all sociology is about ideas and research, you can bring methods into every topic because each topic poses very particular issues and problems for the sociologist wanting to research them. This is a good way to increase depth in your answers and evaluate the methods used.

1.16 How will I be examined for AQA sociology?

It is never too early to be focused on the exam.

At the end of the AS course you will be sitting either two or three examinations for the AS in sociology.

These exams could be any of the following, depending on what topic areas your teachers have decided to teach you:

- Unit 1: Either Family, Health or Media.
  Each section contains one data response question. You will need to choose one section and answer that question.

- Unit 2: Either Education, Wealth or Work.
  Each section contains one data response question. You will need to choose one section and answer that question.

- Unit 3: Methods. You will either be asked to sit an exam paper or conduct a piece of coursework based on writing a research report and evaluation.
  The exam will consist of one compulsory data response question.
  If you are writing the research paper, it should be no more than 1200 words.

How does the qualification work?

All AS qualifications are made up of three units, and all A2 qualifications are made up of a further three units, making a whole two-year course of six units in all.

The points or marks that you get for each unit are weighted by the exam board, and are added together to make a final score for the AS grade. These marks are then added together with the weighted A2 marks for an overall grade. This means that if you take re-sits you can increase your grade (if your school or college allows you to do this).

When are the exams?

Exams take place in January and also in May/June. This means that you may be taught a topic and then sit the exam in it, or sit all the exams at the end of the year.

What does the exam look like?

The exam paper follows the same format for each of the three exams.

* The exam for units 1 and 2 is 1 hour and 15 minutes.

* The exam for unit 3 (if you are doing the exam) is 1 hour.

Papers 1 and 2 are both worth 35 per cent of the AS mark, and paper 3 is worth 30 per cent.

Each exam provides two pieces of source material, and the questions get longer and harder as the exam goes on. You have to answer all parts of the question on one topic per exam.

For consideration:

1   Do you know what topics you will be sitting?
2   Do you know how your teachers have decided you should approach the course. Will you be doing exams in January or May/June or both? Will you be able to take re-sits?

1.17 What is AQA sociology like at A2 level?

A2 sociology

As well as the AS qualification, you also have the opportunity to take the subject further and do the A2 course in sociology for a further year. The A2 qualification extends the knowledge you gained at AS level. The final exam you sit at A2 level is referred to as the synoptic paper, meaning that it is an opportunity to draw together all that you have learned across the full two years of the AS/A2 course.

At A2 level, you have a choice from the following:

- Unit 4: Power and politics, Religion or world sociology.
- Unit 5: Methods (either a piece of coursework or an exam).
- Unit 6: The synoptic unit (either Crime and deviance or Stratification and differentiation).

What are the exams like?

The A2 exams have less short answer questions than at AS level, and ask you to develop full essay writing skills. The A2 year also places a joint emphasis on evaluation and knowledge and understanding.

- Units 4 and 6: there is an 8-mark and a 12-mark question based around a single source item. You are also asked to write an essay. In the final Unit 6 exam you will not get a choice of essay question.
- Unit 5: if you are not doing the coursework option, this paper asks you to answer a short data response question plus an essay.

All the exams last for 1 hour and 30 minutes.

What is the A2 coursework like?

The coursework option at A2 level asks you to conduct an original piece of research using an appropriate sociological tool in order to gather your data. This research could produce primary data (your own) or use the primary data of someone else (making it secondary data for you). It could link to the research report at AS level (if you did it) or could be on something separate.

What is the synoptic unit?

For AQA sociology you will be doing either Crime and deviance or Stratification and differentiation as the synoptic unit. This exam asks you to think about sociology as a whole and to spell out links between the following:

* The topics themselves.

* Theories within and between topics.

* Methods and topics.

* The AS and the A2 year.

Is A2 more difficult than AS level?

The answer to this question is yes and no.

* Yes: there are another two topics to learn, plus you might still be taking some AS re-takes. You will also be required to further develop essay skills and evaluation skills. The A2 exam has some complicated theories to learn, which reflect more about sociology today than those that you may have learned at AS level.

* No: you already have a good understanding of theory and basic sociological ideas. You will also have the basic skills which you will be building on.

For consideration:

1 What do you think will be the most difficult issues at A2 level?
2 How do you think that sociology can help us to better understand social problems?

● **Synoptic Link**

Try to link what you are studying in each topic to issues of inequality and power.

✓ **Top Exam Hint**

Use the theory from the AS year in the A2 year.

1.18 What is successful revision?

What makes good revision?

Many students take revision for granted. They assume that they know what to revise and how to do it. You should think hard about revision; what is the purpose of it, and what are the best ways of going about it?

In order to make the most of your revision, think about how best you learn:

- Do you find writing things down makes them easier to remember?

- Do you need to colour-code revision notes to help you to think about them?

- Do you need to shorten your notes?

We are all different learners, and it is important to find out what works for you by experimenting with different types and techniques of revision.

Some dos

- Undertake active revision, i.e. write things down; do not just read passively.

- Shorten all your notes from your folder and put them onto little index cards ready to revise from.

- Think about evaluation skills while you revise. Practice making lists of how theories and thinkers would criticise each other.

- Practice past paper questions. Get these from your teachers.

Some don'ts

- Do not rely on reading as revision. It is not effective as it is too passive.

- Do not leave sorting out and shortening your notes until the end of the course.

- Do not see revision as a process of putting things into your head. See it as a process of taking things out of your head and putting them into paper. This is what you will be doing in the exam, so it is what should be doing in the revision too.

Experiment with all these ideas and try and find what works best. Make sure you do this early on in your course. Do not leave revision until the very end of your course. You do not want to be experimenting with revision before the real exam. You should already know what works best for you.

Conclusion

Revise early – don't leave it until the last minute. Usually the AS exams take place from the middle of May onwards – much earlier than the GCSE and A2 exams. This means that you basically have a shorter year to learn AS Sociology than you might think. Given this fact, organise your notes early: make revision notes and, most important of all, make sure you talk to your teachers early on about things you might be a bit unsure about. Use the CD-ROM with this book to kick-start your revision and you'll be okay. Make sure you also pay attention to the 'top exam hint' boxes in the margins of this book.

For consideration:

1 What advice do you think would work best for you and why?
2 How do you already revise, and how does this link to the dos and don'ts above?

1.19 Examination advice

You might think that the start of your course is too early to start to think about the final exam. However, it is important to be as prepared as possible in order to maximise your chance of getting a good grade. The following general advice will help you to work towards the exams throughout the whole of your course.

- Get a copy of the specification you are following at the start of your course. Make sure that your folder is divided into the relevant topics, and that you have checked with your teachers what topics or units you will be sitting in the exam. Be as clear as possible from the very start.

- Keep a vocabulary book and refer to it throughout the course. This will help you to keep a track of all the technical language that sociology and sociology teachers use.

- Practice past exam questions all the way through your course. You can get these from the website for your exam board. This will help you to focus on what will be expected of you.

- Think about the synoptic links all the way through your AS course. You could colour-code or highlight topics and ideas that link to the A2 topics that you will study.

- Do not throw your AS notes away as soon as you sit the exam. You might need them for re-takes, coursework and for the synoptic unit.

- Put your studies and named examples onto cards. Bring them into lessons as a memory aid.

- At A2 level, go through your cards from the AS course and pick out those that link to the topics you are doing.

- Use the internet and the CD-ROM that accompanies this book to build-up a series of statistics, studies and other information that you can add to relevant lessons and sections of your folder.

- Read a broadsheet newspaper every week and keep a cuttings file of information and stories that are relevant to your course. This will help keep your answers up-to-date, but will also help with your coursework as you will have a ready-made context for your research.

- Word process all your essays/exam answers/homework if you can.

- Read the relevant pages of this book alongside any lessons you have for added depth and detail.

Conclusion

Probably the most important and useful type of revis[...] practising exam-style questions. You might, nearer the ex[...] yourself as if it was the real exam. This will avoid you gettin[...] surprise in the exam itself. It doesn't even matter if you re-do ol[...] questions that your teacher has given you previously. The point is s[...] that you take the time to practice writing.

Some ideas you could use include:

- Time yourself to make plans for the longer mark questions – 10–15 minutes each. You could do four in one hour.

- Practice whole questions and ask your teacher to mark them.

- Get a friend to choose questions for you at random (you could do the same for them) so it really is an unseen test – just like the exam will be.

Key points to remember

- It is never too early to think about the exams.
- It is never too early to be organised.
- It is never too early to make revision notes.

in order to get the best
xam. These are general ideas
you might be studying.

ciology folder and keep it this
how important this organisation might
out being organised as they are

always up-date this at the end of each
definitions if you are not clear.

ds, use them in homework and in class to
them and can use them in the right

4 ... deas from every chapter (even if you
are not studying it) from the CD-ROM that accompanies this book,
and keep them as a reference guide in your sociology folder.

5 At the end of each topic, spend some time making revision notes
(little index cards are often best for this). You will have to be
organised and well disciplined to keep this up, but it will really help
when you come to revise at the end of the year. Rather than have to
spend time making notes, you can actually get on with the business
of learning them instead.

6 List evaluation points for each topic you study. If you put these onto
cards at the end of each topic then you can start to learn them.

7 Put all your named examples for each topic onto separate revision
cards. You should include what the sociologists did, what they said
and what theory they follow (if you know). You can then use these to
revise from.

8 Make sure that for every theory you learn you can:

- make 10 bullet-pointed statements about the theory;
- identify ten key words the theory would use;
- think of four studies to support the theory;
- think of four criticisms of the theory;
- think of comparisons and contrasts with other theories.

this then you will be able to answer any exam question in-depth.

n you can do is
m, try and time
a nasty
exam
mply

52

uate

Introduction

Key points to remember

- Make sure you are organised right from the start.

- Keep a vocabulary book and use key words as a way of writing in depth.

Frequently asked questions

Q. Why is there so much theory in sociology?

A. Sociology needs theory so that we can try and think about society in new and interesting ways. Theory enables us not to be confused or mislead by what we think is true. We use theories, and 'bounce them off of each other' and by doing this we can try and open up our minds. We all have views; theory is just a way of making them more detailed and then testing them.

Q. What use is sociology in the 'real world'?

A. You have two options open to you; believe what you are told about the world, or find out for yourself. Sociology helps you to do the later, to think about questions and issues you might never have had to think about before. It might seem that all this has nothing to do with the real world, but what you see as the real world might not be 'real'.

Q. Why do sociologists disagree?

A. It is very frustrating when you realise that there are all these theories and they all seem to be saying different things; surely one must be correct? This is how it is with most subjects; there is usually more than one answer and more than one interpretation. It is just that sociology starts people thinking like this much earlier than other subjects do. The disagreement allows us to think about lots of different ideas and this is how the subject moves forward, by disagreement and discussion.

Chapter 2

Sociological research skills and methods

Key issues in research and methods

Why are sociologists interested in research?

Sociology is not just about ideas or ways of thinking about the world; it is also about testing ideas and trying to uncover evidence that might show that some ideas are better than others. In this sense, sociology is not just about theory, but it is also about research. The value of sociology is that it seeks out observations that might not at first seem apparent.

Different sociologists use research in different ways and carry out research for very different reasons.

- Some sociologists collect what we call quantitative data (e.g. numbers, statistics or anything that can be measured). For them, research is about looking at the big picture, making generalisations and trying to find out facts that might relate to a large proportion of society.
- Other sociologists might produce qualitative data (e.g. in-depth meanings or descriptions of peoples' thoughts and feelings). These sociologists are interested in the smaller picture, such as how something is perceived by an individual or a small group of people at a particular moment in time.

What are the key debates in research and methods?

The key debates in understanding why and how sociologists use methods include the following:

- What is data? Why do sociologists want to produce data?
- When should quantitative/qualitative data be collected/used?
- Is sociology a science?
- Is social research value free?
- Should research try and identify trends, or should it look at individual thoughts and feelings?
- What decisions affect research design?
- Why and how do sociologists choose the methods they use?
- What is sampling and why is it important?
- How can sociologists use secondary sources of data?

What are the key ideas and concepts?

There are three key concepts that need to be understood when undertaking research:

✍ Coursework Suggestion

If you do coursework either at AS or at A2 make sure that you use the evaluative tools (is the research valid, reliable and representative?) and be highly critical of what you are doing. Predict any problems you might have in advance, and explain how you will solve them.

1 Theories: ideas and hypotheses put forward to explain something. They are supported by facts, observations and assumptions and can be tested.
2 Methods: the individual tools or techniques of data collection, for example, questionnaires or interviews.
3 Methodologies: the underpinning reasons and philosophies behind how and why a particular sociologist follows the research tradition they adopt.

Positivists such as Comte are interested in looking at research in a scientific way. They aim to uncover social facts and make generalisations or laws (see section 18). Phenomenologists (or interpretevists) such as Weber are interested in *verstehen,* a German word meaning to try to 'see the world through the eyes of those involved' (see section 19).

Many researchers adopt a position half way between these two extremes.

What are the key problems in the sociology of research and methods?

In order to do well in research you must critically evaluate everything. There is no such thing as a perfect method; when looking at a piece of research you should think about how it was undertaken and if the claims being made actually match the evidence and the conditions under which the research was carried out. In order to evaluate research and methods, you can use the following tools.

- Is the research valid? (How true to life are the data collected?)
- Is the research reliable? (Are you confident that the research shows what it thinks it shows? Has it uncovered what it set out to do?)
- Is the research representative? (Can the results of the research be extended to the whole of society?)

There are many problems that a researcher might encounter when undertaking research:

- Practical problems
- Ethical problems
- Theoretical problems
- Sensitivity problems.

These problems are known as PETS. Some might affect the research results, but some might be overcome. You will need to consider any possible problems when making judgements about how successful you think a piece of research is. Remember, as research is about dealing with people, and sometimes a lot of people, it often does not go according to plan, and it is often not perfect.

66 99 Key Definition

Verstehen is the term used by Max Weber to refer to the fact that whereas natural science seeks to test laws and predictions, social science is very different as it tries, in his view, to 'see the world through the eyes of those involved'. Weber was German and *verstehen* is the German word for understanding, or for empathy. In modern-day sociology this idea of verstehen is the aim of micro sociology.

✓ Top Exam Hint

Use the evaluative terms (is the research valid, reliable and representative?) as tools to help you to think about the successfulness of research.

What do we need to know about sociological research?

What does the specification say about methods?

The AQA specification identifies three main aspects of research methods that should be understood:

1 Why would a sociologist undertake research?

2 What types of methods are useful in sociological research?

3 What problems might the sociologist encounter when doing research, and how might they be solved?

You will need to be able to discuss these issues and to use examples of studies made by sociologists to illustrate your points.

How will I be examined in this topic?

There are two options:

1 Examination. This will last for 1 hour and you will be required to use source items. The first few questions test knowledge and the last two are more extended pieces of writing. The very last question is more evaluative. You will be required to answer all the questions in the time provided.

2 Coursework. This will involve you writing up a research proposal of 1200 words. The proposal is written from the point of view of someone about to start a real piece of research, so you will need to write what, how and why you are going to do it. The headings of the proposal are: hypothesis, context and concepts, main research method and reasons, potential problems.

How well does this topic relate to coursework?

All the ideas, skills and concepts you learn in this topic will relate directly to your coursework. Equally, all the ideas about methods you learn at AS level will link to A2 level as well.

How well does this topic help with synopticity?

At A2 level you will be required to 'think around the subject', i.e. to make links between all the different topic areas. Learning about methods is an ideal way to do this as the methods used will be common to all branches of sociology. All sociologists are faced with the same set of problems, the same challenges, the same need to find out about society in a convincing way. This means that the act of research raises common issues that can be used as a way to think about studies and will allow you to compare them.

Conclusion

For the exams, not matter what subject, you might like to think about trying to use methods issues – but only if they are actually relevant! Try and think about *why* sociologists say what they say, and *how* they might come to the conclusions that they do. In other words, try and think about both theory and methods. After all, the whole of sociology is based on them.

Key points to remember

- At AS level the topic of methods focuses on how to carry out research.
- You are required to understand how all research contains problems and challenges to be solved.

How can we find out about the world through research?

How have sociologists used methods to measure the world?

Sociology is not just about having ideas but also about testing them. In order to test ideas, and in order to find out about the world, different methods are used by different sociologists at different times for different reasons.

- Some methods are better suited to studying certain aspects of society than others. For example, participant observation, where the actual process of research is hidden, might be used to study people's everyday behaviour or crime.

- Specialist methods such as content analysis or semiotics are needed to study the media's content.

- Sensitive issues might be best studied using an interview in order to build up trust, or an anonymous questionnaire might mean people do not feel embarrassed to answer questions truthfully.

Using methods to find things out about society involves lots of difficult decisions, and often the method chosen ends up shaping the direction that the research takes. Methods that produce quantitative data (based on numbers) such as questionnaires, will produce different results to methods that are qualitative (in depth discussions).

What methods do sociologists use?

We can identify a wide range of methods that sociologists use in order to try and investigate what society is like:

- Questionnaires: these can be postal, face to face, by telephone or by e-mail.

- Interviews: these can be structured or semi-structured, allowing the researcher to 'go off the point' and allow the person being interviewed to raise issues of their own.

- Group interviews: these are called focus groups, where people are asked to participate in a group discussion about a focused topic.

- Content analysis and semiology: this is where media text and pictures are analysed in order to try and understand the messages within them and meanings behind them.

- Observation: this can be either covert (hidden) or overt (open) and the observer can either participate with those being studied, or can stand back from them.

Many sociologists today mix methods together, using one main method and backing it up with a second method, carried out in less detail, in order to help support or evaluate the findings of the first. Sociologists often make good use of secondary sources which can be either quantitative, such as official statistics from the government, or qualitative such as diaries, letters, etc. A researcher might try and combine both quantitative and qualitative methods together in order to get a much fuller picture, adopting a scientific and also a more interpretive approach within the same study. Much modern day research is undertaken from a position in between the two extremes of sociology, namely positivist and phenomenologist.

Key points to remember

- All methods have both their strengths and weaknesses.

- Good research involves predicting problems and trying to solve them, and making sure that the best, most suitable method is chosen in relation to the topic studied.

- Many sociologists today mix methods together.

✳ Key Idea

Mixing methods together is sometimes called 'methodological pluralism' or 'triangulation'. In other words, it is about using one set of results to compare with, support and evaluate another set. A great deal of modern research works like this, to the extent that the traditional divide between being either 'scientific' or 'non-scientific' is often blurred.

✍ Coursework Suggestion

During your coursework always try to predict problems you may encounter before they happen. Then explain all the possible solutions you can think of to these perceived problems. Good sociological research will comes up with inventive practical solutions to the problems of finding out about people and their lives.

Why do we do research in sociology?

What does this mean?

Research is the process of exploring and gathering evidence. There are two main reasons for a sociologist to undertake research:

1   To build theories: in this type of research the sociologist seeks to uncover data that will help in the creation of an idea of a theory. The sociologist usually has an idea about what is going on, but they will seek data that point towards an explanation for why things are as they are.

2   To test theories: in this type of research, the theory or idea has already been suggested, and the data are gathered in order to see if the idea is true.

Theories allow us to think about the world we inhabit. They allow us to think through why things are as they are, or why things might be different from how they actually seem. Theories are critical; they seek to question, to assess and to ask why. Sociologists undertake research in order to support theories, to prove them, disprove them, and to find out why and how society works.

What is the role of the sociologist in research?

If we consider the role of the person undertaking the research, there are two broad approaches to sociological research:

1   The sociologist as 'expert': in this approach the sociologist gathers the data and is able to uncover the truth as to why things are as they are. The sociologist sees what others in society cannot see because they have the big, overall picture. The sociologist in this view is often seen as a scientist or a detective, trying to find out what is really going on, despite what people in society might think.

2   The sociologist as 'reporter': in this approach the sociologist allows those studied to be the experts on their own lives, and the sociologist takes a back seat, promoting, asking questions, and letting people explain how they see their own lives and the world around them.

Is the sociologist inside or outside?

When undertaking research, you must think about the relationship of the researcher to those they are researching. Is the sociologist 'inside' the group, i.e. part of them and their lives, or is the sociologist separate, i.e. researching from a distance?

- Inside: the sociologist is part of what is being studied. Sociologists are human, and they study humans, so they cannot detach themselves totally from their customs, values and culture. This is often helpful as it means you are quick to understand those being studied and can build relationships with them. This might also be a problem since you might let your own up-bringing affect how you view the evidence.

- Outside: the sociologist is often described as 'outside' as they are researching people from different backgrounds to themselves. This can be helpful as you have to sit back and let your subjects tell you what they think. However, can anyone ever truly understand someone else's life? People are often too distanced to fully appreciate how others live and feel. Equally, if you are too dissimilar to those you are studying they might not trust you, and you might not be able to build up the sort of relationship needed to fully understand them.

The central problem to overcome is whether to be inside or outside your research. It should be easy to find out what others think because you are human like them, but it is often difficult for this very reason.

Conclusion

All sociological research rests ultimately on the assumption that the world of society, of other people's thoughts, of what people do in their daily lives is worth investigating, and also that it is actually possible to 'know' what the world is like. In order to investigate the world, different sociologists adopt very different ways of finding things out, i.e. they use different methods in their research.

For consideration:

1 How does research make sociological ideas more justified?
2 What do you think the problems of research might be for a sociologist, given they are part of the world being studied?

✳ Key Ideas

- Sociologist Ray Pawson talks of the existence of an 'imposition problem' in social research, i.e. you might end up interpreting what you want in your data without realising it. This is because it is very difficult to distance yourself from the process of research. You set the questions, decide who to talk to, and in the end, because of this, decide in part on what the results will look like.

- We use the word 'epistemology' to refer to the idea that something can be 'known' and that there might be a wide range of different ways to find out about it.

What are validity and reliability?

What is validity?

When sociologists talk of research being 'valid' they mean that the measurement or technique (method) used to collect the data actually measures what it sets out to measure. Some sociologists make a distinction in research between two types of **validity**:

1 Criteria validity: this is when a concept used in a piece of research should closely link to the real life events it is supposed to relate to. For example, if you were to study 'class' and ask people about their levels of income, this would be valid since these two factors (class and income) would sensibly be related in the real world. However, if you were to measure class by asking people about their favourite football team, this has no validity since football supporting is not a sensible measurement of one's class.

2 Construct validity: this is when measurement of an aspect of social life allows you to make correlations between this and other aspects of social life that you would think are related. For example, you might predict that it would be possible (if your data and measurements were valid) to correlate class with one's lifestyle, type of house and type of car, as class would cause (determine) these things.

In order to check for validity, it is vital that **operationalisation** of concepts takes place early on in the research process.

A key problem with the validity of any piece of research is that often the same question asked to different people (be it from a questionnaire or an interview) might be interpreted to mean a different thing. Can you therefore guarantee that you are comparing the same thing? Are you studying the same thing, or are you assuming a likeness that does not exist in real life?

What is reliability?

If something is 'reliable' it means that the results would have been produced in the way they were no matter who did the actual carrying out of the research. In other words, the research could be carried out again by someone else and the same results produced. As with validity, there are two ways to measure **reliability**:

1 Temporal reliability: this is when the same research is carried out after a period of time, and the same results are produced.

66 99 Key Definitions

- **Operationalisation** is the process whereby key concepts are clearly explained and defined so that it is obvious to other people what the sociologist means by the concept. For example, if you were to study class, what do you mean by this? What you mean by the term will shape how you study it.

- **Reliability** means a piece of research that can be repeated with the same results.

- **Validity** means true to life.

2   Comparative reliability: this is when two different studies are compared using the same method on the same or different samples, or different methods are used on the same or different samples, and yet still the results are the same.

How do reliability and validity relate to data gathering?

In general, quantitative data are presumed to be high in reliability and low in validity, whereas qualitative data are usually high in validity and low in reliability. In other words, methods that seek to produce a large amount of data tend to be best judged by the replication of the data to see if it holds true, whereas methods that seek small-scale but high depth data tend to be best judged as to whether or not the research is a true reflection of the lives of those involved at the time.

Conclusion

Many sociologists seek to combine methods in order to produce both quantitative and qualitative data, thus trying to make their research stand up to both standards of validity and reliability.

For consideration:

1   Which do you think is more important, validity or reliability?
2   What issues or aspects of society do you think would create the most problems for validity and reliability?

2.6 What types of data do sociologists produce?

What does this mean?

Data are simply pieces of information. This information is gathered through the act of doing research; it is the end product of using a research tool such as a questionnaire or an interview. There are two different types of data that research might produce:

1 Quantitative data

2 Qualitative data

When applied to research traditions, quantitative data are used by positivists (who look at society at a macro level), and qualitative data are used by phenomenologists (interpretivists) who look at micro sociology.

Using different types of data

As we have seen, quantitative data are associated with techniques that are high in reliability and low in validity, i.e. techniques that produce results that can easily be repeated by another researcher. Since these data are produced in number form, they are often associated with what positivists call 'social facts' (underlying patterns of social reality that exist as real things). Quantitative data are produced by techniques such as questionnaires and structured interviews and often sociologists use official statistics produced by the government to back-up their research. **Sampling** is very important in this type of research as the researcher needs to be able to generalise from their findings.

Qualitative data are associated with techniques that are high in validity and low in reliability, i.e. techniques that explore the world 'as it is' and discover meanings and motives.

Many sociologists try and combine the use of both quantitative and qualitative data together. This approach is often called methodological pluralism or **triangulation**. The benefits of this are that a sociologist can use one type of data to support their findings from the other type. For example, in a famous study looking at the Moonies (a religious movement) Eileen Barker (1984) mixed together the methods of questionnaires, in-depth interviews and observation. Equally, sociologist Valerie Hey's (1997) work on female friendship groups in school uses a mixture of focus group interviews, participant observation and the use of qualitative secondary sources such as life documents (diaries and classroom notes).

66 99 Key Definitions

- **Sampling** is the process of selecting a part in order to judge the characteristics of the whole.

- **Triangulation** is the idea that sociologists can mix methods together from different traditions in order to achieve a fuller, more rounded picture of society.

✳ Key Idea

Meaning and motives are major elements in the micro sociology. All human action is seen to be meaningful or based upon an underlying motive (a reason behind the action). The aim of qualitative sociology is to get at these meanings and to see how people make sense of their world.

Evaluating types of data

Feminist sociologists place a great deal of importance upon the creation of qualitative data. Many feminists such as Ann Oakley have argued that in order to make sure we support what we study, we should reject quantitative research in favour of more qualitative research. This is because quantitative research reduces individual people to numbers and statistics rather than trying to genuinely understand each person's experiences in their own right.

Some qualitative techniques raise ethical and sensitivity issues in a way that quantitative methods might not. For example, in-depth interviews might explore the private feelings of an individual, making them feel open, vulnerable and even exploited.

Conclusion

Data is essential and central to all that sociologists do. Data is what we use to think about the world. Our data might either be used to create new ideas, or to test existing ideas. Often, as social research is a 'messy' business, the data we get isn't quite what we expected it to be. On the other hand, sometimes we find what we went looking for since we have structured the research in the first place.

For consideration:

1   Which do you think is the best type of data to produce, quantitative or qualitative? Why?
2   How might the nature of the topic being studied affect the type of data a sociologist produces?

● **Synoptic Link**

Using the feminist view on quantitative data you can make some important evaluations of macro theories in whatever topic area you are studying. This will not only improve your evaluation skills but also allow you to link different parts of the course together.

✓ **Top Exam Hint**

Evaluate research studies by thinking about the ethical and sensitivity issues they might raise.

How and why do sociologists use questionnaires?

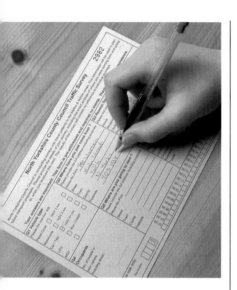

Why do sociologists use questionnaires to gather data?

What does this mean?

Questionnaires are lists of questions administered either face to face with an interviewer, by telephone, by e-mail or by post. Sometime questionnaires might be given to people to complete on their own, or sometimes an interviewer might ask the questions and the responses are written down on a standardised form. All the people taking part in the research will be asked the same questions so that comparisons can be made. Postal surveys have a high non-response rate, whereas questionnaires where interviewers need to be employed cost more money but have a higher response rate.

There are four main types of questionnaires in social research:

1. Factual surveys: these gather information about features of people's lives, rather than asking for opinions or thoughts.
2. Attitudinal surveys: these ask people about their views on certain issues.
3. Social psychological surveys: these developed out of attitudinal surveys and concentrate on asking people about their thoughts in order to try and group people into personality types.
4. Explanatory surveys: these are surveys that are designed to test a **hypothesis** which suggests a relationship exists between two factors. This type of research tries to use questionnaires to show how one set of factors causes something else to happen (causality).

Why are questionnaires used to collect data?

There are six main reasons why questionnaires prove popular with sociologists who want to produce quantitative data:

1. Questionnaires can be used to test theoretical ideas using a hypothesis.
2. Statistics can be produced and analysed thus making sociology more 'scientific'.
3. Generalisation from the sample can take place.
4. Causality between variables can be measured.
5. Standardisation of question allows for measurement and comparison between responses.
6. The findings can be replicated and bias can be checked.

What types of questions can be asked?

Different questionnaires use different types of questions:

- Open questions are where people are asked for their view and have a blank space to say/write what they feel.
- Closed questions are where people are restricted in the type of answer they can give. The question may require a simple 'yes' or 'no', or it might ask for a 'graded response' for example, strongly agree/agree/disagree/strongly disagree, etc.

There are four main types of questions asked in questionnaires, and they are used for different reasons:

1 Classification questions: these are questions about who the person is, so that they can be classified and their answers compared with others of a similar type. These questions might ask about occupation, age, income, etc. and allow the sociologist to gather information for their **explanatory variables**.
2 Factual questions: these are questions that ask for answers that do not involve an opinion, i.e. How many times do you go to church each week? What TV programmes did you watch last night? etc.
3 Opinion questions: these are questions that ask someone what they think about something, i.e. Which TV programme do you think is the best? What clothes do you like the most?
4 Attitude scales: these are statements that the respondent can agree or disagree with. They are used in order to test and compare views and attitudes to certain issues.

Questions should be simple to understand, clear and well laid-out and should only ask about things that can be accurately measured.

Weaknesses of questionnaires

- Questions are set by the sociologist and so might 'impose' their biases onto the research.
- The questions used might simplify important issues by reducing thoughts and feelings to a 'tick box' answer.
- Questionnaires might not be returned if they are self-completion without an interviewer present.
- People might interpret the same question differently; one person's 'strongly agree' might be very different to another's.

> **66 99 Key Definition**
>
> **Explanatory variables** are characteristics that might cause or explain why the person answers a question as they have. These are key sociological concepts such as class, gender, age, location, ethnicity, etc. This type of data is collected through the type of questions we call 'classification questions'.

> **✳ Key Idea**
>
> Questionnaires often suffer from an 'imposition problem'. This is because as the sociologist chooses the questions in the first place, they are imposing their own views on the answers people can give. They are limiting some responses, ignoring others by simply not asking questions about certain things, and therefore they are finding the answers they want because they are asking the questions they want to in the first place.

For consideration:

1 Do the strengths outweigh the weaknesses of the questionnaire method?
2 What areas of social life would most suit using questionnaires?

How and why do sociologists conduct interviews?

What are interviews?

An interview involves someone being asked questions. They are usually taped as the answers might go into a lot of depth. Different types of interviews can be classified as follows:

- Structured interviews (formal interviews): a formal set of questions are asked and the interviewer cannot ask extra questions. This means that comparisons can be made because there is standardisation of questions.
- Unstructured interviews (informal interviews): no lists of formally pre-arranged questions exist, and the interview itself is open and flexible. The person being interviewed (the interviewee) is able to say what they feel, as directed by the interviewer. This type of interview usually lasts a long time, and might occur over more than one session. These interviews must be taped in order for the researcher to be able to fully concentrate on what is being said at the time, thus making sure that they can keep the questioning relevant.

  It is debatable that a totally unstructured interview can actually exist as the researcher will usually have some initial idea of what sorts of things to listen out for. They will also have decided which question to ask first, in order to start the interview in the first place. Many researchers use semi-structured interviews; a set pattern of questions are asked, but the interviewer can allow answers to bring up new questions not previously thought about.

- Focus groups: a number of people are interviewed at the same time, forming a group discussion. A focus is given to the discussion and an interviewer is usually present to direct and guide participants.

Structured interviews are usually associated with quantitative data and the standardised approach means that patterns can be identified. Unstructured interviews are more qualitative, and they are more difficult to analyse as it is often tricky to isolate key variables. Computer programmes are currently available that can turn qualitative interview data into quantitative data by searching for key words or phrases used in answers.

Why are interviews used?

- Many researchers use interviews as a way to generate qualitative data, exploring in more detail people's thoughts and feelings.

- Feminist sociologists often use interviews as they feel that questionnaires are too **masculinist**, i.e. they categorise people and reduce complex personal feelings to statistics.
- Feminist and more interpretive sociologists use interviews as a form of empowerment, i.e. as a way of helping people to understand their own lives and helping them to reflect upon their own experiences.
- Interpretive sociologists use interviews in order to try and achieve *verstehen*, (to see the world from other people's eyes).
- When dealing with sensitive issues, a degree of trust might need to be established between the interviewer and the interviewee (this would not be achieved with a questionnaire).
- Interviews are often used to support other methods of research: more quantitative methods might be supported by interviews which add a bit more depth to the research.

Strengths and weaknesses of interviews

Interviews are a useful research tool as the interviewer might be able to explain questions to the interviewee and ensure that all the questions are answered. People can have their own say, i.e. they can say what they think is important about their lives, rather than their answers being guided by a researcher.

The interviewer and interviewee can develop rapport, allowing for an honest exchange of material based upon trust. Interviewing should be about building an equal relationship between both the interviewer and the interviewee. There should be a bond of trust that breaks down the obvious unequal power relationship within the interview situation, where the interviewer traditionally has power over the interviewee. The interviewee should also be allowed to ask questions as well as the other way around.

Interviews may be less useful where there is interviewer bias, i.e. where the interviewer directs answers with leading questions, ensuring they get what they wanted to find. Interviewers may 'bully' the interviewee into providing the answer they want to hear. In addition, the ethnicity of the interviewer has been shown to have a dramatic effect on the interviewee. Interviews might not be comparable if different questions are asked as there would be no standardisation. As it takes such a long time to conduct an interview, they are often expensive and this means that not many interviews can actually take place (when compared with numbers of questionnaires that can be collected).

> ### For consideration:
>
> 1 Why are interviews a useful research method to use?
> 2 Do you think that interviews allow sociologists to give power to those they study?

66 99 Key Definition

Masculinist is a word used by feminist sociologists to describe non-feminist sociology that is often quantitative and positivist in nature. It is research that categorises people and tries to see patterns in society beyond the experience of the individuals who make up the sample used in the research. Feminist sociology tries to build up personal relationships with those they study since this is seen as less exploitative.

✍ **Coursework Suggestion**

You can use interviews for coursework at A2 course. If you do, make sure you give consideration to any power inequalities in the interview; are you really letting people speak for themselves? This will help you to evaluate what you are doing.

Thinking like a Sociologist

When you conduct or use interviews in your research, discuss the following points:

- The way the interviews allow for *verstehen*.
- The feminist use of interviews.
- How ethnicity might affect the outcome of the interview.

How and why do sociologists observe?

What does this mean?

Observation is the term given to the situation when a sociologist watches what goes on, and makes notes about the relationships, actions and events that are seen. Observations can be either quantitative or qualitative.

- Quantitative observation: this is where use is made either of a pre-coded checklist or the creation of a **sociogram**. A record is made of what happens and this record is linked to categories that the researcher has pre-decided upon. These observations can then be presented as quantitative data, and observations can be compared. The danger with this method is that different observers might 'see' the same observations in different ways, making comparison less objective.
- Qualitative observation: this is where a narrative or story of the situation is created, often associating events with the time they took place.

Traditionally observation is associated with the interpretive sociological perspective. This form of sociology aims to understand, from people's own view points, what they do and how and why they do it. Interpretivists feel that since society does not exist separately from people (but is actually created by people's thoughts and feelings and how they interact with others) this interaction should be studied first hand.

Types of observation

Different sociologists use observation in different ways:

- Participant observation: this is where the observer joins in with those being studied.
- Non-participant observation: this is where the observer steps back and observes those being studied from the outside.
- Covert observation: this is secret observation where those being studied do not know that they are being observed. This is often seen as an unethical research method as those who are taking part are not aware that they are doing so, and as a consequence cannot give their **informed consent** to the research.
- Overt observation: in this situation, those being studied are aware of the fact that they are being observed. The researcher may take the part of a member of a focus group (this often happens with ethnographic research), or may remain at a distance making notes such as in classroom observations. A well known problem with overt observation is what we call the **Hawthorne effect**.

66 99 Key Definitions

- A **Sociogram** is a diagram that shows the lines of interaction and communication between people. It allows you to see who talks to who and how often.

- **Informed consent** is when people know that research is taking place and are aware of what it is about, what it will be used for and what their level of involvement will be. They have the right to refuse to take part.

- The **Hawthorne effect** refers to the idea that the presence of an observer will alter the outcome of that being observed, if those being observed are aware of it. This problem has been given this name after a piece of research on the Hawthorne factory plant in the USA by sociologist Elton Mayo (1933) who found that workers' productivity increased dramatically when they knew they were being observed.

✳ Key Idea

The British Sociological Association (BSA) state that research should involve informed consent. They also state that researchers have a responsibility towards research participants to ensure that their well-being is protected at all times. The problem with covert methods of observation is that after the event, some people may feel lied to, spied on and cheated. In all types of research, sociologists enter into personal relationships with those they study. These relationships should be genuine and not based upon deceit.

- Experimental observation (artificial): this is where the situation being studied is created by the researcher themselves, with the sole purpose of allowing observation to take place. This might involve the use of two different groups to observe; the control group who are allowed to act freely, and the experimental group who have been controlled or changed in some way. A comparison can then take place between the two. This observational situation is often criticised for being too artificial as it does not tell us about how people behave in the real world.
- Field observation (natural): this type of observation occurs in social situations where the sociologist makes use of interactions and group encounters that would normally exist in society, without the sociologist having to actually create them in the first place. This gives the sociologist a direct understanding of real life situations, although the nature of what takes place might still be influenced by the presence of an observer if the method is overt.

Strengths and weaknesses of observation

The strengths of observation methods include the following:

- They provide a means for the sociologist to see first hand what people do and how they do it.
- Sociologists can achieve a sense of *verstehen* through observation. They can feel what it feels like to be a member of a group.
- If using covert methods, researchers can observe natural behaviour.
- The methods usually produce valid data.

The weaknesses of observation methods include the following:

- If the method is covert in nature, some observation might be dangerous for the researcher (especially if those in the group are engaged in dangerous or criminal behaviour).
- The researcher might 'go native', i.e. it might be hard to distance oneself from the group and therefore not be able to observe in an independent way.
- It might take time and lots of funding to maintain observation.
- The method raises serious ethical questions, do we have the right to observe particular situations?
- It might be very difficult to record information (especially if covert methods are used).

✍ Coursework Suggestion

If appropriate in your coursework, discuss the BSA ethical guidelines as part of your evaluation of observation methods.

For consideration:

1 Why is observation a useful method for sociologists?
2 Do you think that informed consent with covert observation is an important ethical rule or not?

2.10 How and why do sociologists use secondary sources?

What does this mean?

There are two types of data:

1 Primary data: these are data collected by the sociologist themselves; without this original research the data would not exist.
2 Secondary data: these are data that exist prior to and independent from the sociologist's own research, and that would still exist even if the sociologist did not do their own research in the first place. Secondary data can be either quantitative or qualitative in nature.

Secondary data can come from a variety of sources:

- Official statistics: these are statistics produced by government bodies.
- Unofficial statistics: these are statistics produced by charities etc.
- The mass media: news stories can be used as a source of information, or research can be conducted into the content of the news and media in general.
- Life documents: these are personal records of thoughts and feelings such as diaries, etc.

Why are secondary sources useful?

Secondary sources can be used as a source of data to support the findings of a piece of research or can be studied in their own right as the sole purpose of a piece of research. Secondary sources can offer a quick and easy way for sociologists producing one type of data to compare their findings with other data, either more quantitative or more qualitative than their own study.

Some sociologists use secondary sources because it is interesting to explore how and why they were created as data in the first place. For example, interpretative sociologists associated with an anti-positivist, phenomenological methodology might use secondary statistical data, but they would use it in a very different way to quantitative positivists. While the positivists would use the data as facts to indicate general patterns and trends, the phenomenologists would ask critical questions of the data, such as the following:

- Where does the data come from?
- How was it collected?
- Who collected it and what did they intend to do with it?

- Why did the sociologist draw the conclusions they did from the data they had?

Phenomenologists would agree that statistical secondary data does tell us something useful about society; they allow us to see how people construct data. This tells us about what the people who made the data were thinking.

Most, if not all research uses secondary data of some sort, since most research is not done in a vacuum, either a vacuum from society or from sociology:

- **Society:** all sociologists start with a problem or research question they wish to explore, these thoughts do not just simply appear out of nothing. Media, statistics from the government, etc. would point towards an interesting topic for investigation, therefore secondary data and sources provide the initial idea to start a piece of research.
- **Sociology:** all sociologists think about what research other people have done into the topic that they themselves are researching into. A major requirement of all research (and of your coursework) is to undertake a 'literature review' which forms the context or the background to what you do. In this sense, therefore, all research involves a consideration of other research, i.e. of secondary data.

Strengths and weaknesses of secondary sources

The strengths of using secondary data sources include the following:

- They are cheap and easy to collect.
- They are a useful way to obtain a historical perspective on research you are doing.
- You can use these data to compare with your own primary data for added depth.
- They may help to make cross-society comparisons with your own data.

The weaknesses of using secondary data sources include the following:

- If you do not know how the data were collected, then it is very difficult to know how valid and reliable the data is.
- You will not know how biased the researcher might have been.
- You will not know if personal life documents really are true or are simply one interpretation of events that might have happened.
- Much research takes place with its own political biases; you may not know if the research was originally intended to attack the government or support them.
- You may not know who funded the research and how this might have influenced its creation.

> **For consideration:**
>
> 1 How useful do you think secondary sources really are?
> 2 What warnings come with the use of secondary sources?

✓ **Top Exam Hint**

The critical questions that interpretative sociologists ask of quantitative secondary data highlight the sociologist's mistrust of data, and the idea that sociologists should question everything around them, including so-called facts produced by other sociologists. Try to be this critical in your exam; question everything, every piece of research and every piece of data you come across.

● **Synoptic Link**

Use the idea that you can question how statistics are created in the crime and deviance or stratification topic area at A2 level.

✎ **Coursework Suggestion**

Use a secondary source in your coursework to 'sell your idea' to the examiner, i.e. to make it seem like it is an up-to-date and worthy idea for research in the first place. Make it link to the real world in some way.

2.11 What are the problems of official statistics?

What does this mean?

Official statistics are statistics that have been produced by an official body, usually a government department, or an organisation associated with the government. Non-official statistics might come from such organisations as pressure groups, charities, etc. Sociologists themselves may be involved in the creation of these official statistics, since they might be funded by and employed by the government. Many sociologists use official statistics as a secondary source.

How can sociologists use official statistics?

There are a number of reasons why sociologists might need official statistics as a secondary source:

- Sociologists use official statistics as a comparison with research they themselves have produced. It might help to be able to compare the findings of a micro piece of research with a larger macro set of results.

- Sociologists use official statistics as a way to compare their own quantitative research with that from another source.

- Official statistics can be used in the comparative method; sociologists can obtain data from a wide variety of nations and can then seek trends and patterns between them.

- Many qualitative sociologists use official statistics, but in a very particular way. They argue that since these statistics are not facts, but are **social constructions**; we can use them to understand more about the assumptions behind their making, but they do not tell us anything about society. They tell us about the views of the people who made them and who claim they are real in the first place.

Strengths and weaknesses of official statistics

The strengths of using official statistics include the following:

- They are often easily available.

- They can give the sociologist a sense of historical perspective.

- They are inexpensive to use.

- They will allow easy comparisons to be made between different societies.

66 99 Key Definition

A **social construction** is not a fact, it is not real, it is something that only seems real because it has been made to appear so in the first place. Things we take for granted in society and see as normal only seem this way because society and culture says it should be like this in the first place.

- They allow hypotheses to be tested.

- Sociologists might be able to get information about aspects of society that they would otherwise not have any information about.

The weaknesses of using official statistics include the following:

- You do not know the circumstances under which the statistics were created (this is often true for secondary sources).

- Statistics which come from governmental sources might be politically motivated, for example, the figures might be changed in order to make the government look better than they are.

- Statistics do not readily show us about how they were constructed in the first place. How valid and reliable are they?

- You do not know how the statistics were collated, how large the sample was, or even how the sampling took place.

- The method used to measure official statistics might change over time. This might alter the patterns and trends being claimed. This is especially true of government statistics, for example, unemployment figures or crime figures.

Qualitative (interpretive) sociologists make the point that official statistics are in fact useful, but only if we use them in the right way and for the right reasons. They do not tell us about 'factual social reality'. Instead, they give us an insight into the complex basis upon which such statistics are actually created in the first place, and how and why they are created.

Conclusion

Official statistics, like any secondary source, have advantages and disadvantages to their use. As long as you are aware of these, they will provide a useful tool for the sociologist. In fact, the many problems with such statistics are themselves objects of sociological investigation.

For consideration:

1 Why are official statistics criticised by some sociologists?
2 Why are official statistics still potentially useful to the sociologist, despite the criticisms?

How can sociologists use life documents?

What does this mean?

Life documents are secondary sources that involve the expression of feelings, emotions and thoughts that are used in everyday life. They are personal documents and sources that have been created not for the purpose of research, but during the course of ordinary life. Examples of life documents include the following:

- Diaries
- E-mails
- Love letters
- Post cards from holidays
- Shopping lists
- School-children's classroom notes
- Photographs
- Graffiti
- Letters from readers written to newspapers and magazines.

Life documents tend to be qualitative in nature as they are about what people think, and often how they feel. They are expressions of ideas that might allow a researcher to understand what it means to be someone. In this way, using life documents might be seen to allow *verstehen*.

Strengths and weaknesses of life documents

The strengths of using life documents include the following:

- They are an interesting and unusual source, adding variety to a piece of research.
- They are valid. They are a rich and ever-present source of documentation of ordinary social life that allows a researcher to see 'how it really is'.
- They pre-exist the sociologist, and therefore are not expensive to collect.
- They are created normally in social life, not simply as part of a piece of research. They are therefore authentic, not artificial.
- They are a good source of qualitative data, they tell us about emotions.
- They allow for *verstehen*, i.e. to see how people think about the world they live in.
- If combined with other methods, they help to provide a fuller picture. For example, if combined with questionnaires, they add a sense of personal feelings and depth not obtainable through questionnaires.
- They allow historical comparison.

✳ Key Idea

Life documents allow sociologists to explore qualitative data; data that is concerned with thoughts expressed in depth. This allows validity, a true to life expression of how people think, and how they view the world around them. This is very important to phenomenologists who try to understand what it means to live in society and to make sense of society in order to live one's life successfully.

The weaknesses of using life documents include the following:

- They may be difficult to obtain.
- You might not know the conditions under which they were written.
- They might not be true (sometimes people write fantasies in diaries rather than actual experiences).
- They are a selective perception. Did it really happen in the exact way expressed, or is it a matter of interpretation?
- Since they are so individual it is difficult to use them for generalisation.

Using life-documents

Max Weber (1905), in his study of Calvinist Protestants, made good use of diaries in order to try and explore the feelings and thoughts of this religious group. This allowed Weber to gain some important historical data, which may otherwise have been lost. In *The Protestant Ethic and the Spirit of Capitalism* he concluded that this group accidentally laid the foundations for the creation of capitalist values in Europe. They believed that through hard work people would receive signs from God suggesting that they were chosen to go to Heaven. They also thought that Catholic groups were too decadent, i.e. they spent too much money. This combination of hard work, seeking profit in business, and then re-investment into the business to avoid spending on personal luxury, created the capitalist values of profit-seeking and reinvestment. Weber explored these ideas by being able to 'get into the minds' of this historical group through their diaries.

A more contemporary use of life documents can be found in the ethnographic study by Valerie Hey (1997) *The Company She Keeps*. Hey was interested in exploring the ways in which school girls thought about and created friendship groups. She wanted to understand how gender and sexual identities were expressed and created through interaction and the sharing of thoughts and feelings amongst 'friends'. In order to explore this very personal issue, Hey used a mixture of methods including participant observation, interviews and the collection of notes passed between girls in lessons behind the teachers' backs. Hey suggests that these notes were important as they were the physical expression of how the girls tried to explore and think about sexuality, gender, being a girl and friendship (these were the most common themes found in the notes). In order to be able to collect these data Hey had to gain the trust and friendship of the girls, and even swapped her own personal diaries in order to share thoughts and feelings.

Secret notes might make interesting life documents.

✎ Coursework Suggestion

You can use life documents to investigate school-children's thoughts about school. Use diaries, graffiti and classroom notes to see what images of life at school children have. What are their concerns? What themes can you identity? How will you collect your data?

For consideration:

1 How useful do you think using life documents are?
2 Do you think life documents really tell us anything? Are they just meaningless or are they important pieces of data?

2.13 Is sociology a science?

Is it realistic to think of sociology as a science in the same way as we think of chemistry and physics?

What does this mean?

The philosopher Paul Feyerabend (1993) argues that there is simply no agreed method that research follows, despite what sociologists and scientists might tell you. Most of the time, research is about solving unexpected problems and rarely ever goes smoothly or according to plan. This means that our search for the 'truth' of society is solely dependent upon the methods we use in the first place; what we find out is a product of how we look, and where we go looking. As long as we recognise this, and as long as we are open about what we did and how we did it, then this is all that matters.

The science of sociology?

The question 'Is sociology a science?' is a long running debate in sociology. There are a number of opinions on this issue:

- Sociology is a science. It can test theories and create laws, and it can seek to uncover **causal relationships**. This view is associated with sociological positivism.

- Sociology cannot be a science because the subject matter of sociology, humans, is very different from the natural world of matter and gases etc. Humans have consciousness and as such they cannot be generalised about. Phenomenologists tend to hold this view.

- Sociology should try and be scientific since science is the best form of knowledge. However, it is impossible for sociology to be so as it tends to simply prove its theories right, and it is reluctant to reject its ideas in the face of the evidence. This view is held by the positivist Karl Popper who argues that sociology is not a science because it does not falsify (reject) theories and seek to disprove them (see section 18).

- Sociology should not be a science as science is a masculinist form of knowledge concerned with categorisation and generalisation, not with trying to understand people (and in particular women) and in doing so, help them and their life situation. This is a feminist view; feminists often reject science as being **malestream**.

- Sociology can be considered scientific, but it depends on what you mean by the idea of science in the first place. Sociology provides a method of choosing between theories by matching theories to evidence and research. As long as research allows you to test theories against each other and it is done in a systematic way, then sociology can be scientific. This is a **realist** position.

Do scientific facts actually exist?

For positivists, scientific sociology is about finding laws, patterns and generalisations. This is done in a detached or value-free way (see section 18). The sociologist is often seen as a detective, seeking to uncover trends and relationships, but one who tests ideas fairly and is not involved with those being studied.

Many sociologists have criticised this positivist approach. For example, phenomenologist or interpretive sociologists argue that facts that cause others things to happen do not exist in society, and they cannot be studied as if they are external to the people in society. Instead, what exists in society are simply ideas which we have as people in the first place. Therefore, it is nonsense to seek causality as if it is separate from people. People think about life and come up with the ideas that we think are 'real' in the first place. Therefore, we should give up macro ideas of generalisation and prediction and concentrate on describing what people make of their own actions, thoughts and their feelings.

A recent, popular view, is that of postmodernism, which argues that the idea that sociology should be a science, and even the idea that being 'scientific' is somehow of value, is a left over idea of a past age. This view says that claims of science being able to seek out a 'truth' that is absolute is a false idea. There are many truths, many viewpoints, and it is impossible to point to one explanation for things happening in society and say that this is the only real reason. If we agree with this idea, the question is what is there left to do? Why do research at all, if its just a matter of interpretation and opinion?

Key Definition

Realism is the view that sociology can be a science, but only if this means finding ways to test theories against each other. Realists argue that there are real, unseen structures that shape society, but action must be studied as this is what we see. They see sociology as an open system science, i.e. society is unpredictable so generalisations and certainties are difficult to create.

For consideration:

1   If postmodernists are right, and there are no 'facts' then what is the point of research and what is the aim of sociology?
2   Why do you think the debate on whether sociology is a science is so popular for sociologists?

2.14 Is sociology value-free?

What does this mean?

If a sociologist (or anyone) is 'value-free' it means, quite literally, being free from values, views or beliefs. A more detailed, sociological way of saying this would be to say that they would not allow their views and beliefs to alter or affect the research they do. So, being value-free is the same as making sure your research is as unbiased as possible.

If your research is not value-free, your results may be incorrect. The whole point of sociology is to try and uncover or get to the reality of social life. You cannot do this if you are not sure that the results of your research are true and genuine.

Types of values

There are different types of values and beliefs that might affect a sociologist when they do their research:

- Personal values: these are the beliefs you have as an individual; beliefs and ideas that are special to you.

- Cultural values: these are the norms and values you have as a member of society. They might affect how you see your results and even what you think might be worth studying in the first place.

- Political values: many sociological theories are based on political views. They are either left wing (e.g. Marxism) or right wing (e.g. functionalism).

- Academic values: sociology has its fashion and trends just like anything else. Things popular to study in sociology today are different from the past, and will be different again in the future. The sociologist will probably try and fit in with the current trends of sociology, otherwise they may not be funded.

- Research values: as a sociologist you might have a personal preference for a particular method over another. Alternatively, you might belong to a group of researchers who all favour a particular approach that you would then need to follow.

As you can see, there are many types of values to try and be free from and this clearly makes it very difficult to undertake objective research. The image of research as being true and correct is not always valid as there are many influences upon research. There is a belief in our society that science is always right as it is based on research and it tests its ideas. However, how do we know that such research is value-free?

Sociologists have particular problems in trying to be value-free, more so than natural scientists such as chemists, since sociologists are part of the thing they are studying. Sociologists seek to understand society, yet they are members of that society. This makes it hard to be objective, detached or distanced from the values of the culture they were socialised into.

Is it possible to be value-free?

All sociologists want those who do research to be honest about their results. Personal values and cultural values concern sociologists the most. This is because they are often hidden. We can see the methods sociologists may have chosen, and if different sociologists use different methods, this gives us a variety of results to compare. However, the reasons behind why the topic was chosen in the first place, and how and why the research ignores some results and interprets others changes what the research means, but it is a process that is hidden from us.

Conclusion

Howard Becker in an essay called *Whose side are you on*? argued that sociologists should give up the idea of trying to be neutral, and instead should try and actually help the disadvantaged in society. He says we should 'side with the underdog' as he feels sociology should help those who lack power. This view has been adopted by those who follow the theories of Marxism and feminism. They seek to identify who the disadvantaged are and to support them. This is clearly not value-free research.

For consideration:

1 Do you think it is possible to be totally value-free in research?
2 Why do you think many sociologists would want to be seen as being value-free?

✓ **Top Exam Hint**

It is a good idea to focus on practical issues when trying to evaluate sociological research. For example, with the issue of value-free research you might say that the practicalities of doing research would get in the way of avoiding unbiased results. Time, money, resources, etc. might all affect what you choose to do and how you do it. Equally, those who pay for your research might wish for a particular result to be 'found' and there might be pressure on the sociologist to agree with those who pay their wages.

✳ **Key Idea**

Max Weber suggests that values come into play the most when the sociologist tries to identify what to study in the first place, and at the end of research when they try and figure out what it all means; to interpret their results. He suggests that all we can do is to announce clearly at the start of our research what our personal values or views might be, and be open about these.

✎ **Coursework Suggestion**

Think about the issue of value-free research when you do coursework. It is a good way of evaluating sources and is vital for good marks.

What ethical problems do sociologists face?

What does this mean?

Ethical problems in research are problems of morality, where the sociologist doing the research potentially violates or breaks people's trust or affects them through the research in some way. Examples of ethical problems include the following:

- Lying to gain access to people to include in research.
- Not telling the truth about the research you are conducting. This is particularly true for covert research where the sociologist is 'undercover'.
- Putting those you study at personal risk and harm.
- Causing upset and emotional trauma.

Ethical problems are more serious than sensitive issues. For example, a sensitivity problem might involve asking people personal questions that may upset them, whereas an ethical problem would be putting people in danger, or exposing someone's private life to their family.

The problem with informed consent

Sociology would not be possible without people to study as it is the study of society. If society is unwilling to be studied, or if society ends up not trusting sociologists, then damage has been done, to society and to the aims and goals of sociology. The BSA suggests that all research wherever possible should be conducted with informed consent, and those involved in research should:

- Choose freely to be involved.
- Not be harmed in any way.
- Have their privacy respected.
- Understand what they are volunteering for.
- Understand they can say 'no' at anytime.
- Understand what the point of the research is.

The problem with this is that sometimes, by knowing you are being studied, you might behave very differently. This creates a real tension in research; having to inform people what you are doing will contradict with not letting them know so you can obtain the 'truth'.

Do we have the right to know?

The problem with ethics in sociology is that sociologists are self-appointed searchers for the truth. Someone usually funds research, and sometimes charities and the government might ask a sociologist to find something out for them, but society as a whole has not asked the sociologist. You have chosen to study sociology, but why should this give you the right to uncover people's personal and private lives? Why should you be allowed to pry? Do you have the right to find out what you want to know?

✓ **Top Exam Hint**

Discuss ethical issues in order to evaluate any research that uses covert methods such as observation. This will help you to score evaluation marks in the exam.

✍ **Coursework Suggestion**

Make sure you include a discussion on ethical issues when you do coursework. Think about the idea of informed consent. How will you manage this?

Covert research methods have particularly been criticised for their lack of ethical consideration. To find out some things, sociologists might have to ensure that those being studied do not know about it, to gather the clearest data. But is this morally right? Why should someone use other people (without asking) in order to further their own career? Sociologists who use covert methods respond by arguing that sociology makes a positive contribution to the knowledge society has about itself, and therefore as long as anonymity is maintained the ends justify the means.

Other sociologists suggest that if informed consent is not present at the start of a study, then a full de-brief should be present at the end. But is this good enough or has the damage been done already?

What do you think?

Consider the following study, published in 1970, by American researcher Laud Humphreys. Humphreys conducted an infamous study that created a lot of press attention at the time called *The Tea Room Trade*. 'Tea-room' was, at the time, a sub-cultural word used by gay men to refer to the public toilets where gay men would meet each other and engage in sexual activity. At the time, homosexual acts were illegal in the USA. Humphreys covertly studied these activities, at the same time taking on the role of the 'watch-queen', the lookout in case the men got caught. He also noted the men's car number plates, managed to find out where they lived, followed them home, interviewed them on the pretence of it being about something else and published his study.

There were a number of different responses to this research:

- Humphreys gave a voice to people whose sexuality was illegal and in doing so, raised attention to this discrimination.
- Humphreys should not have lied to these people since he was studying them breaking the law.
- Humphreys should not have taken it on himself to help these people, they did not ask him.
- Kimmel says about Humphreys' research 'the research was applauded by members of the gay community and some social scientists for shedding light on a little known segment of society, and for dispelling stereotypes and myths'.
- Warwick says about Humphreys' research 'social research involving deception and manipulation ultimately helps produce a society of cynics, liars and manipulators, and undermines the trust which is essential to a just social order'.

Do you think Humphreys conducted his research in an ethical way?

For consideration:

1 Why might ethical problems affect research that is more qualitative than quantitative?
2 Do sociologists really have the right to find out? Should covert methods ever be used?

2.16 What is sampling and why is it important?

How are people selected to take part in research?

What does this mean?

Sampling is the process of selecting those who you will study in your research. The **sample** refers to the selection of people who actually take part, and is seen to represent those in the rest of society who share the same characteristics as those selected to study. Everyone else not studied but to whom the research will apply, are called the **relevant population**.

Sampling occurs because sociologists simply cannot study everyone. They need to make choices as to who to look at, how many people to study and how long the research will actually take. The size and type of the sample will depend on a number of factors such as the following:

- How long the research might take.

- How much funding the research has.

- Whether interviewers/deliverers of questionnaires need to be trained and paid or if the sociologist is going to have to see every person in the sample themselves.

- The method used; questionnaires can be delivered to many more people than in-depth interviews can in the same period. However, questionnaires may have a much higher **non-response** rate than interviews.

- Whether the sociologist wishes to generalise or not.

- Whether qualitative or quantitative data are being collected. If quantitative data are required then the sample size is usually much larger, as generalisation is being attempted.

Sampling methods

- Simple random sampling: in this method, everyone has an equal chance of getting asked/involved in the research. For example, names are chosen at random from a **sampling frame**, maybe by a computer program that is designed to generate random numbers.

- Systematic sampling: in this method a sampling frame is used, and names are chosen at regular intervals, for example, every tenth name.

- Quota sampling: this is when people are selected according to specific characteristics they have, but the way they actually get chosen is still random. For example, you might need 10 males under the age of 30 and 10 females under the age of 30. Often the amount of people studied in each category (each quota) represents the amount of that type of person there is in the relevant population in the first place.

- Stratified random sampling: this method divides people from the relevant population into layers or groups, and then specific names are chosen. Like quota sampling people are put into categories, but like systematic sampling, actual individuals are identified, rather than being selected randomly.

- Snowballing sampling: this method is usually favoured by qualitative sociologists who are not trying to generalise or to have a representative sample. It refers to the way that if you roll a snowball down a hill it gets bigger and bigger as time goes on. In this method, each respondent introduces you to another, and so the sample gets bigger. This is useful if you need access to a difficult group, or if you are researching a sensitive issue where you need to build up trust and personal relationships. This is a 'self-selected sample' which means that people volunteer.

Conclusion

Sampling is important for quantitative sociologists so that generalisations can be made. Clearly, the whole of the relevant population cannot always be studied, and research is usually limited by time and funding. The process of sampling makes the collection of meaningful data manageable, and more data can be collected on less people because you have time to do so. If a sociologist is going to generalise from their sample, then standardisation of the method is important, i.e. the same questions must be asked to the same sorts of people in the same way, otherwise comparisons will not be possible.

For consideration:

1 Why is sampling important in research?
2 Why is generalisation more important for quantitative research?

⁑ Key Idea

Sometimes, if sampling goes wrong, you might have an unrepresentative sample that does not represent the relevant population. When this happens, any generalisations you make may be incorrect, as those you have studied are not like those you want them to represent. This is a problem for random sampling and for self-selected samples.

How much personal involvement is there in research?

What does this mean?

We can think of sociology as one of two extremes:

1   Sociologists should be experts, detached from personal involvement in those they study

2   Sociologists need to get involved to be able to truly explore what people think.

Some argue that the sociologist must get involved personally with those they study, in order to be able to build up the sorts of relationships needed to explore in-depth what people think. This argument is often used by feminists who argue that qualitative methods allow female researchers to build-up bonds with female respondents. For example, Ann Oakley (1999) states that involvement is necessary to develop the bond of trust '…personal involvement is more than a dangerous bias – it is the condition under which people come to know each other and admit each other to their lives'.

Feminists feel that so-called 'detached' methods are masculinist, i.e. too clinical, and involve the researcher acting as an expert having power over those they study. Many interpretative researchers and feminists wish to **empower** those they study.

In the study *The Company She Keeps* Valerie Hey (1997) built up bonds of friendship with the school girls she studied that went beyond the traditional researcher-respondent relationship (see section 12). She visited their houses, and they visited hers, she went out with them at the weekend and exchanged notes and personal letters with them to explore each others' feelings. She even skipped school with them. The point of her research was to explore what being at school and making friends meant to these girls. Hey judged that in order to best do this, she would need to develop close relationships with the girls.

Personal experience and research

Sometimes the decision to start a piece of research is due to personal involvement, or a personal experience. Some sociologists argue that this enables the researcher to explore in detail an aspect of society that allows us to develop a detailed understanding of people's emotions, thoughts and feelings by being able to identify with those we study.

66 99 Key Definition

Empowerment means making the process and experience of being involved in research beneficial to those taking part. This is called 'action' research and is associated with qualitative methods, where those being studied, by reflecting on their lives, are moved forward in their lives from where they started.

Others ague that this makes us too involved in the research, and not detached enough to be able to 'step back'. Potentially this can make the research biased, and the observations and conclusions from the research may be suspect. They may be a fair reflection of reality, but they may be the sociologists' personal view.

An example of research that was triggered by a personal experience is the book *The Making of Men* by Mairtin Mac an Ghaill (1994). This study was ethnographic, exploring how male gender identity was created by boys in school, and the role heterosexuality, homosexuality and homophobia played in the creation of these identities. The study opens with a description of an experience Mac an Ghaill was involved in.

Early on in his teaching career, prior to becoming a researcher, Mac an Ghaill worked at a school where a pupil gave him flowers as a present in the way that pupils often do to thank teachers after exams. The difference in this case was that it was a male pupil giving flowers to a male teacher. Having seen this, some of the other pupils in the school bullied the pupil and this resulted in a fight. Mac an Ghaill was called into the head-teacher's office to explain his role in this situation. It turned out that the head-teacher knew nothing of the fight, he was telling off Mac an Ghaill for receiving the flowers. The fight was ignored. This led Mac an Ghaill to conclude that schools are heterosexual institutions and that they allow homophobia to develop. This incident led him to consider issues of masculinity, sexuality and homophobia. He may not have conducted this research if it was not for this personal experience.

Quantitative (positivist) sociologists would be critical of using personal experiences in research. They would argue that if the researcher is not detached from the study, then their ability to see the facts will be clouded. However, what positivists say, and what actually happens can be very different. For example, Durkheim is considered to be a 'scientific' sociologist; detached and value-free. His study on suicide (1897) is often presented as a scientific study, as it deals with facts in a detached fashion. He even says in the introduction that his study will make people see sociology as a true science. He might have been detached, but what he does not tell us is that a close personal friend of his committed suicide just prior to him making the decision to carry out the study. So, how detached and scientific was he?

✍ Coursework Suggestion

In your coursework, think about how personally involved you might get with those you study. Is it a good thing or not? Does it aid research, or get in the way? If you discuss these issues you will gain evaluation marks.

For consideration:

1 Should sociologists be allowed to draw on personal experience in research?
2 How attached should sociologists become to those they study?

2.18 What is positivism?

What does this mean?

Positivists are sociologists who believe that sociology is a science. They produce quantitative data and seek generalisation from these data. It is usually seen as the opposite of the interpretive approach that focuses on individual meaning rather than on external facts that are seen to affect how society works, creating patterns and trends that can be analysed over time.

Positivism is first credited to have started with Auguste Comte and then later, with his student, Durkheim. For Comte, writing during the Industrial Revolution in Europe, as societies progress, the basis for knowledge used in society changes. He believed in a 'law of three stages':

- Stage 1: the theological stage where knowledge is based on magic and superstition.

- Stage 2: the metaphysical stage where knowledge is based on the belief in abstract forces that might shape the world, i.e. the idea of gravity; we can not see it, but it has a measurable effect. This second stage is a criticism of the first type of knowledge and represents the rise of early science.

- Stage 3: the final stage is a continuation of the second; the rise of scientific thinking. This means it is not a negative development, but it is 'positive' hence positivism.

How does positivism work?

Positivists today try to undertake the following:

- Produce quantitative data.

- Generalise from findings, looking at patterns and trends.

- Seek laws.

- Be 'value-free'.

- Prove or disprove hypotheses.

- Believe facts exist and the process of research is to uncover the facts that are 'out there'.

- Ignore the small-scale world of people's thoughts and feelings which they feel are unable to be measured in a reliable fashion.

- Make sure their findings are representative of those in society they are studying.

Auguste Comte (1798–1857)

☞ Who is this Person?

Auguste Comte, the French philosopher usually credited with coining the term 'sociology' was originally going to call this new subject 'social physics' in order to emphasise its scientific nature.

❝❞ Key Definition

Positivists are sociologists who believe that there is 'a single common method that all scientific subjects follow'. Positivism is the belief, therefore, that in sociology, the social world can be studied with the same approach we might use to study the natural world.

◆ What, When and Why?

Positivism had its origins in the Industrial Revolution in Europe in the late 1800s and is very much a product of its time. During the Industrial Revolution many thinkers came to believe that science was the solution to all of humankind's problems. Science would be able to predict and solve the governing of society. Comte stated that sociology was both a way of measuring the world, and a way to control it. He thought that social scientists would run society as they were best placed to understand what was happening in it.

We call positivism a scientific approach to sociology as it is concerned with approaching research in a systematic way. Positivists have a clearly identifiable approach to research that seeks to test ideas and be value-free, just like scientists.

Positivists use methods that allow for the collection of large amounts of data, but with limited personal involvement on behalf of the researcher with those being studied. They believe that in this way trends can be identified, but that the research will be detached from their own values. For example, questionnaires might be given to thousands of people all over the country and the same questions allow easy comparisons. Interviews are also used, but they would have to be highly structured to allow for a standard set of questions to be asked.

Conclusion

The word 'science' (associated with positivism) might at first seem simple to understand, but sociology has tried to show that science is a very powerful idea. If you can claim that something is scientific in today's world, then lots of people will believe you. Science has what we call a powerful legitimisation claim. This might be one reason why the 'is sociology a science' debate is so important to some sociologists; if your subject is seen as a science it might make people believe you more.

For consideration:

1   Why might sociologists wish to be seen as scientific?
2   How would you criticise the idea that we can apply scientific methods to the study of humans?

What is interpretive sociology?

George Herbert Mead (1863–1931)

☞ Who is this Person?

American philosopher, George Herbert Mead was one of the key founders of interpretive sociology.

✍ Coursework Suggestion

Try to follow the interpretive approach in your coursework. You could adopt the aim of developing *verstehen* and use an in-depth interview technique to do this. Like all interpretivists you would be trying to understand how people themselves understand their life.

What does this mean?

Interpretivism is one of the many names given to the micro approach to sociology. This micro approach determines how sociologists think about what society is (theory) and how they might try and find out about society through research (methods). Other names associated with this view are interactionism, symbolic interactionism and phenomenology. The key point behind this view is that the social world is not seen to exist as a 'thing' having independence from humans and shaping their actions, but instead, society is the sum of the interactions between those who make-up society. All such interactional encounters are motivated by thought, meanings and motives. Therefore, in order to study society from this viewpoint, we should seek to try and understand how people think and how they see themselves. We can then interpret their actions and make sense of the situations they find themselves in.

How does interpretivism work?

Interpretivism is often seen as the complete opposite of positivism. Interpretive sociology is anti-scientific in the sense that it wishes to explore in detail people's feelings and emotions rather than trying to explore large-scale laws, patterns, generalisations and causality. One of the original sources of the interpretive view is the notion of *verstehen* used by founder Max Weber. This is the idea that the aim of research is to see the world through the eyes of those involved. This approach is highly qualitative and it tries to be valid rather than reliable (see section 1). It deals with depth and detail; words, quotes and observations rather than numbers.

Interpretivism recommends the use of techniques that provide ways of getting people to open up and to explore what they do, and why they think they do it. Researchers use semi-structured and unstructured interviews, focus groups and observational methods. The method most associated with this view is that of participant observation where the researcher joins in with the 'real life' activities of a group (either openly or in secret) in order to try and achieve a degree of empathy, i.e. to try and understand how groups work and how they interact with each other.

Interpretive sociology criticises the positivist approach for seeing patterns that do not exist. For example, positivists, because of their use of statistical data would argue that large-scale data provide us with patterns and trends that give us an understanding of how society as a whole works.

These statistics provide us with an insight into social facts, i.e. truths about society. On the other hand, the interpretive view suggests that these so-called facts are really the made-up **social constructions** of those who put the statistics together in the first place. They do not reflect reality, but might come, in time, to be seen as reality. These facts are really human-made. They are highly selective and the product of people using their meanings in the first place, e.g. sociologists writing questionnaires, governments choosing what statistics to look at and publish and people filling in questionnaires when stopped on the street. Instead, interpretive sociologists look at how people behave.

Is interpretivism better than positivism?

This is an unanswerable question. Both approaches do very different things and are therefore both very useful. Many sociologists today combine both approaches together.

Conclusion

The strength of the micro approach in sociology is to focus our research on the small and 'ordinary' things in life – the ordinary ways in which ordinary people go about their lives. This is often missed by the more macro approach.

For consideration:

1   What do you think are the main strengths of the interpretivist approach?
2   Which do you favour, interpretivism or positivism and why?

66 99 Key Definition

Social construction is is an interpretive word meaning the way in which society is created by people and their thoughts and culture. Things that appear real are only real because society says so.

✓ **Top Exam Hint**

Although textbooks present positivism and interpretive sociology as total opposites it is important to remember that many sociologists combine both approaches together (see section 3). The reality of current research is that people do interesting and exciting research in a structured way. They do not necessarily follow a trend or a narrow position.

What is the link between theory and methods?

What does this mean?

Theories are ideas that we have, ways of thinking about the world and society around us, whereas methods are the ways we go about collecting evidence or data. Methods are used to do the actual research in order to test if theories are correct or not. In this sense, both are important, we cannot really have one without the other:

- Theory with no methods means we have not tested our ideas and assumptions. How do we know if our theory is correct? How do we know if our image of the world is true or not? Are we just choosing theories because they are our favourites, not because we can find evidence to support them?

- Methods with no theory behind them become an exercise in collecting data for no real reason and not being able to do anything with it.

Which comes first, theory or method?

- Some sociologists who adopt an empiricist approach to research argue that we can do research without theory and that after collecting data the 'facts will speak for themselves'. In other words, data collection will point towards the theory and conclusions rather than needing them first.

- More sociologists adopt a position called rationalism. This means that we think about social life first, come up with theories and then we test them with research.

Some have suggested that it is impossible to collect data without some sort of theory. It is impossible to be so detached and value-free that we can simply go out and find facts. All research is directed in some way, from the questions asked to those who get chosen to take part. This means there must be something guiding research, some idea of what is interesting to look at, or some idea of what the researcher might wish to find out. Therefore, theory will exist before the method in this case.

Testing theories

Karl Popper argued that research should take place through a twin-process of what he calls **conjecture** and **refutation**:

Sir Karl Popper (1902–1994)

☞ Who is this Person?

Karl Popper was born in Vienna in 1902. A famous philosopher and positivist, he was a Marxist in terms of his political views. He invented the idea of **falsification**, the idea that we can only prove things wrong, allowing us to reject theories. Popper was very critical of both Marxism and sociology claiming they were unscientific since they never tried to genuinely test their theories, but held on to them as if they were untestable truths. He was knighted while resident in the UK in 1965 and was professor of Logic and Scientific Method at the London School of Economics. He died in 1994.

66 99 Key Definitions

- **Falsification** is, according to Popper, the process of proving ideas and theories wrong. Popper uses the example of the hypothesis 'all swans are white'. We could never prove that this is true because how many observations are enough? Even if we saw 100 or 1000 swans, we could never say for certain that the next one will also be white.

- **Conjecture** and **refutation** is the twin process of creating a theory to test and then trying to prove the theory wrong.

- First, an idea or theory is devised. This is a conjecture, i.e. making interesting and bold statements to then test.

- Second, you should seek to test the ideas and try and prove them wrong (refute them). This is because, Popper argues, you can only ever say for certain that 'so far you have found something out'. You can never for certain ever say 'this is always true' because you never know what the next test might show.

In this way, it does not matter where the theory originally comes from or even how biased it might be as if it is wrong you have to say so. This will still help your research, because knowing something is not true is still knowledge. The methods allow us to test theories and to discard them away if we need to.

Macro or micro?

Traditionally, sociologists have adopted either a way of looking at society on a large-scale (macro) or a way of looking on a much smaller-scale (micro). The theory adopted then directly influences the methods chosen. For example, those who wish to study the whole of the social structure, the way society links together as a whole unit, would use large-scale methods that produce quantitative data. Those who are interested in the small-scale level of individual actions and in trying to explain what and how people think would wish to adopt micro methods that produce qualitative data such as interviews and observation. In this way, the type of theory and the approach the sociologist uses to understand what is real in society links directly to the methods used to find out about social life.

It could also be the case that rather than theory influencing methods, methods may influence theory. For example, for some, only methods that give power to the individual to express themselves should be used in sociology as this is more humane and ethical. We should not see research as something we do to people, but as something they join in with in an active fashion. If you think this, as many feminist sociologists do, then you are drawn to a very micro set of methods, which in turn will shape what you can and cannot actually find out. This will then ultimately affect the theory you adopt.

A great deal of research today mixes both macro and micro approaches. In these cases, the links between theories and methods are still there, but can be much more open than the rigid and rather unrealistic macro/micro divide of traditional sociology.

For consideration:

1 Do you agree that facts can speak for themselves without theory to direct research? Explain your view.
2 Why might the traditional link between theory and methods be limiting for sociologists?

How has sociological research changed over time?

What does this mean?

Like everything else, sociology has its fashions and fads. It changes and evolves over time, and the ways of doing social research also change. Different techniques and issues popular at one particular time will be replaced with other ideas over time.

Late 19th century

When sociology was developed by Comte as a distinctive way of seeing the world, it was associated with the ideas Comte himself had on positivism. This was a very macro, very scientific approach. General laws about human behaviour were made. This is the same image that Durkheim held in his classic study on suicide (1897). Sociology was seen as a means by which the truth about the whole of society could be uncovered.

Early 20th century

The ideas of Weber on *verstehen* sociology were first developed in the early 1900s, but became popular in sociology during the 1920s when taken up by the Chicago School, a group of sociologists associated with the more interpretive approach. This change from macro sociology to micro sociology has developed a key debate within modern-day sociology, and a debate that still exists today: what is the best type of data to produce? What are the most useful techniques to use to understand society?

The ideas associated with the Chicago School, the use of participant observation in particular and their view of people as active and creative, seeking the meaning of their actions, challenged the previously dominant macro approach of early sociology. These views claimed that sociology is not value-free and not scientific. Instead, the sociologist is part of what they study, and seeks to try and explore how people make sense of what they do

Late 20th century

Since the 1960s and 1970s the aims of positivist sociologists became significantly different from the early positivism associated with Comte

◆ What, When and Why?

When sociology was first invented it was heavily scientific in nature. It was believed that sociologists could obtain absolute truth and that facts could be established about the social world. Since this time, many sociologists have questioned the ability for anyone doing any sort of research to be able to certainly say that facts exist.

✳ Key Idea

The Chicago School are closely associated with the development of both the theory of symbolic interactionism, and the use of the method of participant observation. As the name suggests, the Chicago school was the sociology department at Chicago University in the USA in the 1920s. It was heavily influenced by the ideas of Max Weber on *verstehen*, plus it was the first official English speaking sociology department in the world. The aim of the Chicago School was to use the local micro environment as a tool for research; to study how the city worked and how its people lived their day-to-day lives. In doing this the School pioneered the development of micro methods, and also made some major contributions to the subject of geography; in particular the idea that cities are based upon a series of concentric circles of land use.

and Durkheim. Rather than seeking absolute 'truths' or general laws of society, the aims of quantitative sociologists today are much less absolute. Many seek to produce statistical overviews and to seek causality, in other words to try and find a connection between two variables, such as class and health. This is called a **correlation**, where two or more things have a relationship to each other that can be identified. This is usually the point of those pieces of research that try and use quantitative methods such as questionnaires.

Feminists have greatly contributed to the methods debate in modern times. Feminists have tended to adopt more qualitative approaches in social research as they see these as not being 'masculinist' in the ways that quantitative methods are. Feminists have argued that quantitative methods objectify the research participants, i.e. take advantage of people and then throw them to one side once they are finished with.

Most modern sociologists are not interested in the macro/micro divide. Researchers are interested in ways that they might combine both quantitative and qualitative methods together, using them to support each other's findings. Modern sociology is also less scientific than that of the founders. Definitions of what science is and how it works are continuously changing over time. For example, realists argue that sociology can be scientific, but only in the sense that theories can be combined together and can be tested; not in that absolutes can be established. Another trend that realists often adopt is 'grounded theory': the idea that theories can come from research data, but through using these data we can locate or 'ground' what sociologists find in the ideas and reality of people themselves.

Conclusion

In all, much research today is about practical considerations. Research is about problem solving; how can sociologists get the data they need? What methods are the best? Remember, there is no such thing as a perfect method, it depends what you do, and how you do it.

For consideration:

1   Why do you think sociological ideas change over time?
2   Why might it be important to know the time that an idea was popular?

66 99 Key Definition

Correlation means the degree of relationship between two variables.

How and why do some sociologists mix methods together?

✳ Key Idea

Methodological pluralism is the term we use to describe mixing methods. These methods could produce both quantitative or qualitative data or could both produce the same type of data. Alternatively, you might mix both primary and secondary sources or have a main method and then a secondary method that you can use to test the first.

Paul Willis

☞ Who is this Person?

In his classic study Learning to Labour (1977), Paul Willis mixed a number of methods together in order to understand what it meant to be a working-class boy in an education system set-up to disadvantage you in the future.

66 99 Key Definition

Ethnography is an approach to sociological research that concentrates on the collection of small-scale data through a number of qualitative techniques. These allow the researcher to understand what it means to be a member of a small group, usually a sub cultural group. It is used to try and allow the researcher to fully 'submerge' themselves within the strange new world they are studying, yet unlike covert participant observation, it still allows the researcher to ask questions from the viewpoint of someone who is an outsider, trying to understand enough to become an insider.

What does this mean?

For many modern-day sociologists, the traditional divide between being either a positivist or an interpretivist is not realistic nor is it sensible. For many, good sociology, and good sociological research is simply that which works, that which gets meaningful results. Often, to get an interesting result, to find things out about society that you would not have known before, you have to adopt an interesting approach. Sometimes mixing methods (methodological pluralism) is the only way to get a fuller picture.

Examples of methodological pluralism

A classic example of a study that has combined methods together is Paul Willis' *Learning to Labour*, originally published in the late 1970s. Willis combined a number of qualitative methods together (observation and interviews). These methods, added within the method of 'hanging around' with people and groups (a much used approach to qualitative data gathering) is known as an **ethnographic** approach.

A more modern mixed approach that focuses upon the qualitative, is the research entitled *The Making of Men* by Mac an Ghaill (1994) (see section 17). He was interested in how a sense of masculine identity was created within schools, and to investigate this conducted a three year piece of research using daily observations at a school he worked at. He also used questionnaires and diaries, plus formal and informal group interviews with both pupils and staff at the school.

Is mixing methods a good idea?

French sociologist Pierre Bourdieu has suggested that ethnographic data collection is not enough on its own. We need to see the general trends (often presented as a series of statistics) and use the ethnographic data to explain what the statistics mean; how they were created, what they mean for ordinary people and their lives and how the broad trends operate in day-to-day practice.

It is dangerous to assume that mixing methods is always a good thing. It has become very fashionable in social research to mix methods, but like anything fashionable, you should do it because it is the best thing to do, not simply because everyone else is. A weak method and a poor research plan will still have their problems no matter how many methods you use. Mixing methods can have real benefits, but only if it is planned and thoroughly executed.

The reality of going out and getting data is often very different from the simple, neat and clean way in which methods are presented in textbooks. There are always problems, and the solution to the problem might take the researcher off in a very different direction to the original aim of the research. When mixing methods you might be led along very different paths, and the different methods might produce very different results to each other.

Conclusion

What happens if your different methods produce results that do not support each other, but actually contradict each other? The study *Negotiating Family Responsibility* by Finch and Mason (1993) starts with the view that the results you get are a product of the methods you use in the first place. This means that different methods will naturally produce different results, but this is fine as it allows us to compare results and account for the differences. In this case, research becomes about exploring the differences between data rather than simply having one viewpoint only.

For consideration:

1 Why should you not always use methodological pluralism?
2 How and why might research be different to the way it is presented in textbooks? What does this mean for how research actually happens?

Examination advice

This section provides some practical advice in order to get the best possible grade you can in your sociology exam.

Learn key terms and know when to use them

- In the AS exam, the first question will ask you to define a key term or concept and explain it. This means that you can arm yourself before you go into the exam with definitions of key concepts. Keep a key vocabulary dictionary throughout your course to help you to revise this aspect.

- Use key terms in longer exam answers, especially those at the very end of the exam (which you must leave enough time for). Using key terms adds important depth and detail to your answers and it demonstrated your knowledge to the examiner.

Evaluate sources critically

- Some key ideas in the methods topic area can link well to evaluative points you might like to make. For example, consider the following list:

  - Validity

  - Reliability

  - Representativeness

  - Malestream

  - Verstehen

  All these key ideas can be used to assess the worth of a piece of research or a study. If you can comment on each for a particular source you will be successfully evaluating the usefulness or success of the study.

- In any longer methods exam questions (and in your coursework as well) there are always assessments to be made about studies and methods regarding practical issues, ethical issues, theoretical issues and sensitivity issues (PETS) name these and try and use them.

- Every method has both strengths and weaknesses. Make sure that you always present both of these, this is an easy way to be more evaluative in your work.

- Value-freedom is an important debate within methods, and again, provides a way of evaluating a source. You might like to explore the extent to which a study might be value-free or not, and why this might be a problem. You could also look at how a particular method might present issues of value-freedom. You could link this to quantitative and qualitative methods; how do different methods that produce different types of data have different types of problems?

- Some methods raise ethical issues, especially the more qualitative methods based upon observation. Use these ethical issues as a way to think about whether sociologists have the right to do their research or not.

- You could evaluate a study by asking yourself the question 'What value has this study contributed to sociological knowledge?' In other words, why has a study been useful?

- Try to think about the 'influences' on research. These will help you to consider why a piece of research was done the way it was.

- Think about the relationship between theories and methods. What people do and how they do it is often a consequence of what they think about society in the first place.

Key points to remember

- Use PETS.

- Learn key words and key ideas relating to methods off by heart.

- Always think about both strengths and weaknesses of sources.

Pushing your grades up higher

This section provides some practical advice in order to get the best possible grade you can in your sociology exam.

✓ **Top Exam Hint**

Do not forget that methods and theories are always linked; you can discuss both in every topic in order to show how sociology really works.

🍵 **Thinking like a Sociologist**

In order to evaluate a source discuss the following key ideas in relation to it:

- Reliability
- Validity
- Representativeness.

1   Refer to methods used in other exam questions if you can make a link to the method in the source you are studying. If you know the research technique used in a particular study, you can make evaluative points about the findings of a study.

2   Use the idea of macro/micro sociology or positivism/phenomenology in exam questions on methods. Most research techniques, types of data, etc. can be related back to these opposite approaches to sociology, and by talking about them then you can achieve a more detailed answer.

3   Use the idea of malestream sociology in order to evaluate positivism and quantitative sociology from a feminist viewpoint. Feminists argue that quantitative sociology is masculinist as it is about facts and not about feelings. As such, feminists use micro methods since they are interested in supporting and respecting those they study.

4   Discuss the idea of *verstehen* when you discuss qualitative techniques. It is a very important idea and one that will allow you to analyse qualitative techniques in a clear and concise way.

5   Learn some case studies that will enable you to use them more than once in your exam. For example, if you learn about a particular study relating to Family and households about housework, learn about the methods used in the study as well, then you can use it in questions relating to both topics.

6   Learn a case study for every method possible and learn a list of strengths and weaknesses for each one.

7   For the A2 course you will be required to be synoptic; this means making lots of links between all the different topics. Talking about methods is an excellent way of doing this.

- Make sure you are able to describe the macro and micro traditions in-depth – you will probably use these in most exams.

- Make sure you can demonstrate that research is 'messy' – that there are lots of problems and the challenge of research is to find ways to solve these problems.

Key points to remember

- Learn the methods used in case studies for all topics.
- If possible discuss both positivism and phenomenology in your answers.
- Use the idea of malestream sociology as a good way to evaluate sources.

Frequently asked questions

Q. Why are methods so important?

A. Methods are vital to research. Without them we would have only theory, and no evidence. Methods allow sociologists to seek answers, whereas theories allow them to imagine what society might be like. Sociology is both a theoretical and an empirical discipline. It needs to undertake research in order to find out what society is really like, rather than taking for granted what others might tell us, or what we might have been socialised to believe.

Q. Should I try to discuss methods in all my exam answers?

A. Yes, if it is relevant. You must make sure that you answer the question you were originally asked, but methods are a good way of evaluating sources. You could question the usefulness of a method, or argue that a study is out of date so more research is needed. Also, you could say that generalisations are not possible from small-scale research. All these methods-related comments would help you to be more critical of the named examples and theories you learn in all topics in both the AS and A2 course. Discussing methods in the A2 exam will help you be synoptic, allowing you to pull all your sociology knowledge together.

Q. Which method is the best?

A. This is impossible to answer. It is important to remember that all methods have their strengths but also their weaknesses. Your choice of method depends on who and what you are studying, what data you wish to collect and also what type of theory you have. Some sociologists might have favoured methods, but they would only use them if the topic in question was relevant.

Research skills and methods

Family

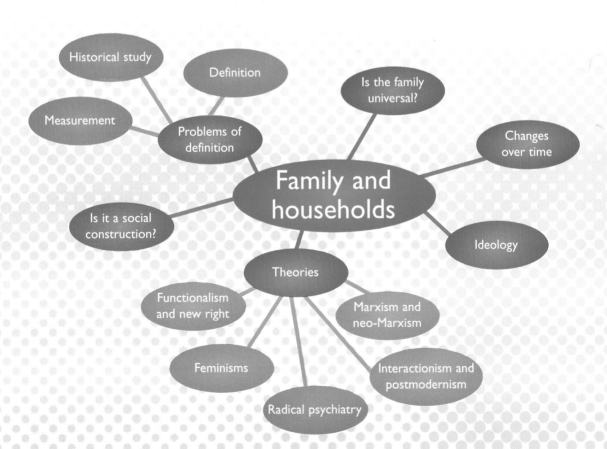

Key issues in family sociology

Why are sociologists interested in the family?

Sociologists are interested in the family since it is seen to be central to how society works. Families offer:

- socialisation of the norms and values of society
- an opportunity to develop self-identity
- an environment in which babies and young children can be protected and cared for.

Families are central to society, and therefore, they are central to sociology. Many issues that sociologists are interested in stem from or link to the family in different ways. For example:

- gender roles
- crime and violence
- inequality
- social control.

All these issues can link to the family; therefore this makes the family an important topic to think about. It is also the case that other aspects of society link to the family.

- Education might be affected in a positive or negative way by the family you live in.
- Your identity might be affected by how you are brought up.
- Crime might link to the family. Some families might expose children and young people to crime and criminal values more than others.
- Your family will be affected by the class you have – and your class will be initially given to you by your family!
- Your health will likewise be affected by your family's habits and their attitudes to money. Again, this is perhaps a product of class.

As we can see, therefore, most aspects of society can link to each other, yet the family is particularly central to these links.

What are the key debates in family sociology?

In terms of family sociology, the key debates we need to think about are:

- What problems do we have in defining the family?
- What does the media say about the family?
- What do politicians think about families?
- How have families changed over time?
- What are the problems with looking at the family in history?
- What do functionalists think about the family?
- What do Marxists think about the family?
- What do feminists think about the family?
- What do interpretive sociologists think about the family?
- Why is the family important for socialisation and social stability?
- What are the changing patterns of marriage and divorce today?
- Do families need fathers?
- Do we have family diversity?
- Will diversity lead to the breakdown of society?
- Does the family have a dark side?
- Do we have postmodern families?
- What might the future of the family be?
- Is childhood a social construction?

What are the key ideas and concepts in family sociology?

Sociologists are interested in how families have changed over time, and in how they affect those who live within them. They are also interested in what families do for society: how do families 'fit in' to the overall structure of society? What does 'the family' as an aspect of society do, and does the family do the same thing across all societies?

✓ **Top Exam Hint**

Try to show how the family fits into wider society. Show the links between the family and other aspects of sociology and society that you are studying. This way you can start to get depth in your answers.

● **Synoptic link**

If you can spell out the ways in which the family links with other aspects of society, then you are actually being 'synoptic'. You are demonstrating how different bits of society all join up and interrelate to each other.

✍ **Coursework Suggestion**

Many students choose family sociology as the basis for their coursework, either at AS or at A2. Don't forget that if you do choose family sociology then you should try and link what you do to other aspects of sociological study.

3.2 What do we need to find out about family sociology?

✓ Top Exam Hint

Use these bullet points as headings to help you to organise your notes and your revision.

✎ Coursework Suggestion

You could study the roles in the home, or between different ethnic groups as your A2 coursework project.

What does the specification say about the family?

We can break down the specification into the following ideas, which this chapter will look at.

- Changes in family life over time and the patterns of living they lead to

- Ways of thinking about different family types: ways of 'classifying' families to make comparisons and contrasts

- Family diversity

- Power and roles in the family

- What families do – for the individual and for the wider society

How will you be examined in this topic area?

You will have an exam which lasts one hour and 15 minutes, this will be the paper 1 topic. Like the paper 2 topic that you are studying, the questions will be linked to two source items and will increase in marks and in difficulty as the question paper goes on. The questions are worth 2, 4, 6, 8, 10 and 20 marks – the last two questions being longer response questions than the first four.

How well does this topic relate to coursework?

The family is a very popular topic for coursework. This is probably because as an AS exam subject it is one of the first pieces of sociology you will actually get to grips with, but secondly, since we all have families it gives us something real to focus upon. Remember, however, because we all have one, it might be very difficult to be detached when doing research – a real problem for all sociologists looking into this area.

How well does this topic help with synopticity?

In a sense, the family as a topic in sociology has the aspect of synopticity already built in. This is because, as mentioned in the previous section, the family is seen to play a central role in society, and therefore, also in sociology. We all have a family of one sort or another (depending upon the definition you might be using), and we are all able to recognise the importance of families in society. We all think about and maybe talk about our 'family' on a regular if not daily basis. The relationships we build with those in our family are vital, and they affect how we live our lives. Since we all go back home to our family each night, the family has a massive impact on our lives, and therefore has a massive impact upon all else that we do. In other words it is very synoptic.

What is important to try to remember is that the synoptic links that sociology encourages you to make can all be seen to impact from or impact on the family. In other words, the family can cause things to happen and to change in society, or can be influenced by society in the ways in which it is structured or made up.

- Culture – families give us our culture, yet their structure and 'type' is a product of our culture or sub-culture.

- **Socialisation** – families give us the most important socialisation of all, primary or early socialisation, yet in turn, we are socialised by society (and by the family) to believe that the family is the 'right' way to live!

- **Identity** – our 'identity', in other words, who we think we are is the product to a large extent of how we have been brought up, yet at the same time how we have been brought up will shape the sorts of relationships we make, and maybe even the sorts of family structures and patterns of living that we ourselves create when we have the chance to, later in life.

Whatever we do, the family is always there – behind the scenes, shaping our life, patterning society. Therefore, it is very important that we study it in sociology.

Key points to remember

- The family is a popular topic for coursework because it appears 'familiar' to us.

- The family is a really useful synoptic tool.

- Studying the family requires us to try very hard to give up our common-sense assumptions.

66 99 Key Definitions

- **Socialisation** means learning the norms and values of society.

- **Identity** is used in sociology to simply mean knowing who you are. The family is important in this process.

● Synoptic link

Try to use these concepts in your family exam for added depth.

How can we find out about the family?

As with all areas of sociological investigation, studying the family poses some general and some quite specific problems.

1   **General problems** – sociologists will need to make a very careful decision about what research method to choose, and what sample to create and this is true for all research. The sociologist will also need to make a decision about what type of data to produce, to create either quantitative or qualitative data, or maybe to somehow combine the two.

2   **Specific problems** – first, gaining access to families might be an issue. After all, if you think about it, most of our time spent in families is 'behind closed doors'. How can we gain access to this most private of all aspects of society? Another quite important problem is the fact that since family lives are very personal (if not the most personal) things in our life, we might not actually welcome sociologists questioning us about them. After all, how would you feel? This is an important point to remember when doing coursework if you have the opportunity. Do we as sociologists really have the right to know? Do we really have the right to pry?

As you can see, in some senses studying the family is simple – they are everywhere! Look out the windows of your house, go to the supermarket or the park; you will see families going about their lives and living their routines. But, at the same time, they are also very secret and very private!

How have sociologists tried to measure the family?

Through this chapter you will come to see that different sociologists have attempted either quantitative or qualitative measurements of the family and the sorts of things that families do.

*   **Quantitative family studies** – these often look at size or structure, and they often try to measure how family and marriage might change over time. There are, however, huge problems with historical records about the family. In the past, having children outside marriage was a serious act of deviance, and so records are often incorrect as families often covered such things up. Equally, although divorce has been legal for a long time, arguably, it is more socially acceptable today than before. Some families could therefore be considered 'empty-shell' families, that is, the family members stay together, but without a warm or close relationship.

✓ **Top Exam Hints**

*   Try to think about methods in relation to studies on the family. It is actually very difficult to study the family since it is so private. Give a sense of this in the exam for added evaluation marks.

*   Always try if you can to question the reliability and validity of quantitative secondary data. How do we know these 'facts' are true?

- **Qualitative family studies** – these often look at the feelings and emotions of those in family relationships. What does it mean to have the role of 'father' or 'mother'? How might different ethnicities and classes have very different experiences of family life? These studies try and achieve what we call '*verstehen*' i.e. they try and 'see the world through the eyes of those involved'.

What methods do sociologists tend to use to study the family?

Some methods are probably more appropriate than others when it comes to the family.

1 Covert (hidden or undercover) methods would be very difficult to use unless you were to study your own family. And, if you did that, you probably wouldn't be detached anyway – not a good idea for a sociologist.

2 Questionnaires could be used, but, as with all studies that produce quantitative data, these would not tell us much about what it would feel like to be a family member. Quite often, however, questionnaires are very useful if we want to study family size, or even to look at issues such as housework i.e. issues that involve adding things up, or measuring time spent doing things.

3 In order to understand the feelings of belonging to a family, many sociologists use the interview method. However, it is important that such interviews are conducted with great sensitivity and care.

What problems with definition are encountered in family sociology?

The fact of the matter is that the family is not actually a single, clearly identifiable thing. We all have one, we can all recognise them when we see them, but they are very different from one another – and certainly very different from the sorts of families we might see on TV, on advertisements. This is because there is such a wide variety of family types; we call this 'diversity'. It is very difficult to measure and study something that can't be easily defined. But, what is interesting is that this is only clear when you try and think about it. Before this, if someone said you to 'I don't know what a family is', you would probably think them silly. But now?

Key points to remember

- Like any topic, studying the family poses some specific problems for research.

- It is very difficult to clearly define the idea of a 'family'.

- Quantitative and qualitative studies of the family are very different.

What problems do we have in defining the family?

Why are there so many different types of family?

What does this mean?

Families are central to all that we do. From when you wake up to when you go to bed, you will probably have seen your family, or maybe tried hard not to see them, spoken about them or thought about them. Even if you haven't done this with your own family, you almost certainly will have seen someone else's, if not in real life, then maybe on TV. Go to the bus stop, the park and you will see families. Walk down an average road and behind all the closed doors will be whole families or parts of families, people who are family to each other and to others living elsewhere. They are an essential part of life – an essential part of living.

But what are they? This is a difficult question, since it asks us to really try as sociologists to take a step back, and to think about possibly the most obvious feature of social life in a fresh light. Think about the following questions:

* Are all families the same?

* Do families do the same things as each other?

* Do we all feel the same way about our roles and positions in our family?

* Does everyone like their family?

It is probably more useful to think about the family as a symbol, rather than as a real thing. It is obviously true that families are 'real' – you can see them after all. However, what you can actually see are people, and the reality of this thing called 'family' is in our and their heads: it is a symbol for a set of relationships and a series of interactions. It is a product of culture.

Is the family 'natural'?

This is a very important sociological argument, and one that causes great academic debate. Are humans the products of their upbringing, their culture, or are they the product of natural genetic pre-programmed chemical responses?

1 Sociologists in the main feel that that what humans do is down to 'nurture', that is, we are the products of the environment we live in and the culture into which we have been born. At its most extreme, this view sees humans almost as 'blank sheets of paper' upon which our culture (and in particular our language) writes. We are not born who

we are, we are born with the potential to become whatever we are brought up to be. When applied to the family this viewpoint argues that families are created by culture, and this is why there are so many different types, and also why different cultures around the globe 'do' family life in a wide variety of ways.

2   The opposite view to the nurture view is that of **sociobiology** which holds that it is not nurture that shapes us but 'nature'. When applied to the family this view asserts that it is natural to want to live in the thing we call 'family'. Sociobiologists Tiger and Fox (1972) suggest that humans are pre-programmed to form family relationships; there is something within our natural make-up that directs us towards certain patterns and ways of living. TV documentary-maker Desmond Morris (1968) also argued in his book and TV series 'The Naked Ape' that humans create cultures based upon the natural responses and urges they have. There might be cultural diversity in the ways in which we live, but the needs and desires we have are all located in our genetic make-up, directing the path our lives take as a species. We are basically apes without fur – naked apes, that can create and develop new ways of living, but they are always locked into or based upon natural patterns of biological need.

What is the family?

If we think about the family as a 'symbol', then it might help to see the family as an '**imagined community**'. This means that it is a set of abstract relationships that we learn through socialisation and that take on meaning for us as we develop the skills to understand and to use language to describe our surroundings and our thoughts. It is an imagined set of feelings. All our families are different, but we can all use the word to refer to what is familiar about the relationships we have with certain significant people. In this view, a very 'interpretive' one, we are taught what families are by socialisation and so they are not natural.

Conclusion

Zygmunt Bauman (1990) describes the family as an 'insider group' which is a way for us to tell who we are or are not. They are a way of developing an identity and of giving security. Again, however, this is what they are in the abstract. It is very difficult to generalise about what families are, what they are like and what they do. For many people, families are not a source of security – quite the opposite. They can be very damaging, causing great physical and mental harm. As sociologists, we must remember that people are different, and therefore so too are their families.

For consideration:

1   Do you think families are natural or cultural and why?
2   Why and how might we be able to claim that families are 'not real'?

✓ **Top Exam Hint**

It is always good practice to start the longer mark questions by defining and explaining the words in the title of the question. In the case of the family exam, your introduction to these answers could focus on how it is difficult to define the concept, making it hard to get sociologists to agree how to measure it.

◆ **What, When and Why?**

The ideas of **sociobiology** go back to those of Charles Darwin on the process of evolution. These ideas have been very influential in the 'nature vs nurture' argument, although many sociologists reject such claims and instead take an alternatively extreme position know as cultural relativism. This is the idea that as humans we are nothing except that which our culture makes us.

❋ **Key Ideas**

- Perhaps the best way to think about the family is to think about other words that the word 'family' is like. It is like the word familiar, and in fact, both come from the same Latin original source: *familia*. This means that the family is something 'familiar', something that is part of ordinary life, something that we take for granted. A habit, almost.

- The phrase 'imagined community' is the idea that the relationships we have with people and the bonds that tie us together are essentially abstract symbols that we make real by acting as if they are real. By doing this we come to know who we are, and where we belong.

3.5 What types of family structure do we have?

Is this still a typical family today?

What does this mean?

The term 'structure' refers to how something is patterned or how it might be made up or constructed. How are different families constructed differently? This is an important question as we must understand that not all families are the same.

Can we define the term family?

Diana Gittins (1993) suggests that the family is an idea rather than a physically real thing, and in fact that the reality of family life is very different from the idea. We all speak of 'the family' as if it is a single, common object, but in reality it is a wide variety of different practices. It has different sizes, different roles and different relationships within. When we talk about the family in ordinary language ('common-sense thought') we often miss this important point.

What is the ideology of the family?

Some sociologists like Gittins, talk about the 'ideology of the family', which is sometimes referred to using Ann Oakley's term 'cereal packet family' since it is the view we might have gained about family life from the advertising media's representation of the family. In particular, think about breakfast cereal adverts, that is, two parents, children, around a table, happily sharing the family breakfast. How true is this really?

What types of family exist?

As sociologists, we use a great variety of terms to describe the family.

1   Traditional extended family – three generations or more in the same house.
2   Peter Willmott (1986) has added to the idea of a traditional extended family with the following three further distinctions:
    *   Local extended family – separate nuclear families who are related, and see each other often since they live in close proximity to each other.
    *   Dispersed extended family – nuclear families that are related and who see each other quite frequently but do not live together.
    *   Attenuated extended family – nuclear families that are related and see each other or have some sort of contact infrequently.
3   Nuclear family – the sort of family type we often see on TV, that is, two generations living together. This is the image of the family in common-sense thought.

4   Reconstituted family – reconstituted means making something more out of previous pieces. In other words, families that have step relationships.
5   Lone parent/single parent family
6   Symmetrical family – Young and Willmott (1975) use this term to describe families that have joint roles between the partners in terms of the duties and chores they perform.
7   Dual-worker families – families where both partners contribute to the family income. This would certainly make the type of family life different from families where only one partner works, in terms of childcare and disposable income amongst others.
8   Cohabitation families – where partners live together without being married.
9   Same-sex families – families based upon lesbian or homosexual relationships.

What are households?

As we can see, families might be different from one another for reasons such as: size; roles; number of generations; marital status; number of partners.

There is also a very important distinction to make between:

*   family – symbolic shared practices
*   households – where you live, the dwelling you live in, and its size and structure
*   roles – the relationships between the people who live together
*   kinship – feelings of belonging with others; feelings of being part of the same family as others.

Conclusion

Households and families are not necessarily the same thing, and this further confuses the picture of what family life is like. For example, we might not be related to the people we share a house with; think of student halls of residence, for example, or people sharing a flat. Equally, if households are close by, this might actually change the type of family life you have. You might live in a cohabitation family, a nuclear family or a single parent family, but have other kin living so close by you see them often. If this is the case, what sort of family do you really have? Equally, families change with time; you might be a member of lots of different types of family structures in your lifetime.

For consideration:

1   Why do you think there are so many family types?
2   What implications might such family variety have for social research?

◆ **What, When and Why?**
Neo-conventional family – this idea, associated with Robert Chester (1985) suggests that although we might construct nuclear families in different ways (through maybe divorce and re-marriage or through cohabitation) it is still a nuclear-type structure that most people try to strive for most of the time. This is the 'new-norm', or the new convention.

3.6 What is the ideology of the family?

What does this mean?

An **ideology** is a word associated with more 'critical' or 'radical' theories such as Marxism and feminism. It means ideas that are used to justify how things are. Or, sometimes, it can be seen as a way of thinking about society that encourages us not to see power inequality.

Marxists and feminists argue that those who have power in society are able to control how society thinks about itself. In order to do so, they present social ideologies (ways of thinking) that hide or cover up inequality and the fact that those in power run society for their own benefit. This idea is summed up in the classic Marxist phrase,

> 'The ruling ideas are, in every historical epoch, the ideas of the ruling class.'

In other words, those who rule society continue their rule by shaping the ideas of the population. Michel Foucault (1977, 1979) has said a similar thing. He says that,

> 'Things are not powerful because they are true, but they are true because they are powerful.'

Sociologists such as Abbott and Wallace (1997) and Diana Gittins (1993) talk about an ideology of the family which can be seen in the views of politicians, doctors and religious leaders. They also argue that this ideology about the family is present in the media. An ideological view of the family is one which is believed by people to be 'common-sense' so it is simply accepted and not questioned. In fact, its so-called 'truth' may be very different from the reality. For example, we might use the term 'cereal packet family' to refer to how the media tends to suggest that nuclear families are the norm, whereas in fact what exists in society is wide family diversity.

Why is the ideology of the family a problem?

Feminists and Marxists argue that the ideology of the family that exists in modern UK society is damaging, controlling and limiting. It hides the true nature of family life. This is often to protect traditions and assumptions that themselves might affect how people think about the society they live in. For example, many tabloid newspapers regularly criticise single-parent families, and many politicians blame such families for so-called rises in criminal behaviour (not that we can know for sure that crime is on the increase since it tends to be hidden).

<figure>

✳ Key Ideas

An **ideology** is a way of seeing society. Many sociologists think that the powerful use ideologies to control how the powerless think about society.

✓ Top Exam Hint

Learn these two quotes off by heart. You can use them in a number of ways in a number of different topics – in fact, anywhere and everywhere that you talk about ideology and power; these concepts are the essence of sociology!

</figure>

Barrett and McIntosh (1991) have argued that in common-sense thought, we tend to see single parents as 'bad' and the nuclear family as 'good'. They refer to the nuclear family as an '**anti-social** family' as the ideology (the common-sense view) makes other types of families seem worse, and the nuclear family as the best sort. But is it really? We need to look at the sociological evidence before we make our minds up.

What ideological assumptions exist in society?

This ideology of the family (seen in the media amongst other places) makes a number of assumptions about family life which people in society take for granted and might not question. These assumptions become seen as fact, but they are really untested.

The ideology of the family says:

- families are natural
- family life is normal
- families should have opposite sex parents
- women should care for children
- the nuclear family is best
- too many single-parent families will lead to a crisis in society.

How often do people believe these statements do you think? How often are they questioned? How often do you see these views in the media? As sociologists we must ask ourselves how true these statements really are. And how can we tell? Where is the evidence?

Conclusion

Interestingly, some sociological and political ideas, as we shall see throughout this chapter, share this ideological image. In particular, the New Right, the New Left and the functionalist view can be attacked by feminists as having an ideological image. In this view the nuclear family is seen as the best family of all, the perfect way to build a stable and functioning society. Is this really true? Many feel that the family has a 'dark side' – a massive set of negative consequences.

For consideration:

1 Do you think an ideology of the family exists in modern society?
2 How can you tell?

✳ Key Idea

Barrett and McIntosh have described the nuclear family as being 'anti-social'. They do not mean by this that those in a nuclear family behave in an anti-social fashion, but rather, that the ideology of the nuclear family is such that it makes us believe in the so-called 'common-sense' idea that the nuclear family is the 'best sort', thus making other family types seem inferior and not as good for society – quite untrue!

✍ Coursework Suggestion

You could investigate how the media has an ideological image of the family for A2 coursework. Study adverts on the TV using the methods of semiology and content analysis.

3.7 What do politicians think about the family?

✳ Key Ideas

Gittins (1993) says,

'Family households are a vital and integral part of any society in some shape or form. Family ideology is not. There is no ideal family. When politicians articulate a fear that there is a crisis in the family, they are not worried about divorce or rape or incest as such, but rather that the ideology is being challenged.' (1993, p. 168)

The New Labour government of Tony Blair said in the 1997 election that families were the building blocks for society. What does this mean?

◆ What, When and Why?

Consider these examples:

- In 1997 the Conservative Party election manifesto said: *'The family is the most important instit'... ...in our lives. It offers sec'... ...'ity in a fast-chan'...*

- ... ...abour said: ... ...'re a basic ... ...'he ... ...'his has ... ...' must

What does this mean?

Many sociologists – quite often from the Marxist or feminist traditions – have criticised political views on the family as being 'ideological', that is, based upon false, untested assumptions.

In recent years we have seen both Conservative and New Labour governments openly state that single parents are damaging for society and that this crisis in the family (and in 'traditional values and morality' in general) will lead to a crisis in society due to a lack of stability.

In the Conservative, or the New Right view in sociology, the family is a basic building block of society. It is at the heart of society, ensuring that people learn the 'right' values to ensure stability. Marxists would attack this, suggesting that this is ideology – a way of controlling what people think in order to maintain an unequal society.

Many feminists such as Gittins see family diversity as a really positive feature of society since it will allow freedom of choice. In this view the ideas of politicians limit choice, since they proclaim that some types of family are 'better' than others.

What do politicians say about the family?

Politicians tend to share the idea that society is changing, but that the family should remain the same to protect us from these changes. In this way, society will make sense to us, and we are able to build a smooth-running society.

Anthony Giddens (1994) notes that many politicians, as shown above, often talk about 'traditional family values'. Giddens notes that this claim is very unrealistic. We know today that families are not always a source of comfort for everyone and, equally, that in the past women and children were often treated badly in the family, lacking power, decision-making ability and often the victims of physical abuse. Such abuse also continues today, irrespective of the sort of family structure that might exist. It is therefore very difficult to say that a certain type of family is better than another or that we should return back to an age when the family was 'perfect': it simply never was.

The ideas of Giddens and the work of Janet Finch (1989) would both suggest that this type of thinking is little more than what is known as a 'golden age'. There are assumptions made about the past and the present state of families, but without any real hard evidence.

- The past is seen as an age of strong morality. Strong roles were in place and the family is seen to have functioned to maintain moral standards through the socialisation of norms and values. (This is similar to the functionalist argument in sociology as we shall see later in this chapter.)
- In this way of thinking, the present is seen as having reached a crisis point. Strong morality does not exist and society is collapsing since the family is unable to perform the functions it once did.

This is a 'golden age' since it is a completely unrealistic image of the past as some perfect time that we should return to.

Giddens suggests the opposite. He claims that individuals (and in particular women and children) have more freedom than ever before, freedom to decide who they are and how they wish to live their lives. This is referred to as a 'plastic identity'. Who we think we are is mouldable. We are able to take control of our lives, our lifestyles and, unlike ever before, the sort of family choices we wish to make. He refers to society as being post-traditional, unlike those on the New Right in the Conservative Party, who wish to return to traditions that are assumed to have existed, but which might not have been as 'perfect' as we might think. This raises some serious questions about our knowledge of the past development of the family. How can we really tell anything about the lives of those before us?

Conclusion

Often politicians are responsible, along with the media, for creating what we call '**moral panics**' about the family – an exaggerated sense of fear about a largely fictitious threat. Modern-day family moral panics have included:

- concern about 'absent fathers'
- concern about homosexual families
- concern about single parent families
- concern about a lack of discipline among the young due to a breakdown in family socialisation
- concern about a change in the gender roles in the family
- increased sexual abuse of children

For consideration:

1 Why do you think we have so many moral panics about family life?
2 Why do you think some people see the past as being much better than it might actually have been?

66 99 Key Definition

Moral panic – an unrealistic or hyped fear

Folk devil – the largely exaggerated or even fictitious group we have moral panics about

✳ Key Idea

Joan Smith (1997) sees these moral panics as further evidence of the existence of what feminists have termed 'patriarchy' in society – male dominance and the control of women. These panics serve to increase the control of women by labelling some women and men as 'dangerous' and as 'deviant'. The feminist view in general argues that the New Right views on the family are especially patriarchal since they advocate that women and men should return to 'traditional' roles, otherwise society will collapse.

How have families changed over time?

What does this mean?

In order to study what families do and how and why they do it, many sociologists are interested in looking at how the family has changed over time. Like any aspect of society it is important to see the family as in flux, that is changing, not fixed or static. Society is constantly changing, and so too are the ways in which people live their lives.

What is the theory of transition?

This view is associated with the ideas of functionalist thinkers Talcott Parsons (1955) and Ronald Fletcher (1966). This view sees the family as changing to meet the needs of the society that it serves. Like a view often expressed by politicians, the family in this functionalist image is seen to be at the heart of both society and social stability. Parsons and Fletcher suggest that as society becomes more complex and industrial, the family loses functions. Other institutions take functions away from the family (such as education and health care, now provided by the state), allowing the family to better perform the essential functions that it is left with, that is, socialisation and stabilisation. This process of the loss of functions and the specialisation of others is known as 'structural differentiation'.

William Goode (1963), another functionalist thinker, has suggested that the process of 'transition' is a global trend. The extended family is being replaced by the nuclear family as the better and more suitable type. Many feminists attack this idea claiming that it is little more than an ideological view of the family.

How has the family changed due to industrialisation?

1   A key debate involved in the issue of how families might change and develop over time is that of the role that industrialisation might have played in changing the family. The classical functionalist view is that industrialisation caused the decline of the extended family, and the creation of the nuclear family. This is because workers moved into the newly created towns, leaving their extended families behind them. In recent years, this view has increasingly come under attack.

2   Starkey, and others such as Peter Laslett (1965) and Michael Anderson (1971), suggest that rather than creating the nuclear family, industrialisation actually increased the likelihood of the extended family. This is because as people moved to newly created towns, they moved in with relatives in order to find comfort and security. We see

✳ Key Ideas

Transition means changing, or 'evolving' over time; adapting.

✓ Top Exam Hint

Try to show that what sociologists often say is actually a product of the times they were writing in.

◆ What, When and Why?

David Starkey at a sociology conference in 1995 described this classical functionalist view as 'nonsense, sentimentalism and not founded in historical fact'. He is referring to the idea that this view represents a rather generalised view of history, with little attention paid to actual historical data.

this today with patterns of migration around the globe. People often move near to, and even move in with, people they know before they establish themselves in a new place. Starkey goes further and argues that due to the crowded living conditions in the newly created towns, the time of industrialisation was probably the only period in the UK when the extended family was in high numbers.

3   Extended families are, however, often seen to be related to the class of the families themselves. It is important to remember that factors such as age, class, ethnicity and location will all increase the likelihood of family diversity. In a study of Bethnal Green in East London, Young and Willmott (1962) argued that kinship patterns in working-class communities tended to be based more upon extended style family structures than isolated nuclear structures, which in turn are more associated with middle class or affluent families.

4   Finally, Young and Willmott (1975) also suggested that as the nuclear family develops, we will see a changing of the roles between the partners within the family. They describe what they call a 'symmetrical family', which can be seen as very similar to the functionalist view of 'transition', as follows:

- Stage 1: Pre-industrial families – families worked together as a unit of production.
- Stage 2: Early industrial families – the extended family is broken down by geographical mobility due to the rise of towns and urban areas. Traditional gender roles develop as men become 'breadwinners' in the home.
- Stage 3: Symmetrical families – as time develops, life in the nuclear family becomes more 'home-centred' and the roles become increasing shared, hence the term symmetrical.

Conclusion

As we can see, the history of sociological debates on the family is based upon the idea that industrialisation had a massive impact on how we lived our lives, and on the types of families we created for ourselves. However, we often have to question the reliability of the historical picture we are painting.

For consideration:

1   Why do you think sociologists tend to focus upon the industrialisation era in history when discussing the family?
2   How easy or hard do you think it might be to study historical changes in the family?

What are the problems with looking at the family in history?

How have families changed over time? What is a typical family today, and how can we really know what happened in families in the past?

What does this mean?

Studies of the family and how it might change over time are often only as good as the historical evidence and data the researcher has at their disposal. Such data is often patchy and incomplete, or at least, quite open to interpretation.

What problems exist with historical data?

- **Problems about size** – it is difficult to tell exactly how big families were in the past. Since divorce was illegal until this century, and not easy to obtain until changes in the law in 1971, many families stayed together but in name only. Equally, illegal abortions often occurred when children were conceived outside of marriage, or illegitimate children were given to work houses or orphanages. Occasionally, these children were taken into the family under the guise of being the offspring of the married couple, who were in fact really the grandparents. Such changes do not easily show up, if at all, in historical data.
- **Problems about relationships and roles** – while we might learn from parish records details about births, deaths, marriages and therefore the size of families, this tells us little about what life was like within the families themselves. Historically, we might be able to use life documents and other secondary sources to complete this picture, and to give us more qualitative historical information. For example, we might be able to use paintings, diaries, love letters, etc.
- **Problems about measurement of structure** – even if we can find out in a reliable fashion how big households were, it still doesn't tell us about the inter-relationships between households. For example, a road might look as if it has 20 nuclear families living in it. Yet, some of these households might have kin in other houses in the same or nearby streets. What might look like a nuclear family might actually be a modified extended family instead, but how would quantitative data tell us this?

What can we tell about the past?

Using parish records in England from 1564 – 1821, Laslett (1965) has been able to identify the existence of only about 10 per cent of families that were not nuclear in structure. These results are very different from the previous ideas of Parsons.

1 Anderson (1971) obtained census data from 1851 on Preston, and has noted that extended kinship was strengthened and not weakened with the process of industrialisation.

2 In a similar study to that of Anderson, Liz Stanley (1992) looked at Rochdale in the 1980s and found that the 1980s mirrored the 1880s. There was high female unemployment and wide-ranging family diversity.

3 American sociologist Litwak looked at nuclear families in the 1960s and still found that in 52 per cent of cases such families still had regular contact with wider kin – including at least weekly contact with other family members. This again suggests that what might look like a 'nuclear' family, and what might actually be a nuclear family are very different, but this is difficult to tell from the size of the family alone.

4 In 1993 Finch and Mason conducted a detailed survey in the Greater Manchester area, looking at how families took on and divided up the responsibilities of care and support for ill kin. After interviews with 978 people and a further 88 questionnaires, they found that in over 90 per cent of cases, assistance and mutual support between kin was widespread. Many in the sample had offered or received financial support from kin, or had helped out with childcare or the care of ill relatives. This again indicates that although we might have nuclear families, we still have a great deal of modified extended support networks.

What about now?

It is possible to point to a number of changes that the family seems to be going through in modern times:

- divorce is on the increase
- marriages are taking place much later in life
- those that get divorced are more likely to get remarried than people getting married for the first time.
- there is an increase in cohabitation relationships
- there is an increase in births outside of marriage and in single parenthood
- family members are living much longer today than ever before
- family size is decreasing – we are having fewer children
- increasing numbers of women are having children later in life
- step relationships are increasing.

Brigitte and Peter Berger (1983) maintain that although in recent years society has accepted that the nuclear family has a considerable dark side (which is more frequently discussed and revealed than ever before) we still have not found a real alternative.

For consideration:

1 What methods do you think are best to get at the reality of family lives?

2 What changes do you think the family will go through next?

✓ **Top Exam Hint**

As part of your revision put all the names from this chapter onto revision cards and then every time you practise a past exam question try to see which names would link and why – this way you will be able to use these ideas in a unique fashion, rather than assuming they can only be used in the way that we have presented them to you here.

✎ **Coursework Suggestion**

You could, for A2 coursework, study people's attitudes to the future of the family. Try to find out what their anxieties about the family consist of.

✳ **Key Idea**

Robert Chester (1985) has suggested that such changes only serve to indicate that we have a new norm. We have a new form of the nuclear family, but one more flexible than before, based on cohabitation and maybe re-marriage and step relations, rather than nuclear in the tradition sense. Humans still, after all, enter into relationships and partnerships with each other, and will always continue to do so.

3.10 What do functionalists think about the family?

What does this mean?

Functionalism is a theory in sociology associated with the views of founder Emile Durkheim (who died in 1917), and with sociologists such as Talcott Parsons (1955) and Ronald Fletcher (1966), who both wrote in the 1960s. Functionalism was a very popular 'macro' sociological theory during the 1960s, but is often seen to have been replaced in the history of sociological ideas by neo-Marxism and feminism in the 1970s and 1980s. Having said this, the ideas on the family held by functionalists are important to the sociology of the family as a whole, and although they are rather old ideas, they are reflected in many modern-day views held by the New Right, the New Left and by many politicians.

What is functionalism?

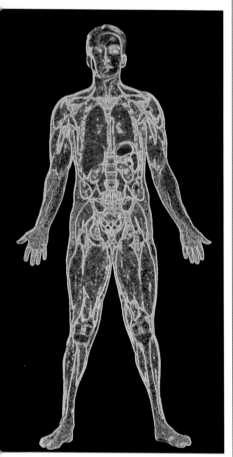

Functionalists compare society to a living body; all the parts connect to make up the whole

- The starting point for all functionalist analysis is to ask 'how does this aspect of society function?' They start with the assumption that things that exist in society exist for a reason and contribute to the whole, or the larger pattern in some way.
- At the heart of how functionalists see society in general is a notion called the 'organic analogy'. This idea helps functionalists to focus on how the parts of the society all inter-relate together and combine in various ways. They argue that society can be seen as a living, growing and evolving entity, like a body. The parts of the body contribute something to how the whole thing works and each has a function to perform.
- This is an example of what we call a 'consensus theory'. The basic functionalist starting point is that society's normal state is one of balance, of harmony between the parts that make up the whole.
- The family is seen as a key institution in society to help keep society in balance.

What functions does the family perform?

1 George Murdock (1949) – In a cross-cultural study of 250 societies, Murdock identified what he claimed to be four universal functions of the family for every society:
- sexual – the family provides new members to allow society to continue
- reproductive – the family allows sexual expression to be stable, by regulating and creating laws and guidelines about who we can

enter into sexual relationships with and when

- economic – the family provides for its members
- educational – the family teaches new members the values of society, allowing for balance to be maintained over time.

In this view, the family is universal. Every society needs the structure of a family since every society needs the above four functions to occur in order to stay 'healthy' and in balance.

2   Talcott Parsons (1955) – After Murdock, Parsons has suggested that modern-day families have lost some functions, but have specialised in those they have retained. Parsons suggests there are two essential functions families now perform, but again, like Murdock, these functions are seen to be vital for continuing social stability:

- primary socialisation of children
- the stabilisation of the adult personality

For Parsons if these two functions are not adequately met, then we will have a dysfunctional society. Functionalists refer to this situation as 'anomie' meaning normlessness. This is like sickness in the human body if we continue the idea of the organic analogy.

Parsons has argued that the nuclear family is the most functional family type of all in modern society since it is most ably suited to perform these two basic and 'irreducible functions' needed to ensure **social order**. Many see this claim as a product of its times (the 1960s) and as a highly ideological view of the family.

3   Ronald Fletcher (1966) has suggested, like Parsons, that the family has lost functions, noting that the non-essential secondary functions families once performed are now largely performed for society by the state instead – functions such as health care provision, education etc.

The family is left with three essential functions that it now performs:

- stable satisfaction of sexuality
- production and rearing of children
- home provision.

✳ Key Idea

Social order – functionalists think social order is vital. Without it we would have instability and society would be 'sick' and dysfunctional.

Conclusion

In this functionalist view, families are essential. They maintain balance and order. They teach us the values and norms of our culture. Without families, society would collapse.

For consideration:

1   What do you think of the functionalist view? Are families like this?
2   How might families cause dysfunctions in society?

3.11 What do Marxists think about the family?

What does this mean?

The sociological theory of Marxism comes from the ideas of Karl Marx (died 1883), his writing companion Fredrick Engels and their modern-day followers, many of whom might describe themselves as neo-Marxists since there have been considerable changes and up-dates to the traditional macro Marxist view as sociology has developed.

The Marxist view is often seen as the opposite to the consensus-based theory of Durkheim and the functionalists. Marxism itself is often described as a radical or conflict theory since it sees society as based upon power inequalities due to the existence of a class hierarchy.

Having said this, however, there are many similarities between these two so-called opposites.

- Both are macro theories, i.e. they look at how society is patterned as a whole.
- Both are interested to look at how and why people follow the rules of society.
- Both believe that there is strong social control and order in society.

Where they differ is that whereas for functionalists social control is largely positive, creating a balanced and orderly world to live in, Marxists see social control as the ability of a ruling powerful group to control the rest of society, creating inequality.

"" Key Definition

Class is defined in the traditional Marxist view as the relationship one has to the means of production, i.e. everything needed in society to make an end product, to produce the goods of society. For Marx, there are only two possible relationships: either you own the means of production and therefore have power, or you don't, and you work for those that do.

What do Marxists think about society?

- Marx starts with the general observation that society is divided in terms of class, since it is what he refers to as a 'capitalist' society. By this he means that in modern society there are two main groups that have a conflicting relationship with each other – the ruling class and the working class.
- Society is therefore seen as unequal and as exploitative. Those in power keep the rewards of society for themselves, controlling the actions of those below them in the structure of society.
- Like functionalists, Marxists believe that society has order, but that this order hides the true nature of society. Order is really about the control over those who have no power in society, allowing such an exploitative society to continue over time.

What do Marxists think about the family?

1 Early Marxist views on the family come not so much from Marx, surprisingly enough, but from Engels. Engels (1972) argued that the family is shaped by the economic structure of the society in which it exists. This is a classic Marxist idea called **economic determinism**: those who hold and own the means of production can control all else in society, and can control how features of society are shaped. Engels suggests, in a view that actually crosses over with early feminist writings, that the family as we know it was 'invented' at the same time in history as private property and the state. Monogamy (one man married to one woman at one time) was invented to control women in order to establish legitimate lines of inheritance for private property. The reasoning behind this idea was that fathers needed a stable sense of who their offspring actually were in order to ensure that property was passed on to their own kin. This also invented patriarchy – the notion that men dominate women in the family and in society.

2 Eli Zaretsky (1976) suggests that the family serves an unequal society by providing emotional support for ordinary people who are exploited in such a society. It is what is known as a safety valve. It allows for comfort and security, making people feel that society is fine and permitting their exploitation and powerlessness to continue. In this way, it contributes to '**false consciousness**' – it makes society seem better than it really might be.

3 Neo-Marxist Louis Althusser (1971) makes an important distinction between:
   - repression – controlling people physically or with the threat of force
   - ideology – controlling people by affecting how they think about society

   He suggests that the family appears to be a private institution, but is really the subject of much state control. Within the family, ideologies are socialised into each new generation, making them accept how society is.

4 Jacques Donzelot (1985) argues that the family is not as 'private' as it might seem. Although we might feel safe from the problems of society behind the closed doors of our family lives, the family is actually in the middle of a complex series of power relationships including the regulation and monitoring by the state, doctors, the police, teachers, social workers, etc.

Conclusion

In the Marxist view, the family is a source of social control, unlike the functionalist view which sees it as the building block of society and more like social cement.

For consideration:

1 Which approach do you find more realistic – Marxism or functionalism?
2 How can the family teach us to be uncritical of the society we live in?

※ **Key Ideas**

- Economic determinism – this idea can be used to describe most Marxist views on how the whole of society operates. It simply means that the class system, and the inequalities that it produces are the most important features of all society – and that class allows some to shape the whole of society in their interests.

- Marxists make a distinction between false and true consciousness: **false consciousness** means you are a victim of ideological control and do not really see the 'truth' – you do not see how those in power make society unequal.

- Marxists in general also look at the role played by the family in the reproduction of capitalist and ruling values over time. They argue that families do teach values to the next generation, as functionalists also do. However, these values are termed, 'ideologies'. They justify the way things are in society, and stop us from questioning how society really is.

3.12 What is the interpretive view of the family?

What does this mean?

Interpretive sociology goes by many other names. We might call this 'micro sociology' or sometimes interactionism. This sort of sociology is the other side of the coin to the more structural approach of theories such as Marxism and functionalism.

The interpretive approach, as the name suggests:

- looks at roles and relationships between people
- looks on a small-scale level at how people act and interact with each other
- tries to understand how people understand or 'interpret' the world around them and their place in it
- looks at the meanings and motives people have for the actions they undertake
- asks how the world make sense for those in it, or how those in it make it make sense?

As we can see, with its emphasis upon looking at why people do what they do, and how people form relationships and roles, it is a very useful tool for us to use to think about the nature of family life.

What does interpretive sociology say about the family?

- For Berger and Luckmann (1967), what we regard as 'real' in society is the product of 'social constructions'. In other words, what we consider to be real is what our culture tells us is real. What we consider to be 'normal' is shaped and moulded by the norms of the culture that we are brought up in and socialised by. When applied to the family, we can see that in this view, our common-sense dominant image of the family is itself a cultural creation – this is a very different view to that held by sociobiology which argues that the family is a product of natural instincts.
- Erving Goffman (1969) has advocated the adoption of what he refers to as a 'dramaturgical approach' in micro-sociology. He suggests that a useful analogy to use when describing the world is the term 'theatre'. We have roles, we take on parts, we follow scripts depending upon the roles we have. Again, when applied to the family, it is interesting to see how we 'act out' family life, how being in a family gives us many different scripts or roles to follow: father, mother, step-father, sister, son etc. Each role comes 'ready-made' with a meaning attached to it, but we have to live out or act out the role in order to

make it come alive – to make it 'mean' something in our lives and in the lives of those whom we act and interact with.

How does the interpretive approach see marriage?

Due to its emphasis upon looking at what people do and how they act and create and share meaning with those around them, the interpretive approach is a useful way of thinking about what the relationships within the family are like.

- Berger and Kellner (1964) have suggested that the roles learned and adopted in the family are '**ongoing constructions**'. When we first enter into these relationships the roles are not clear, and they need to be learned, and then practised just like learning any script. The relationships we build in the family are very fragile, they need to be negotiated, renegotiated and constructed again and again. They have to be built by those involved.
- David Clark (1991) looks at how we can think about the differences in the reality of how people create married relationships. He asks how married life make senses to those in the process of acting it out. What does it feel like to be married, and does it feel the same to everyone? As we can see, these are very 'micro' concerns – they look at what people think and how they make sense of what they do. For Clark, like all interaction and like all roles we might take on, marriage is something we need to practise – it is something we 'do', rather than simply 'have'.

How can we study power in the family?

David Morgan (1996) argues that food and how it is used in the family can give us an insight into common-sense assumptions about power. It can symbolically represent power inequality in the family.

For example someone has to shop, decide what to eat, unpack the shopping, cook, decide on the meal time and someone has to wash up.

Who is it that does all these things? How is it organised? Is there power inequality in this action?

Conclusion

The micro approach when looking at the family is useful since it allows us to think about the nature of the relationships within the family. It allows us to see families not as fixed or static 'things', but as livings sets of interactions. People make families real by 'doing them'.

For consideration:

1   How useful do you think the interpretive approach is when looking at family life?
2   What does it mean to say that families are not 'things' but are 'practices'?

✴ Key Ideas

- Zygmunt Bauman (1990) has suggested that we can best understand what family life means – what it does for the individual – if we see it as an '**insider group**'. In other words, the family gives us our place in society from the moment we are born; it tells us who we are and it gives us a feeling of security, informing us where we 'belong'.

- David Morgan (1996) talks of 'family practices' which is a very micro idea. In this view, families are not 'things' as such, they only really exist because we give the symbol some meaning in our culture. They are sets of interactions that make sense to us or 'practices'.

✔ Top Exam Hints

- Use the idea of a dramaturgical approach to looking at sociology and society. It can be applied to most areas of life, and really helps us to make clear how interpretive sociologists think about society, and how this is very different from the more 'structural' or 'macro' approaches.

- Use David Clark's idea combined with a feminist perspective when discussing issues of inequality in the family.

- Try to show that the macro and the micro approaches to the family are two sides to the same coin; don't always simply present them as complete opposites. Sociology needs them both and so, therefore, do you, and your exam answers.

♟ Thinking like a Sociologist

The micro sociological approach has been adopted by many other sociologists since it allows us to produce qualitative data and to try to really see what family life is like. Often, this approach, like feminism, considers issues of power and decision-making in the home. An excellent example of this is to consider the role played by food and meal times in family life, and to look at what this might 'mean'.

What do feminists think about the family?

In what ways is the family a source of control for women?

✳ Key Idea

In terms of thinking about sociology, many feminists see sociology as 'malestream'. It is often dominated by discussions about class, at the expense of discussions about gender, which if they exist, are often added on, but not taken seriously. It is true to say that without the feminist perspective, sociology's knowledge about the family would be rather lacking. Feminists have often focused upon the family as an object of study since it is seen as a major feature of the oppression and control of women in society.

What does this mean?

First, it is important to note that there is no such thing as a single feminist sociology. Instead, there are many varieties of feminist theory. However, as noted by Barrie Thorne (1982) they all share in common the following ideas about the family:

- society is male dominated – it is patriarchal
- the psychological experience of being in a family is different for men and for women
- the family is a source for the control of women
- families socialise us with gender roles that themselves reflect and continue patriarchal ideologies
- families are not 'private' – they are controlled by the state, and women in particular are the subjects of massive social control
- there is no biological need for the family – it is a product of culture rather of nature

What do feminists think about society?

In general, the starting point for most feminist analysis of society is to see society as being made up of unequal structures of power between men and women. We call this **patriarchy**, which literally means 'rule of the father', but in general usage this term is used to refer to the ways in which society is male-dominated. This is seen to be a product of culture – it is not natural. This is very different from the sociobiological view that would argue that the family is a biological product of our natural needs.

What do feminists think about the family?

Beechey (1986) notes that in common-sense thought in society, the family is often taken for granted as natural, without any real questioning of this, and is also thought about in a gendered fashion: families seem to require different things from men and from women. We are seen to need and to want to live in families, they are seen as the best way to bring up children, and women are seen to have the main role in this childcare. This is an ideological view of the family as far as Beechey and other feminists are concerned. It is untested and it allows male dominance to continue. Men are seen to benefit from the family more than women.

Feminists point out the following 'dark side' of the modern-day family:

1   The family contains a large amount of psychological harm for women
2   Women do the majority of housework, even today
3   Women do the majority of emotional work
4   There are lots of instances of sexual and domestic abuse of women in the family context

- **Marxist-feminism** – this view, held by writers such as Barrett and McIntosh (1982), claims that the family serves the needs of capitalism; patriarchy in the home allows capitalism to continue in wider society. The exploitation of women and the care women provide men in the home allows feelings of alienation and exploitation from work to be reduced, allowing society to go unquestioned. Equally, women are needed by capitalism to raise the next generation of workers.
- **Radical feminism** – this view held by Shulamith Firestone (1979) argues that male power is based upon natural biological physical strength. Family life serves to benefit men as it is designed to allow men to benefit from the care work provided by women. This inequality is underpinned by the use or the threat of male violence against women.
- **Black feminism** – the writers Amos and Parmar (1984) are keen to point out that ethnicity has a massive effect upon the nature of family life, and therefore on women's experience of the family.
- **Post-feminism** – this view suggests that women's lives are freer than ever before. It claims that the need for feminism is over, since patriarchy in the family has been massively reduced. Women can now choose what they want.

Conclusion

The ideas of Sylvia Walby (1990) and the approach sometimes called '**triple systems feminism**' are of great use when thinking about how the family links with patriarchy in society as a whole. Walby identifies six main ways in which patriarchy works in society:

1   domestic labour serves men
2   paid work – women are still bounded by 'traditional values'
3   the state – promotes an ideological image of the family and marriage which is patriarchal
4   physical violence by men often occurs in the home
5   women's and girls' sexuality are limited and controlled by the family more than men's
6   the media presents a highly ideological image of women's family roles.

For consideration:

1   What do you think is the most valuable insight about the family made by feminism?

◆ **What, When and Why?**

According to the 1996 British Crime Survey, it is estimated that 6.6 million people in the UK have experienced some sort of domestic violence, including threats of violence as well as actual physical harm. Interestingly in this study, 23 per cent of women claimed to have been physically harmed by a partner, but so too did 15 per cent of men in the sample of 11,000 people nationwide.

✓ **Top Exam Hints**

- Make sure you show, for added depth, that you understand that there is a whole variety of feminist approaches in sociology.

- The ideas of post-feminism have some things in common with the ideas of Giddens and also with the theory of postmodernism. They all see that there is increased freedom of choice in society. Try to show comparisons like this in the exam where possible.

3.14 What are conjugal roles?

What does this mean?

The term 'conjugal roles' refers to the roles shared by the partners in the family. The term conjugal itself means the specific relationship between two people who are married. We use this term in sociology to refer to the ways in which housework, childcare, etc. are divided up and distributed, and whether this is done on a 'fair' basis or not. Another way of expressing this is to talk about the 'division of domestic labour'.

How are roles in the home divided?

The feminist view tends to argue that segregated roles are much more widespread than joint roles. In the majority of cases for example it is women who provide housework, and not men.

Many contemporary feminists talk of a 'triple shift' in the experience of women's lives. Many women go out to work, yet many women still perform the majority of housework. Also, many women provide emotional work for the family, caring for relatives when they are sick, etc.

In this view, women's lives are three times harder and paid work outside the home has not 'liberated' women in the ways we might think.

Why do we have inequality over domestic tasks?

According to the functionalist Talcott Parsons (1955), there are segregated roles in the family because these are 'natural'.

Men have **'instrumental roles'**, bringing in resources from the public world of work, and women have **'expressive roles'** based on emotional support and childcare.

This is a highly sociobiological argument, and is reflected in many of the ideas held by the New Right on the family today. Parsons argues that men and women simply have naturally different roles and that both are needed for the family to run in a smooth fashion. This is also similar to the ideas of New Left thinkers Dennis and Erdos (1992) who have suggested that families need fathers. The father's role as an authority figure is needed in order to maintain standards of discipline and control throughout society as a whole.

The New Right have suggested that single parent families are 'damaging' for society since they lack adequate socialisation. The traditional nuclear family, with a traditional gender role division, is seen in this view as 'most suited' to society.

✳ Key Idea

One of the earliest descriptions of conjugal roles comes from Elizabeth Bott (1957) who suggested that there are two main types of roles that couples in the family might adopt:

- **Segregated roles** – based upon a traditional gendered separation; the male is the breadwinner, doing DIY etc., the woman tends to the home and provides emotional support and child care

- **Joint roles** – based on an equal sharing of decision-making and tasks and responsibilities between the couple.

◆ What, When and Why?

According to the 2001 Labour Market Trends survey, there are 12.5 million women in paid work in the UK – this is roughly 73 per cent of women aged 16–59. However, this survey also shows that the factor that influences women's paid work the most is the presence of dependent children in the family home, suggesting that women still put childcare before paid employment. However, there is a significant increase in 'working mums' than ten years ago.

What do feminists think?

Hannah Gavron (1966) describes women as being 'captive wives'. She suggests, as many other feminists have done since, that the psychological experience of being in a marriage is different for women and men. Women have high expectations of marriage, and there is a great deal of pressure and expectations put on the relationship by women and men. The interviews in Gavron's research revealed that women had a high expectation of freedom, yet were then even more affected by the reality of the unequal division of domestic labour. This led to feelings of being 'captive'; of marriage feeling like a prison, confining the women and determining who they were by the traditional roles they took on.

- A classic feminist study on housework and housewives, comes from Ann Oakley (1974). She takes a critical stance against the claim made by Young and Willmott that families are becoming increasingly 'symmetrical' as time goes on. For Young and Willmott, roles between the partners are increasingly likely to become shared and to be based upon joint decisions and a sharing of tasks and responsibilities. Oakley's research shows this not to be the case. She identified the existence of strong segregated roles, and that women did the overwhelming majority of housework.
- There is an assumption that families are more likely to be 'symmetrical' if they are middle-class. The research of Stephen Edgell (1980) suggests that this is still not the case. Even middle-class families are likely to have segregated relationships.
- Mary Boulton (1983) goes further and argues that large-scale quantitative surveys, if anything, are more likely to exaggerate and increase the amount of housework men do. Questions about who does what often do not take into consideration time spent, and they certainly do not show the psychological experience of being in a relationship where the woman takes responsibility for caring, nurturing and developing children for the whole of their lives. This is a very difficult relationship and 'burden' to show, by simply asking who does what tasks in the home.

Conclusion

The overwhelming evidence seems to suggest that families are no longer symmetrical, but that women are working in paid work more than ever before, and that there is increased democracy for women.

The rise of modified extended families, especially amongst some ethnic groups in the modern UK, also raises questions about the idea of conjugal roles. It could be the case that the roles and responsibilities performed by family members are not solely confined to the married couple anymore.

For consideration:

1 Do you think traditional conjugal roles still exist in the majority of families? Explain your view.
2 Do you think families will ever be 'symmetrical'? Explain your view.

☀ Key Ideas

- A recent study by Ermisch and Francesconi suggests that if women work in full-time paid employment while bringing up children there might be an effect on the education of the child. This is a longitudinal survey of people born in the 1970s, based upon a sample of 1,263. Using data from the British Household Panel Survey, these authors have argued that where mothers work full time, children are less likely to gain A Level qualifications, more likely to be unemployed later in life and more likely to suffer from psychological disorders associated with stress. (This research was published by the Joseph Rowntree Foundation in 2000.)

- Many feminists have argued that government welfare policies encourage a very patriarchal view of the family. They encourage marriage, a traditional nuclear family, and work on the assumption that women will do the majority of childcare. For example, there are presently tax credits for those who are married rather than cohabitating together. Plus, with family allowances and tax credits the assumption is that women are encouraged to stay at home with children rather than go to work. In fact, even the TV advert for this scheme shows traditional nuclear family structures, and shows the man as the breadwinner. A very patriarchal view.

- Giddens (1992) provides a different interpretation of family life. He suggests that, unlike ever before, there is an increased 'democracy' in the family, and that women's roles and lives are freer now than at any other point in history. He sees increased opportunity for women to take control of their lives, and increased freedom to make choices.

What are the changing patterns of marriage and divorce today?

What does this mean?

Patterns of marriage vary considerably – across the globe, between classes and regions, and within the same society over time. At a common-sense level you might be aware that many people today are not getting married, but what does this really mean? What does the evidence really say? Many politicians fear the 'death of marriage' and discuss this as a new family crisis. Is this true, or a moral panic?

What types of marriage exist across the globe?

There is great diversity across the world, although the common-sense ideology of the family in Western thoughts tends to tell us that **monogamy** is 'natural'. Often family types and marriage diversity vary according to ethnicity and religion. For example, many people have arranged or even enforced marriage in the UK today, because of their ethnic traditions.

Polygyny is more common than **polyandry**. Sometimes societies use polyandry as a form of birth control since it limits the number of children born to the husbands. For example, traditionally in some parts of Nepal, young women marry more than one man, all of whom are brothers – insuring that there are lots of 'family members' available to look after children.

Do we have a crisis with marriage?

The New Right, the media and politicians in general tend to wish to protect marriage as a way of making society stable. Feminists refer to this as an ideological view of the family. Divorce certainly is on the increase, and family diversity is also increasing, but this does not mean to say we have a crisis.

A particularly dramatic rise in divorce has occurred since the 1971 Divorce Law Reform Act, which arguably made divorce easier and more acceptable. There are a number of possible reasons why divorce might be on the increase.

1 Divorce is more acceptable.
2 People who marry young might grow apart or regret the decision.

What will the future of marriage be in society?

66 99 Key Definition
We can make a distinction between:

*   **Monogamy** – one man married to one woman. In recent years, due to the rise of divorce and re-marriage, we have a situation of serial-monogamy in the West, i.e. we have different partners in a lifetime, but not at the same time.
*   **Polygamy** – one person marrying more than one person at the same time (illegal in many Western countries). There are two types of this:
    polygyny – men marry more than one woman at the same time; and
    polyandry – women marry more than one man at the same time.

3 Young people might have high expectations of marriage which are not fulfilled.
4 Increased freedom and rights for women to take control over their lives.
5 Increased social condemnation of domestic violence.
6 Longer life expectancy means couple have more chance to grow apart.
7 The rise of the nuclear family might mean that some people are increasingly isolated from wider kin and this might increase the psychological pressure on married relationships.

Many sociologists are now claiming that divorce is the norm.

- Robert Chester (1985) has said that the nuclear family will not die out as such; it will change its form and accommodate new ways of living, but will still be based around the two-partner model – such as step families or people living together.
- David Morgan (1996) suggests that divorce is commonplace, and that this change has occurred in just 20 years. It is another stage for many along the life course. However, divorce offers freedom for some, but poses interesting problems and diversity for our family relationships and for our individual identity and the roles we might take on. The more divorce and re-marriage increase, the more we find ourselves part of many different families at the same time, and the more we accommodate different roles and ways of acting which shape who we might think we are.
- Anthony Giddens (1991) suggests that divorce poses challenges and opportunities. It can cause great psychological harm, yet can also offer new opportunities and freedoms. It certainly offers many people the chance to re-assess who they think they are. Giddens refers to this as 'ontological insecurity' – concern over who we think we are; concern over knowing our own identity. Giddens says that divorce and its increase has fundamentally changed the nature of modern-day family life. It is both a reflection of, and a further influence on increasing post-traditionalism, the decline of old ways of living. Giddens refers to this identity which people are given the opportunity to rebuild as a 'plastic identity' since it can be shaped and moulded.

Conclusion

As we have seen, there are great changes taking place in marriage in recent years. We are possibly yet to see their full impact on society and on our daily lives, but many feel that society will no longer be the same. This is very realistic as all human actions change over time, and often change gradually; it is often the case that we don't see or understand the changes until they appear dramatic or overwhelming. Maybe this is why so many people in society are worried about the future or the 'death' of the family?

For consideration:

1 What do you think is the main reason for divorce?
2 How might widespread divorce dramatically change society?

3.16 Do families need fathers?

What does this mean?

Many politicians and New Right sociologists claim that we are witnessing a death of the family: the rise of single-parent families will lead to a massive change in how society operates, and the loss of important social stability. How can we investigate this claim?

Why do we need fathers?

Functionalist Talcott Parsons (1955) suggested that both the traditional gender roles of the parents are vital for the well-being of the family, and this early view is often still reflected today in the ideas of politicians on both the New Right and on the New Left. Parsons argues that due to biology, men and women offer different things to the family, and to the children they bring up. As we can see, this idea reflects the influence of sociobiological thinking on sociological views. For Parsons, men have an 'instrumental role' based upon provision for the family, whereas women have an 'expressive role', based upon providing care and emotional support. This has brought Parsons under attack from many feminist sociologists who see this argument as highly patriarchal.

Muncie and Wetherell (1995) note that such traditional images of male and female parenting roles have existed in the UK state's view on the family for a very long time. For example, the welfare state, created in 1942, assumed that marriage was the goal for all adults and that women would support the family. Even today, on adverts for state benefit we see very traditional parenting roles represented – the mother staying at home, the father as the main provider.

Interestingly, many families in the modern UK have women as the strong discipline figure, not the man as would be traditionally expected. Barrow (1982) for example, has documented the fact that amongst some ethnicities (such as UK West Indian families) the mother is traditionally the strong family figure. Many West Indian families are what are known as 'mother households' – two generations of women plus children living together.

We can also question the extent to which 'house-husbands' might exist in UK society. Research in 1999 by the Joseph Rowntree Foundation indicated that the father role has changed, but the idea of the male as the breadwinner for the family remains very strong. Instead, fathers are having to become 'super-dads' doing much more than ever before. They

Do families need fathers? Do families need mothers?

✓ **Top Exam Hint**

Try to link the ideas of functionalism to the ideas of sociobiology, and then you can attack functionalism with feminism. This is how you can build up evaluation in your answers, by 'bouncing' theories and ideas off each other.

are keeping the traditional father roles, but are adding to this an increased expectation from children and wives to become more 'involved' in the upbringing of children, as well as providing for the family.

For the New Right, however, the traditional male father figure remains an important feature for a stable society. The New Right view on the family is also, like Parsons' view in the 1950s and 1960s, a product of the time it developed in – the late 1980s. Many from the New Right and the New Left claim that we have a death of the family, and 'absent fathers' were seen to be to blame, as well as young women choosing single parenthood as a means to receive welfare – a situation quite exaggerated and impossible to prove.

Conclusion

New Left thinkers Dennis and Erdos (1992) have argued that lone parenthood has a considerable effect on the rise of deviance and crime: the absence of an authority figure causes young children to lack proper respect for the rules of society.

This is a controversial claim, but certainly one that echoes the ideas of Parsons some 45 years ago. We are certainly seeing the rise of government policies that seek to put more responsibility on families for bad behaviour in schools, truanting and delinquency.

For consideration:

1 Do you think the father and mother gender roles are natural? Why?
2 Do you agree that absent fathers lead to social breakdown?

◆ What, When and Why?

Hilary Land (1995), not a New Right sociologist, describes the changes that were taking place in society when this view became popular:

- By 1987 14 per cent of families with children were lone parents in the UK
- In 1989, 644,000 lone parents received state welfare
- By 1989, 27 per cent of births took place outside marriage

✳ Key Idea

State overload – The New Right uses this idea to refer to the crisis point welfare spending has reached (if this is true) because of the fact that some people are taking money from the state. In this view, the state should not provide welfare, and this would force people to 'help themselves'.

3.17 Do we have family diversity?

✓ **Top Exam Hint**

Think about the synoptic ideas of class, gender, ethnicity, location and age as ways in which to think about the diversity of families.

66 99 Key Definition

Cultural capital – this means the ways in which your class background benefits you and allows you to increase your provision of the rewards of society. For example, your accent, language codes and values are part of your culture, and may advantage or disadvantage you and your family.

What does this mean?

Diversity means variety – lots of different types. When applied to the family and to households, we can offer lots of different ways of thinking about how families might be different from each other:

Rhona and Robert Rapoport (1982) identify five different ways in which we can think about diversity:

1 Organisational diversity – families might have different structures and different roles within them.
2 Cultural diversity – ethnicity and religion might make some people have different types of families and ways of living from others.
3 Class diversity – the income that the family has and the '**cultural capital**' of the class background of a family may dramatically affect the lifestyle of the family members.
4 Life course diversity – where different families are along the stages of their life will also affect what sort of family they have, for example, if they are young couples, middle-aged with children, or elderly where children have young families of their own.
5 Cohort diversity – those born at the same time represent a 'cohort': a group of people who have common experiences of the world as they have lived through common historical events. This affects, among other things, your family life. If you lived through the second world war in London, for example, you may have been evacuated away from your family to the countryside for the duration of the war, giving you and your cohort a similar experience of family life.

How might geographical location affect family diversity?

Eversley and Bonnerjea (1982) illustrate that where you live in the country will affect the sort of family you are more likely to have:

• Affluent south of England – mobile two-parent families, children leave at an early age to seek employment or to go to university or to boarding school.
• Coastal areas of England and Wales – retired couples and elderly widowers often move to these areas to 'retirement homes'.

- Industrial areas and inner cities – old working class traditional communities with extended family-type structures and large support networks.
- Recently declining ex-industrial areas in the Midlands and the North of England – large-scale unemployment will put massive pressure on family life.
- Inner cities – wide turnover of population; many people arrive and live in these areas for a short period of time; large differences between very poor and very wealthy; lone parents; single person households and large numbers of multi-adult households.

How can we understand cultural diversity?

The modern UK includes many different ethnic groups, religious groups and therefore many different types of family practices.

Ballard (1982) looked at South Asian families in the UK. Across the generations these families had very different expectations of family life, the older generations being more traditional than the younger ones. The influences of Western culture and traditional family culture increase diversity since they lead to new mixed ways of family living, or might further increase tradition as a response to racism, or feelings of a loss of identity. These types of families made great use of extended family style structures.

Ann Oakley (1982) studied Cypriot families in the UK. As discovered in the findings of Ballard above, such families often used the extended family network as a means to establish community ties and support networks, much needed after migration. These families also tended to fulfil an economic function together, perhaps working alongside each other in family businesses.

Conclusion

Rhona Rapoport (1989) suggests that family diversity is a European experience, not simply a UK experience. However, for Katja Boh (1989) it makes little sense to use the term 'diversity' because we are all being diverse in the ways that we are mixing and combining different family structures and traditions together. Therefore, we may as well talk about 'convergence' – we are all moving towards a new normal, mixed set of family relationships.

For consideration:

1 Why do you think family diversity is important for the sociologist trying to understand the modern-day family?
2 What sort of diversity do you think would have the most impact on making families different? Why?

 What, When and Why?

The average number of people in households is on the decline in the UK from 3.1 in the 1960s, through to 2.4 in 1999. The latter figure was once the average number of children per family, but now is the average number of all persons in all households – a very different picture. The fastest growing type of household is the single male household.

3.18 Does the family have a dark side?

✓ **Top Exam Hint**

Use the ideas in this section to make evaluative criticisms of the functionalist and New Right views of the family in the exam.

What does this mean?

Sociologists use the term 'the dark side' to refer to a negative feature of an aspect of society that is hidden, misunderstood or unspoken about. The ideology of the family paints a picture of 'happy families' caring for each other, but how true is this really? What goes on behind the closed doors of the family?

Often this dark side of family life consists of the fact that some family relationships, as we would expect given how many there are, are dysfunctional . They might be based upon violence, control, inequality and psychological harm.

How does the family control and affect its members?

*   First, the family is not the safe haven that the ideology says it is. Both domestic violence and child abuse take place in some families. In fact, it is probably the case that we know less about this sort of crime than we think because it often goes unreported and undiscovered.

*   Sociologists Dobash and Dobash (1979) conducted interviews with women who had been victims of violent assault within the family. They point out that when women are the victims of rape, murder or assault, it is usually a family member that is the criminal, and more often than not the husband. The family is the most likely source for such crimes, rather than society as a whole, as is more generally feared.

*   Jan Pahl (1980) notes that male physical control of women in the family is usually combined with more economic control. Women are often not able to leave the situation if they wish to, for fear of having no way to supprt themselves.

*   Radical feminist Brownmiller (1976) goes one stage further and argues from a 'separatist' position that all men are rapists. She says that men are biologically violent, and that the act of heterosexual sex is actually an act of violation and domination of men over women.

*   Smart (1976) and Heidenshon (1996) have both noted that women and teenage girls are more likely to be controlled by the family than men and boys. They are more likely to have their freedom limited especially in terms of going out at night and in terms of sexuality.

- Another way we can think about the negativity of families is to think about the inequality in household roles that takes place in many families. Feminists such as Ann Oakley (1974) and Hannah Gavron (1966) illustrate that men do many fewer of the household chores than women do. Traditional gender roles thus oppress women more, making them 'captive' in the home.

- A further way in which we can think about the family is offered by radical psychiatrist R D Laing. He claims that the family is an 'emotional pressure cooker'. Because many people do not have wider kin to turn to on a regular basis the relationships in the family can get very strained. He thinks that such pressure in the family leads to the increase of mental illness in society, in particular the rise of schizophrenia, since family members feel under pressure not to be who they might want to be.

Conclusion

Not all families have the problems outlined above, but some do. This is enough to enable sociologists to reject common-sense and ideological views of the family as always a 'perfect' way to live.

For consideration:

1 Why do you think that in common-sense thought we often ignore the dark side of the family?
2 Why do you think the mass media might exaggerate this dark side?

✐ Coursework Suggestion

For A2 coursework you could look at how families treat male and female children differently. If you looked at families from different classes, ethnicities, and with parents of different ages, you might be able to make some interesting comparisons.

3.19 Do we have postmodern families?

What does this mean?

The postmodern view is a relatively recent addition to sociology. This theory claims that a massive and irreversible change has taken place in society in the past 20 years, making the world a very different place from what it once was. Such is the impact of this change, we are 'beyond the modern'. We have raced into fast forward, experiencing rapid change in all that we know – change at both macro and micro levels. Change that makes us question the nature of our very selves.

What are the features of a postmodern society?

- According to French sociologist Lyotard (1984) the 'postmodern condition' is about the rise of the relativity of truth. What this means is that things we used to believe in, or things that used to be true, are now uncertain. We now question the values, ideas and traditions of the recent past; certainty is becoming uncertain. We used to believe in science, for example, but many are now worried about the effects of science, and feel that we can't really believe what scientists tell us any more.

- In this postmodern view, Baudrillard (1988) claims that the previously stable knowledge we had of the world – the way we saw society and our place in it – has 'decomposed': it has all come crashing down.

- Although he is not a postmodernist, Giddens' ideas are reflected in the view above (1991) with his concept of 'manufactured uncertainty'. Giddens claims that we are increasingly aware of our place in the globe and of the ways in which there are many risks to daily living, many of which humans themselves have caused in the first place. This makes us anxious about what the world is really like and it makes us uncertain what our future might be like.

What are postmodern families?

The central change we have witnessed in terms of the family in recent years is the rapid increase in diversity and choice. This increase results in new ways of living and relating to others, and in turn the withering of older, more traditional values concerning how we should live our lives. Many sociologists agree that this change has occurred, and this certainly seems to match some of the ideas of the postmodern view above.

✓ Top Exam Hint

Try to use the ideas of postmodernism if you can – they are quite up to date and therefore show the examiner that you can do much more than simply give an answer using ideas that are now 50 to 100 years old in some cases.

✳ Key Idea

Giddens uses the term ontological insecurity to refer to the ways in which we worry about who we think we are in today's rapidly changing world.

Postmodern families are 'undecided', 'uncertain' and they are always changing.

Postmodern families:

- allow for more choice

- are not 'fixed' by past traditions

- offer new ways of living and relating to each other

- might offer more freedom to think about who we are and what we want

- might offer increased anxiety – we might decide we no longer know who we are, or what we want; there might be too many choices to make and the world might feel too uncertain.

Conclusion

When looking at the family, we can see two different possible consequences of this postmodernisation process, if it is true.

- The postmodern optimistic view – claims that increased diversity will lead to further choice and increased freedom

- The postmodern pessimistic view – claims that increased choice might lead to less certainty and therefore more anxiety about our world, our lives and our selves.

For consideration:

1 Do you feel the world is undergoing great change? How can you tell?
2 Do you feel families are uncertain?

3.20 What might the future of the family be?

What does this mean?

Sociologists have spent a great deal of time looking at the family in the past, and how it has changed. Some have tried to go one stage further to think about what it might be heading towards. What most sociologists agree on is that it is always changing.

What can we say about the changing family?

We can identify the following trends in the sociological treatment of the family, as seen in this chapter:

- the family feels private – but it might actually be open to quite a lot of public scrutiny

- we have wide family diversity

- many politicians might feel diversity in the family is damaging for society

- many sociologists can identify a clear ideology of the family that exists in society

- historical records on the family are often open to question

- common sense tells us that the family is natural – but how do we know for sure?

- the reality of family life is complex

- families are not things, but they are **practices** – they are ways of thinking about how we act with some people and what our roles mean.

Where does this leave us?

- For the New Right and the New Left the family is to be protected at all costs – the future of the society we live in depends upon it.

- The feminist approach, however, embraces family diversity. They feel that diversity best matches the reality of the modern family in the UK, although many feminists point out that the family is still a massive source of the control of women in society. Diversity might be a way of challenging this, however, since it means that women might have more options than ever before.

✓ **Top Exam Hint**

Use these bullet points as a way of making evaluative conclusions in appropriate exam questions.

✳ **Key Idea**

David Cheal uses the term 'family practices' rather than just 'family' to try to make the point that families are not 'things', but rather they are 'doings' or 'practices'.

- For Giddens the family is more democratic and equal than ever before. We have witnessed massive social change in our personal life and in our personal relationships with others and these changes have increased the opportunities and the challenges open to us. This could be a source of anxiety, or it could be a source for personal liberation and identity formation.

- The postmodern view on the future of the family would be to argue that present-day diversity is both a consequence of and a contribution to the increased postmodernisation of society in general, and of our personal lives, emotions and identities in particular. We are living through a world under rapid change.

Do we have 'brave new families'?

Ulrich Beck and Elisabeth Beck-Gernsheim (1995) argue that in our modern world the family is under question unlike ever before. Clearly the family always changes, but for Beck and for Giddens (1991, 1992) we are now able to think about and reflect upon these changes. We are aware of the changes while they are happening – this makes us uncertain about the future of the family as individuals and as a society.

Postmodern thinker Judith Stacey (1990) suggests that the time we are living in is 'contested' – we are uncertain what will happen. Beck's response to this is to say that we will always have some sort of family as it is, after all, the best symbol we have to describe those closest to us. Quite what it will be, however, only time will tell.

Conclusion

Berger (1963) noted a long time ago that the family is central to who we are. He refered to this as the 'sphere of the intimate'. This means that the family and the relationships we build help us to create our own personal biography, i.e. how we see who we are and the experiences we have had through our life course to date. If the future of the family is uncertain, then who we are is uncertain and who we might end up becoming.

For consideration:

1 What do you think the future of the family will be?
2 Do you think we are living through a period of change? Why?

✓ **Top Exam Hint**

It is interesting to note that in this chapter we have come across a few sociologists who make observations about the family whilst working with their own family members who are also sociologists. There are in fact three examples in this book so far. What might this tell us about our need as humans to understand our own family life?

Is childhood a social construction?

What does this mean?

The 'family' is a social construction since, as we have shown, it is a symbol that we think of as real, that we use in our minds and with others to describe the feelings we have and the relationships we have with those close to us.

Equally, as with other social constructions, the concept of age in general and of 'old age' and of 'childhood' in particular link to our understandings of roles within the family. In this view, childhood does not exist in terms of real biological ages, but rather, the reality of childhood lies in the value and interpretation that our culture places upon it.

What is age?

We often use the idea of a 'life course' to describe the ways in which time, age and the family all relate to each other. We can locate certain key points for our culture along the course of our life:

*   birth
*   early infancy
*   childhood
*   teenage years
*   early adulthood
*   middle age
*   old age.

Different cultures however, interpret the roles and 'scripts' associated with these stages in different ways. Equally, within societies over history, these roles change. Today, we are all too familiar with the idea of a 'stroppy teenager' – like the character of 'Kevin' played by comedian Harry Enfield. However, many sociologists agree that the idea of a 'teenager' was a product of the post-second world war era, with the creation of extended schooling and the rise of youth culture due to the creation of a music industry. Before the second world war, 'teenagers' as we understand them today simply did not exist. Instead, boys, for example, wore shorts at school, and then at fourteen left school, took up a trade if they were working class, started to wear long trousers and become an adult. No difficult transition – no hormones. This therefore suggests that age is a cultural creation if its characteristics can change throughout history.

Is childhood and teenagehood 'real'?

What is childhood?

The role played by children in the family, and the notion today of what we call 'childhood', is again an interesting social construction, as is the notion of old age.

- Childhood is seen as a biological given, yet it is the object of great public concern. The media and politicians frequently discuss how best to deal with deviant children and how best to protect our children from deviant adults. We have massive moral panics about child pornography, yet at the same time have young girls modelling for fashion houses in provocative dress. Archard (1993) notes that in our common-sense thought, childhood is based upon notions of 'separateness' from adulthood. Children are not adults, they are separate from adults, and need to grow up to be able to join the adult world. Children need to be protected from the adult world, yet at the same time taught how best to fit into it.
- This is very different from the Victorian time in the UK when children were 'seen but not heard'. Today we have what various writers describe as 'child-centredness' where many families put the wishes and desires of the children before their own. Brigitte and Peter Berger (1983) have noted that since the general decrease in infant mortality in the nineteenth century, children have become ever-present in the household. This has changed their role in the family quite considerably, from being able to offer an economic contribution, to the present dependence upon family members for the first sixteen years of their life.
- Phillipe Aries (1973) has argued that the idea of children as vulnerable to a harmful adult world is a recent cultural creation. For example, in the Middle Ages, children over five were actually considered to be adults and as such had economic and sexual roles in society – the latter a notion found abhorrent today.

Conclusion

Robert Bocock (1993) has suggested that over the past century we have seen the rise of a consumption role for children, and also in particular for that age we describe as 'teenagehood'. Capitalism needs people to buy the things it produces, in order to keep profits flowing. Children today, unlike ever before, are part of this process. Many products are aimed directly at them, effectively 'creating' or 'constructing' their identity as children – from toys to sweets, from clothes to the singles charts. All of this spending on, by and for children links directly to the ways in which the family is now often centred directly on children. Previously, before the creation of capitalism, children contributed to the family, rather than the family providing for them.

✳ Key Idea

Neil Postman (1985) suggests that childhood is disappearing in modern society; it is being decomposed. Due to the rise of the mass media, children are able to experience things that previously were only available to adults. As such they are growing up more quickly and in time this means our notions of age and of childhood will need to be changed once more.

For consideration:

1 Why do you think notions of childhood might change?
2 Can you see anything contradictory about how our society presently thinks about children, and their roles in the family?

3.22 Is old age a social construction?

What does this mean?

Age, and time for that matter, are both cultural creations. Clearly age does exist in a physical sense since our bodies get older, and eventually we will die. Yet, the meaning of age, and the social roles and expectations associated with different ages are the products of the culture you come from. Again, this is further confused by the fact that as we get older there are some things our bodies can no longer do.

How do we think about age?

- Sociologist and historian Norbert Elias (1992) has shown us that the very ideas of time and age vary quite considerably across the globe. In the West we think about a measurable, calendar age, related to the centrality of time for our cultures. Marxists add to this that capitalism needs a strong concept of time in order to be successful as the economic production process needs people to be able to measure time in a common way. Workers need to have a common sense of time in order to make sure they all arrive for work at the same point.
- In many cultures time might be measured by reference to the passing of historical events, or the passing of natural events such as floods or monsoons. There are many people around the globe who do not know their 'age' in the Western sense that they would know their birthday, the number of years lived, and the calendar age they had reached. This is something that in the West we would find almost incomprehensible, such is the dominance of clock time and calendar time in our culture.
- Time is everywhere, as are watches. Age gives roles to people, it allows people to think about themselves and allows others to think about them.

What is old age?

- In terms of old age, people are living longer today than ever before. This has fundamentally changed our experience of the family. We have more families today who have reached the end of the life course. Their children have moved away, creating the idea of a 'retired family'. Retirement, however, and the way that this affects the family, varies according to the class of the people involved. Retirement for an elderly couple with savings and a private pension will be very different and will offer more choices than it does for a couple with neither.
- Since people are living longer, old age becomes something society ends up thinking about and noticing more. Some suggest that we are

facing a future of an 'aged society' where the number of elderly people dependent upon the state for welfare will outnumber the number of people in full-time work. This is, rather stereotypically, sometimes referred to as the 'greying of society'.

- How society 'treats' the elderly, how ordinary people 'see' those who are old and interact with them, varies. In many cultures the elderly are treated with respect – they are seen as sources of great wisdom, as heads of the household. Many Marxists have pointed out that in modern-day capitalist societies the elderly are often defined as not useful. This is because they do not work and they often cannot buy very much, thus, they do not really make a contribution to the continuation of the capitalist economy. This is why the elderly, like children, are seen as a 'problem' for society, rather than as a rich source of knowledge and status. They are seen as a problem since they are really a problem for capitalism.

- Marxist Chris Phillipson (1982) suggests that the elderly are often defined in capitalist societies in the West as people whose usefulness to society has passed. They are ex-workers, retired from making a financial contribution to society. They are seen as a drain on the financial resources of the state.

- Giddens (1986) notes that in modern society the longer life expectancy of family members has had a massive effect on the nature of family life. Since people are living longer, we are increasingly exposed to a wider variety of relationships within the family. We have the increased likelihood of building relationships with grandparents and even great-grandparents, relationships that previously would never have existed since people would have died before it was possible to build them.

Conclusion

Many postmodern authors in sociology have also argued that as a society our attitude to the elderly is under considerable re-assessment in recent years.

- The elderly are beginning to develop an economic role of consumption – there are more things associated with old age for the elderly to buy.
- There is an increased recognition that the elderly can do things we would never have thought possible, e.g. exercise, wear fashionable clothes, etc. Our notions of old age are undergoing great change.
- There is the development of medical industries aimed at keeping the elderly younger, for example, hormone replacement therapy, plastic surgery and the invention of Viagra.

Meyrowitz (1984) has suggested that age is undergoing a reversal. Children are growing up and are becoming more adult-like, whereas adults are becoming more child-like; they are stopping their aging process.

✳ Key Ideas

- Giddens also argues, as does Elias, that due to the increase in old age, as a society our attitude to death is also under great change. Death is now much more hidden than it once was. As Elias says, 'Never before have people died as noiselessly and hygienically as today' (p.85). As people are living longer, death is becoming more invisible.

- Featherstone and Hepworth (1991) suggest that we are experiencing the rise of a 'mask of aging' brought about by medical and scientific development. We can change and mask the age we are, we can challenge unlike before how others think of us.

For consideration:

1 How do you think notions of old age have changed in society?
2 How does increased life expectancy affect the family?

3.23 Examination advice

In order to do the best you possibly can, follow the advice given over the next two sections of this chapter. You might also wish to think about the advice given at the end of every chapter (even if you don't actually study the topic, there still might be some good general advice you can follow).

- Know the time limits of the exam. Before the exam, practise past papers to the timing of the exam: time yourself so that you can devote the right amount of time for the right sort of questions.

- Understand the rules about word length. Short mark questions require only a sentence – sometimes two. The longer mark questions at the very end of the exam require much more depth; leave the right amount of time for these questions and make sure you write an appropriate amount. Many students every year in exams do not do their best because they simply get the word length wrong.

- Do the right sort of revision: it might help to think about revision as taking things out of your head – rather than as putting things in. It actually doesn't matter how much you know (or rather, 'remember') if you cannot actually get it out of your head onto paper – which, after all, is what the exam is asking you to do!

- There is more to 'learning sociology' than simply being able to remember things. Make sure that you also practise evaluation skills. They are much more important next year, but are still important this year. Think about what studies and theories agree and disagree with each other. Make lists of these agreements and disagreements as part of your revision, this should help with the longer mark questions in the exam.

- Make sure that you see the connections between the concepts and the studies or the named examples. One way of revising this would be to keep a vocabulary book throughout the year, and when it comes to revision make sure that you learn each concept and what it means, and for every concept make sure you have a named example that would agree and a named example that would disagree.

- Theory is an easy way of getting depth. Make sure that in your answers for the longer mark questions you are able to show a sense of the theory (the background) to the specific named example you are using. This is a way of putting the study or even the concept into a wider and more detailed context.

- Try to think about the problems of historical context in the family exam. Is it the case that what a particular sociologist thinks about the family is the product of the time period they were writing in? It probably would have some influence on their views after all.

● Synoptic link

Try to show in the exam that the family influences and in turn is also influenced by other aspects of society such as class, ethnicity, culture, education etc. This is a good way of exploring interesting ideas and of getting depth. You will also be practising important synoptic skills.

✍ Coursework Suggestion

The family is a very popular A2 coursework topic, it is an aspect of society that we are all familiar with after all. You could look at family diversity – how different classes or ethnicities structure their family relationships in different ways. Equally, you could look at roles around the home – who does what, and how does this link to the sociological literature?

✓ Top Exam Hint

Try to explore (but only if relevant) the fact that the family topic area is the victim of a series of massive methodological problems – problems with measuring, defining and gaining access in order to be able to do social research. This will help your answer have both depth and evaluation.

- Try to see if you can work issues of methods into your exam. It is actually very difficult to really know what goes on in families; they are, after all, 'behind closed doors'.

Key points to remember

1   Try to practise timed past papers as part of your revision

2   Try to explore issues of methods in the exam

3   Practise your evaluation skills

3.24 Pushing your grades up higher

If you can try to follow the advice below, then hopefully you will be able to push your grades up as high as possible. None of the following tips are, however, a substitute for good revision, but they will help if combined with good revision.

1   When it comes to answering questions on the family, make sure you can show that there are many problems regarding the measurement and definition of what families are and of what they do. These problems will have a huge effect on how sociologists see the family, and therefore the theories they have about the family. Try to spell out this important evaluation point if you can.

2   A major theme that runs throughout the whole of family sociology is the idea of an ideology of the family. This idea is relevant to a wide range of debates, exam questions and theories. It is also an excellent way to develop important evaluation skills – by questioning what we hold to be 'common-sense' and to be able to illustrate that these ideas might be open to question by sociological analysis.

3   Try to give a sense of the centrality of family life for the whole of society, and as a product of this, the centrality of family sociology to the whole of the subject. In a sense, the topic has in-built 'synoptic skills' since most things can be or are believed to be, related to the family.

4   Make sure that you read a good quality newspaper throughout your sociology course – there are often stories about family welfare policies and family legal changes. Keeping up-to-date with these changes will really help you to be able to apply recent legislation to the ideas and theories that you have learned, in particular the ideas of the New Right and the New Left.

5   The feminist view in the sociology of the family is an excellent tool to be used for evaluation. In a sense this theory has evaluation built into it, since it is highly critical of the common-sense view of the family and highly critical of the ideology of the family that it sees as being present within New Right thinking and the views of politicians.

6   Although it wouldn't be recommended that you do this very often, brief reference to how the media might portray the family and how this might have changed might also help you to build a picture where you can discuss the ideology of the family in some detail. You might be able to refer to a TV advert you have seen in order to discuss modern-day views on housework, etc.

Key points to remember

* try to demonstrate the problems we have with measurement of the family

* brief reference to the media and to current newspaper articles on the family might help you build depth

* try to use the idea of an ideology of the family where possible in order to be able to demonstrate the critical nature of sociology

3.25 Frequently asked questions

Q. Why are sociologists so worried about the family?

A. It is certainly true to say that sociologists are worried about the family; almost every sociology course you could imagine tends to deal with the sociology of the family at some point, and often quite early on in the course. The reason for this is that for many sociologists, the family is seen to be at the centre of society, therefore, it ends up at the centre of sociology as well. The family is a source of socialisation – it is our point of first contact with the world, and it provides our upbringing in this world. It is therefore very central to our thinking about our lives, our identities and our futures.

Q. Are there 'better' types of families than others?

A. No. Although the media, politicians and many on the New Right might try to claim that some families are better than others, sociologists tend to take a very different view. We hear a lot in the media about 'dysfunctional families' which are often associated with single parents, homosexual partnered families and families receiving welfare support, but this is a massive generalisation. In fact, many sociologists would go further than this and say that this type of thinking is an 'ideology' – a way of re-enforcing traditional values in society, values that tend to end up oppressing women.

Q. Why can't sociologists agree on the definition of the word 'family'?

A. The simple reason is that since there is so much family diversity, it is very difficult to say what exactly the family is – there are so many different types! Even to say what families do is difficult, since the different types might actually do different things from each other.

Chapter 4

Mass media

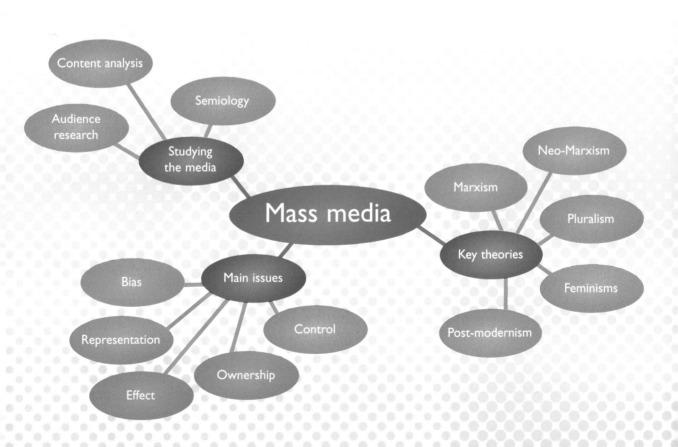

CD-ROM 4.1

Key issues in media sociology

Why are sociologists interested in the sociology of the media?

Sociologists are interested in the mass media because of the enormous power it seems to have over our lives. Sociologists have wanted to address questions such as: How does the media influence the world of politics and how can politics influence the media? How does the media influence our private lives and identities? How important is it that most of our knowledge of the world comes from the mass media?

What are the key debates in the sociology of the media?

The questions above have led to several key debates in the sociology of the mass media.

- Do the media just present the views of powerful social groups, or do all views get a fair hearing in the media? There is debate on this between Marxists and pluralists (see sections 5 and 6).

- Is our behaviour and our sense of personal identity determined by the mass media, or do we have the ability to select and shape our own destiny? If so, to what extent, and how can we be sure of this?

- Are the knowledge and information we gain from the media both objective (true, factual, uninfluenced by emotions) and balanced? Some sociologists argue that influences by powerful social groups and the fact that society is stratified (divided into social levels) may lead to systematic biases in the information that is broadcast by the media. To say that the media reflects systematic biases means that people in the media select what should be shown according to their own personal tastes and prejudices, and that this occurs in patterned ways. For example, a white news editor may think that news items about race are not important, and so may regularly ignore such items.

What are the key ideas and concepts in the sociology of the media?

There are several key concepts that we should start with.

- First, consider the term 'mass media' itself. This refers to any form of communication with a mass audience, e.g. books, newspapers, radio, television, the Internet. Sociologists argue that these media can have important effects on society because of their mass audiences.

- Another important, but debated, concept is **ideology**. Ideologies produce distorted views of reality. Some sociologists believe that the media produces and broadcasts ideologies, and that these work as a form of social control, maintaining social order.

- Lastly, related to these previous concepts, the idea of media effects suggests that the mass media can influence our behaviour in many ways.

What are the key problems in the sociology of the media?

Some of the key problems that arise in studying the mass media are methodological and theoretical. Methodological problems arise from the way in which concepts are defined and studied. Theoretical problems are concerned with the general assumptions that researchers may have, such as whether society is characterised by conflict or cooperation, or in the case of the media, whether audiences are active or passive.

- Many of the concepts we use are hard to define and measure. For example, when looking at whether people's behaviour is influenced by violent or sexual programmes, we have to decide how we define 'violence' or 'sexual'. Sociologists refer to this as **operationalisation** (for an example, see section 15).

- It is hard to disentangle causes and effects. If a person acts violently (whatever that may mean), can we be sure that the media caused the behaviour? It might be only one element in a complex set of causes.

- A key theoretical problem is whether audiences are active or passive. This relates to the different types of theories in sociology: action theories and structural theories (see Introduction). Sociologists have very different views as to whether we can act as we wish or whether our actions are constrained by social structures.

66 99 Key Definitions

- **Ideology** – a set of beliefs that forms the basis of a political or other system, which reflect the social needs and aspirations of an individual or group.

- **Operationalisation** – this refers to the way that sociologists define concepts. If we are trying to measure 'violence' in the media, we need to be able to show how we define it. Does it include things like verbal aggression? This can sometimes be as traumatic as physical violence. Having made a definition, sociologists need to select an indicator. For example, an indicator of class is occupational title. There is often debate about how a concept is defined and whether the indicators chosen are valid.

✍ Coursework Suggestion

If you are doing your coursework on the media it's very important to discuss how you have operationalised and measured key concepts in your project. Discuss why you defined and measured the concepts in the way you did, and why that was better than some of the alternatives you could have used.

✓ Top Exam Hint

You can always use methodological concepts to evaluate theories and findings in sociology. **Operationalisation** is a really good term to use for this. However, lots of students fail to make the most of it, thinking it's enough just to write the word down. Make sure you explain what it means (with an example) and show how it might lead to a completely different way of interpreting a piece of research and often a rejection of the researcher's conclusion.

● Synoptic Link

It's vital to make the connections between key sociological issues, such as the methodological points on operationalisation and the theoretical debates on structure and action. This is because these will influence the answers that sociologists reach and you therefore need to show that you understand how and why researchers come up with different answers. So if you do this, it will show that you are trying – and succeeding – to think sociologically.

What do we need to know about media sociology?

What does the specification say about the media?

The AQA specification identifies four main aspects of the media for students to investigate.

You need to understand the following: how sociologists explain the relationship between ownership and control; how the media content is selected and represented; what role the media plays in representing key social groups; and what sociologists have said about the relationship between the media and its audiences.

Also, don't forget that there are two core themes that you should be aware of: socialisation, culture and identity; and social differentiation, power and stratification. Good candidates will not waste the opportunity to show their understanding of the media's role in socialisation, and will be able to discuss the role of the media in a society stratified by class, race and gender, and characterised by differences in power.

How will I be examined in this topic?

You will have to answer one question on the mass media, which consists of six parts (a to f). You will be able to score a maximum of 60 marks, awarded as follows; a = 2, b = 4, c = 6, d = 8, e and f = 20 marks each.

There will be one data item at the beginning of the question. This is intended to make you think on your feet and so help you to bring a bit of originality to your exam work. It should also discourage students from just regurgitating material learnt parrot-fashion. The item does not have to be a passage of text. It could be a table of statistics, or some other piece of research data, even a photograph.

You will have 75 minutes to answer all of these questions.

How well does this topic relate to coursework?

There is lots of scope for coursework in this topic. Content analysis is a relatively easy research method, and most people have access to the mass media. As gender, race and class identities (as well as issues such as age and disability) are hotly debated now, there is a wide choice of topics to investigate. Also don't forget that these issues can be studied in relation to

---

✓ Top Exam Hint

It is a very good idea to check through the specification for your exam board and obtain copies of past papers and mark schemes. Make sure you know and understand what the exam will test you on, and note down how the marks will be awarded. You will be able to find information about exam board publications and the specification on the following website: www.aqa.org.uk

the Internet, and this itself also raises new questions about technology, media and identity.

How well does this topic help with synopticity?

There are lots of links between the media and other topics.

Family How are our views of social policy and social problems formed by the media? Consider media portrayal of different social groups, for example, underclass, teenage mothers, single parent families (see sections 9, 10, 11, 12, 18).

Education There have been moral panics (for key definition, see section 18) about various educational issues in recent years. These include debates about standards in education, as well as concerns with discipline, and fears about drug use and sexual abuse.

Crime and deviance How does the media influence our view of crime and deviance? (See sections 15, 16, 18.)

Sociological theory Our understanding of the media has to be related to several key theoretical debates, such as: the structure/action debate (agency, active/passive audience), and debates about globalisation (for key definition, see section 21) and postmodernism (for key definition, see section 20). See also sections 14, 15, 17, 18, 19, 22).

Methodology This topic involves some important general methodological problems in sociology, in particular the problem of operationalisation and measurement. Examples from this topic can be used to illustrate your understanding of this key methodological concept. You can also use your understanding of the links between the media and violence, and the wider issue of media effects to highlight the problems in trying to identify the causes of social action (see sections 14, 15, 17, 19).

Key points to remember

- Check your specification, and get copies of past papers and mark schemes.

- Find out how this topic is related to other parts of your sociology course.

- Think about how this topic relates to general sociological concepts (especially theory and method) and remember to use the course themes.

66 99 Key Definition

Synopticity – this refers to the links between different topic areas you have studied in sociology. This is clearly important for examination purposes, but it is also good sociology. Sociologists can only explain social phenomena (things that happen in society) by exploring the links between different aspects of society. You cannot fully understand the media without a good understanding of theory and methods. Similarly, sociologists would say that you cannot fully understand how we think about crime and deviance in our society without also understanding how views about crime are shaped by the media.

How can we find out about the mass media?

How have sociologists tried to measure media effects?

Sociologists use the whole range of research methods available when studying the mass media. Which method they use will depend to a considerable extent on what they are trying to find out. Research on the media tends to fall into two groups.

1 Projects investigating media effects and audiences' response to the media.
2 Studies focusing on investigating media messages and representations.

The former may use well-known research methods such as interviews, questionnaires, focus groups, or experiments. The latter tend to use less common methods like content analysis and semiology (explained below).

The strengths and weaknesses of the research methods used in the first group mentioned above are well known (see Chapter 2, Sociological research skills and methods). Sociologists also have to pay particular attention to issues of operationalisation and validity (does the study give a true picture of reality?) when using these methods to study the media. Content analysis and semiology, although they are very appropriate in studying the media, are less well-known methods, so they will be the main focus here.

What methods do sociologists tend to use to study the mass media?

Content analysis is a quantitative method, which allows sociologists to analyse and measure the content of the media. Observers can, for example, examine and measure the extent of bias in news reports, identify how much time the media spends on certain issues, or see whether characters in adverts or soap operas are stereotyped (e.g. on grounds of race, class, gender, age, and so on).

Researchers select certain programmes or types of programmes to view (using **sampling techniques**), and then analyse the content using a coding scheme. A coding scheme allows the content of the media to be placed into a category. For example, researchers watching prime-time viewing on British television channels could record a category of 'violent characters contained in programme', by noting every time they saw a 'violent' character in a programme. At the end of a programme the researcher would be able to quantify the number of 'violent' characters seen in the programme. Other coding categories in the scheme might allow the recording of further information, e.g. whether the perpetrator of violence was male, their age, race, and so on.

✓ Top Exam Hint

Comments on methodological issues such as the strengths and weaknesses of a particular method, or comments on validity, reliability, or the operationalisation of a concept, are a good way to evaluate and analyse the accuracy of research findings and theories.

66 99 Key Definition

Sampling Techniques – sociologists can use various sampling techniques in order to gain a representative sample of media output. They can use a sampling frame, such as a newspaper list of all the programmes being broadcast. They could then pick every 10th programme, for example, to gain a systematic random sample. Alternatively, they could, by entering all the programmes onto a database, use a computer to pick a number of programmes entirely at random (making the sample truly random).

Semiology is the scientific study of signs and symbols, developed by French thinkers such as Ferdinand de Saussure (1974) and Roland Barthes (1973). Semiologists argue that all societies have a shared understanding of language, including signs and symbols. This means that we can examine the media and analyse the meanings of the language and signs that are used. For example, images of a national flag could signify nationalism, and images of pretty women could signify and reinforce patriarchal ideals of femininity and the female role.

What problems with definition are encountered in studying the media?

The main problem with content analysis is that it can be very hard to ensure that coding schemes are reliable, and interpretation of the coding scheme can become very subjective (see Chapter 2, Sociological research skills and methods). This is a problem with definition. In the previous example, for instance, different researchers (and media audience) may have widely differing views as to whether a character or indeed a programme is 'violent'. This can mean that the research lacks reliability, and it also means that the quantitative data produced by content analysis may not give a true reflection of how a message or representation is received by an audience. Therefore content analysis may lack validity. This means that it may not be giving a true picture of reality because it is highly dependent on the way researchers select and categorise the data. It may also lack reliability because different researchers may reach different decisions, and so they may be collecting and interpreting different information.

As for semiology, critics have argued that signs are always interpreted from various social positions, and that audiences may interpret signs in widely varying ways. As some critics of semiology put it, meanings (for our purposes, being the same as 'definitions') are not fixed; they are polysemic (open to many different interpretations).

Conclusion

Content analysis and semiology assume that the media audience is passive and that media content will inevitably have powerful effects. They seem to neglect the possibility that people will challenge media representations. These methods also involve considerable difficulties in defining the representations and concepts that sociologists are studying. This does not mean we should not use these methods, but we should be aware of the pitfalls.

Key points to remember

- Content analysis depends on coding schemes – and these are open to interpretation.
- Semiology works on the assumption that there are shared views about the meaning of signs – but others argue that signs are polysemic.
- Understanding media content and its effects can only be achieved by looking at the meaning media content has in its social context – and it may be contested.

☞ **Who are these People?**

Ferdinand de Saussure (1857–1913) and Roland Barthes (1915–80) were both important French academics. Both were interested in the way in which symbols are used socially to create meanings and the social effects that such symbolic use has.

● **Synoptic Link**

Remember that you can use this topic to answer synoptic questions about methodology. However, it is always a good principle to demonstrate sociological understanding by showing how theory, methods, and substantive topic areas have to be interrelated for a full understanding.

What have Marxists said about control of the mass media?

✳ Key Idea

Marx's own work best illustrates what could be called '**traditional Marxism**'. Some 20th-century Marxists can also be described in this way, though they vary in their detailed assessments of Marx. Traditional Marxists argue that all aspects of society can be explained in terms of their relationship to the economy. The fact that there are owners and workers, and that these two classes exist in conflict, shapes (or determines) everything else in society.

❝❞ Key Definition

False class-consciousness – this Marxist concept assumes that the proletariat fail to recognise that they are exploited and oppressed. This has been strongly debated, with critics claiming that it is illogical – is it only Marxist sociologists who can correctly identify the existence of exploitation?

☞ Who is this Person?

Karl Marx (1818–1883) was a prolific thinker and writer. Born in Germany, he is famous for writing *The Communist Manifesto* and for being the inventor of communism. He studied philosophy before becoming a journalist and political activist. His political activities made him unwelcome in Germany and France, and he settled in London in 1849. He is important for his writing on the nature of capitalist society.

What does this mean?

Marxist theory has traditionally seen the mass media as a form of social control, as a way in which dominant social classes perpetuate their own dominant ideas. Marxists claim that the media simply transmits the dominant ideology. Dominant ideologies are the ideas that are most powerful, and Marxists argue that these are always the ideas of the capitalist ruling class. This is said to make the working class have a **false class-consciousness**. This means that they have a false understanding of their true position in capitalist society. Marxists would argue that watching a diet of soap operas and game shows on television dupes the majority of the working class into a passive (unquestioning) acceptance of the capitalist system and their own exploitation within that system. This view is known as the manipulative or instrumentalist approach and makes several key claims.

- The capitalist owners of the mass media deliberately aim to popularise ideas that will be to the direct benefit of capitalism and the capitalist class (of which they are members).

- The owners of the mass media have direct control over the ideas communicated through the mass media.

- The mass media is an instrument that allows its owners to ensure that their ideas and interests are the ones that gain most attention.

- The owners manipulate the mass media in the interests of the capitalist class by controlling the material that their editors and journalists publish. This means that they can and will intervene in the day-to-day running of the mass media, promoting the publication of particular items or news that they feel strongly about, and suppressing others.

- The mass media audience are seen as passive consumers of the distorted and partial accounts of news, and of the cheap distracting entertainment, which the media provides them with. The mass audience uncritically accepts what is given to them and so public opinion is easily manipulated by the mass media.

Why have neo-Marxists been so critical of traditional Marxist views?

In the 20th century neo-Marxists, such as Gramsci, were keen to rectify what they saw as the mistakes of traditional Marxism. Neo-Marxists argue that empirical evidence contradicts the idea that the owners of the media always directly control and manipulate the content of the media. Far more important, they argue, is the fact that the majority of managers, editors and journalists share a similar social background (class, race and gender); the media is still dominated by white, middle-class males. They also believe that with the wide variety of media outlets now available, even views critical of capitalism find their way into print and onto the airwaves and the Internet.

These points seem to suggest that the Marxist view is wrong. However, neo-Marxists say that it just means that Marxism has to be modified to take into account the changed circumstances of contemporary society. They argue that ideological dominance works in a more subtle way than traditional Marxism assumed. Ruling-class ideas are dominant in the media because those who run the media have a shared set of assumptions and social backgrounds. Neo-Marxists use the concept of hegemony, which means dominance or leadership. The dominant ideology is seen as being one of many sets of competing ideas, and its dominance or leadership is never complete. Alternative ideas always exist and can challenge it. Manipulative media owners do not suppress alternative and critical views. According to neo-Marxists these views are more effectively marginalised if they are permitted to exist. This has the advantage of reinforcing the legitimacy and fairness of the dominant ideas, since all ideas appear to have had a fair hearing. At the same time, alternative viewpoints can often be easily made to appear naïve or lacking in common sense.

Conclusion

Like many theories, Marxism has been adapted to changed circumstances. However, whilst neo-Marxism may seem subtler than traditional Marxist accounts, it is worth remembering that many non-Marxist sociologists would agree that the content of the media is indeed manipulated by owners and others, at various times for many different reasons.

For consideration:

1 Is Marxist analysis still relevant?
2 Does the neo-Marxist approach underestimate the power of those who own the mass media?

☞ Who is this Person?

Antonio Gramsci was an Italian Marxist and member of the Italian Communist Party in the 1920s. He was imprisoned by Mussolini and eventually died in prison. Gramsci worked as a journalist and political activist. His political experiences led him to reflect on the importance of cultural factors and ideology in preventing the development of revolutionary ideas, and this led him to develop an influential critique of traditional Marxism.

✷ Key Idea

Neo-Marxism was very influential in Britain in the 1970s and 1980s. It seemed to be a good way of dealing with the obvious weaknesses of traditional Marxism, by providing a more sophisticated picture of the relationship between the state, capitalism and the ruling classes. It demonstrated that culture was an important aspect of capitalist society, by showing that the norms or values about race or gender were the result of cultural beliefs and were not caused by economic factors.

✓ Top Exam Hint

You will impress examiners if you show that there are different schools of thought within Marxism. A key difference is that between traditional Marxism and neo-Marxism.

● Synoptic Link

Relate your general theoretical knowledge and understanding to this topic. You could discuss how recently Marxists have dealt with the problem of economic reductionism (seeing everything as being caused by economic factors, e.g. neglects cultural beliefs like religion). You could also gain a lot of credit by relating this to the structure/action debate. Marxism leans heavily towards the structure side in this debate. Say how big a problem you think this is and whether there are any points Marxists can make in reply.

What do pluralists say about control of the media?

Robert Maxwell (1923–1991) succeeded in building a publishing empire that spanned the world.

What does this mean?

Pluralists such as James Whale (1997) argue that the Marxist case neglects important empirical (observed) facts, exaggerates the power of the media, is not based on an accurate idea of the way audiences respond to the mass media, and uses unhelpful concepts such as 'ruling class ideology'. This means that the picture of the role of the mass media in contemporary society presented by Marxists lacks validity.

Pluralists make several key claims.

* They claim that society consists of many competing interest groups. None of these groups inevitably gets its own way in the mass media, and views are continually being contested. Large and powerful interest groups are often challenged and criticised, and sometimes these challenges may be successful.

* Pluralists claim that access to the media is now easy for all to gain. It is in the interests of the media to cater to the needs of minority interest groups; they can after all be another source of profit for media organisations.

* Pluralists also argue that not all media owners try to control media content. In fact, owners who attempt to exert day-to-day control of the content of the media (as did media tycoon Robert Maxwell) are the exception rather than the rule. Pluralists taking this approach can also point to the many cases where top newspaper editors become involved in disputes with owners over control of editorial content.

* Pluralists also argue that media owners and professionals cannot afford to ignore the views and interests of the public, since if the public dislike a newspaper or television/radio station, they will stop buying it or watching/listening to it and this will mean the end of business for that organisation.

* Finally, pluralists argue that the concept of a ruling class ideology provides an unconvincing model of how people act (human agency). People are not stupid, they have consciousness and the ability to think for themselves, and they use the mass media in an active way. Mass audiences pick and choose what they listen to, read, and watch,

and they are also capable of knowing when they are being lied to. Audiences should be seen as '**active audiences**'.

What criticisms can be made in response to the pluralist case?

Several criticisms can be made of the pluralist view.

1 Marxists would argue that there is not equal access to the media. Minority interest groups can easily publish a newsletter or run a website, but they will find it difficult to equal the sales revenues of large media corporations, which is important if they wish to maintain a publication or media outlet for a long period of time to gather and build support.

2 Media owners can try to control the content of the media if they choose. Owners are not always successful in doing this, but they still have more power to do this than most other groups in society.

3 Governments do attempt to manage the media. They are not always successful, but it seems unlikely that they always fail. The pressure to provide what the public wants can lead to a reduction rather than an increase in choice, as it may well become uneconomical to publicise minority views.

4 Finally, the mass media is still dominated by white, male, middle-class professionals, and this influences the content of the mass media.

Conclusion

Pluralists argue that the ownership and control of the mass media do not inevitably lead to bias. However, the pluralist approach is founded upon the highly contested view that all members of society, and all interest groups, have equal power to gain access to the media, and indeed to the truth.

For consideration:

1 How could people's freedom to choose and interpret media representations and images be constrained? How could this influence your assessment of the pluralist view?
2 Has the expansion in the number of television channels led to a significantly wider range of views, opinions and representations in the media?

66 99 Key Definition

Active audience theories argue that media effects are always limited because the audience have to be seen as having the ability to choose and interpret media representations and messages. This assumes that people's behaviour is not completely determined by structures – they have agency.

✓ Top Exam Hint

In evaluating and analysing the pluralist view, it's worth noting that you cannot reach conclusions simply by viewing one sort of evidence. Empirical evidence (this means evidence gained from research) is of course helpful, but its significance has to be interpreted, and this can only be done by using sociological theories. Remember in sociology, theory and method always go together.

● Synoptic Link

It is important to link your understanding and knowledge of theoretical debates about power, structure and agency to this issue.

Who owns the media?

Rupert Murdoch, though Australian-born and a US citizen, has a strong grip on the UK media sector as well as the American and Australian media.

What does this mean?

Media ownership is increasingly complex. Ownership of the mass media tends to be increasingly dominated by a small number of large corporations. For example, in the USA, currently about ten corporations dominate the media, whilst in Britain four companies produce around 85 per cent of national and Sunday newspapers. New patterns of ownership mean that one individual very rarely owns these corporations, and this raises questions as to how such complex corporations can control media content.

Marxist views – ownership equals control

Traditional or classical Marxism argues that there is a direct relationship between the ownership of the media and control of media content. Owners are, in other words, able to ensure that only views that they approve of are published in the media. The media is therefore seen to act in ways that reinforce capitalism and the interests of capitalists.

Neo-Marxists claim that this view no longer accurately reflects media ownership and control. Because there are very few examples of media corporations that are entirely run and owned by one person, neo-Marxist theorists argue that the influence of ownership will be more complex and there will be a more indirect form of control. Neo-Marxists argue that media owners may vary in the degree to which they control media products. Far more important, neo-Marxists argue, is the fact that the media reflects the assumptions and ideas of the dominant social groups. It is the world-view of this elite, which is predominantly white, male, middle-class and middle-aged, which is reinforced by the media. Media ownership is important then, even though ownership is less concentrated in the hands of a few individuals. This means that capitalist influence is even subtler and more powerful than the classical Marxist tradition assumes.

Pluralist views– the public gets what the public wants

Pluralists argue that Marxist views are highly exaggerated and make a number of criticisms of the Marxist approach.

1   Pluralists point out that the public exercise choice in the media products they use. If the media does not provide what the public wants, then they will stop buying newspapers and television licences, satellite television, and so on. Thus ownership does not matter,

because the owners are not all powerful – they have to satisfy public demand.

2 Moreover, pluralists would argue that the power of the media is democratically controlled and accountable, since governments regulate the media and there are anti-monopoly laws in most countries that prevent one owner having too much power.

3 Pluralists would point to the many examples of journalists and editors who act against the wishes of media owners and who work hard to hold the 'powerful' (e.g. politicians, public officials and top business leaders) to account. If ownership really did mean control of media content, then surely this sort of high quality journalism would never get published at all?

4 Lastly, pluralists argue that Marxist approaches mistake the nature of the audience. Audiences are not passive and uniform; they are diverse and critically engage with media output from many different perspectives, and do not simply believe everything they read or hear.

Conclusion

It seems clear that media ownership is increasingly concentrated in the hands of a small number of large corporations. Pluralists are right to point out that new technology means that almost anyone can publicise a particular view or interest that they have. However, this does not mean that all views can gain an equal amount of attention. The crucial aspect of this issue is, then, the effects of restricted media ownership. All sides in this debate make useful points on this matter. Ultimately though, the evidence has to be interpreted in terms of a theoretical perspective. One of the key differences between Marxists and pluralists is their view of power and it is this that leads them to reach very diverse conclusions about the importance of new patterns of media ownership.

For consideration:

1 Has the expansion in the number of media outlets in recent years (digital and cable TV, the Internet, commercial radio) led to a broadening of ownership?
2 Do media owners take sufficient notice of viewers' opinions? What factors encourage owners to listen to public feedback?

 What, When and Why?

Sociological and public debate on the ownership and control of the media reflects the concerns of a particular time. Issues of ownership have not always been so controversial, for example in the earlier part of the 20th century. In recent years though, the growth of cross-media and transnational ownership, and the domination of the media by figures such as Rupert Murdoch, has led to increased debate and concern on the issue.

✓ **Top Exam Hint**

In assessing the importance of ownership and its influence on editorial control, remember to use the theoretical perspectives to interpret and analyse empirical findings.

Who decides what counts as news and how is it selected?

Princess Diana and Mother Teresa died within five days of each other in 1997, yet Princess Diana's death received vast amounts of media coverage compared to Mother Teresa's. What does this tell us about the selection of news?

What does this mean?

Many people would probably agree that what we read in the newspapers or see on the television is called 'the news' precisely because it is novel, unpredictable and exciting to us. It is, in short, new.

However, sociologists have argued that the process by which journalists create the news is a manufacturing process and its production processes are quite predictable.

Philip Schlesinger's (1978) study of news production showed how journalists use a 'news diary' to make their job easier by creating a daily routine. The 'news diary' consists of important national events, such as key political events (Budget Day, for example), around which editors can start to plan coverage. This means that articles can be prepared months, weeks or days in advance of an event. Planning which stories will be covered, and having some advance notice, is vital for journalists who usually have to work to very tight deadlines.

However, journalists do not just randomly pick out what seem to them to be interesting items. They are guided by 'news values' – shared norms and values about what is of importance and interest to the audience. Research by Galtung and Ruge (1981) shows that there are two key sets of factors involved in determining journalists' news values: bureaucratic and cultural.

Bureaucratic factors refer to the routines of journalism and the form that these impose on news items:

- News items must be immediate, and refer to current affairs, not to historical or dated issues or events.
- News has to be brief.
- News has to be simple.

News is also defined by cultural factors and has to be:

- Novel, exciting and different, e.g. disasters.
- It must focus on elite decision-makers, and on personalities rather than issues.
- It is ethnocentric – people are interested in news that they see as most relevant to their life. Ethnocentric means centred on one particular ethnic or cultural group.

Do the media set an agenda for society?

Sociologists would say that since journalists (influenced by news values) manufacture the 'news', the whole process of making the news is socially constructed. Most sociologists who have studied the mass media have drawn the conclusion that since this is true, it follows that media professionals have the power to present agendas (lists of issues) as to what key issues society should be concerning itself with at any particular time. This happens in several ways.

- Stuart Hall (1982) argues that the elite groups of decision-makers and public figures who are regularly featured in the media become the 'primary definers' of public affairs and debates.
- Studies by McQuail (1972), and McCombs and Shaw (1973), say that the media act as 'agenda setters'. What this means is that as media professionals select what is newsworthy, they are in a position to shape the way public debate is conducted, to influence what issues are seen as being most important and worthy of debate, and what issues are seen as being unimportant.
- Herbert Gans (1974) suggests that key figures, such as editors, act as 'gatekeepers'. They are able to make decisions as to which news items are of most significance and thus which should gain access to media space.

This gives the media tremendous power to influence public debate, and this is why government advisers ('spin doctors') are so keen to control the media and get it on their side. It is also why various interest groups and pressure groups employ press officers to liaise with and attempt to influence the media.

The Glasgow University Media Group (GUMG) has become famous for their research in this area. They have shown not only how the media are selective in their choice of which issues deserve reporting, but also in the presentation of the news. In their study 'Bad News' (1976), the GUMG shows how television news has routinely been biased in its portrayal of industrial disputes, through, for example, asking biased questions and focusing on particular issues such as strikes and disputes in large companies (see section 8).

Conclusion

Sociological studies show that what we think of as a spontaneous and unbiased recording of 'news' is in fact socially constructed. Journalists' shared notions of 'news values' guide their activities. Moreover, their ability to **set agendas** and to control access to the media through '**gatekeeping**', means that the media can have a considerable influence on public debate.

For consideration:

1 Does the media set the agenda for public debate, and does it matter if it does?
2 Are media professionals still recruited from a narrow range of social groups?

✓ Top Exam Hint

If a question asks you to evaluate the role of the media in the selection and presentation of the news, it's a very good idea to use the theoretical views discussed in previous sections to help you do this (see sections 4, 5, 6).

66 99 Key Definition

The terms '**gatekeeper**' and '**agenda setting**' refer to the way in which senior editors are able to control access to the media, and thus determine which stories and information are broadcast or published. By selecting only certain information and news items, the media help to form an 'agenda' for debate. An agenda is a list of issues that will be discussed at a meeting.

● Synoptic Link

The ideas of 'news values' and 'agenda setting' are seen as an important influence in the social construction of crime and deviance (see section 16).

4.8 Is the media biased?

What does this mean?

'**Bias**' means prejudice or distortion. Many sociologists have argued that the media is often biased in its representation of social groups and in its presentation of social issues. For example, many news programmes have been seen as giving only one side of the story, or as neglecting some stories as being of no interest to the audience. One of the most famous groups of sociologists who have studied bias in the media is the Glasgow University Media Group (GUMG).

How do organisational factors cause bias?

Sociologists point out that the way the media is organised is itself a cause of bias. In terms of news, for example, the media as we have seen, have to package and present news material within certain restraints, e.g. time, amount of space and news values. In addition, media editors and owners are in a powerful position to influence the coverage of the media through agenda setting, gatekeeping, and norm setting. However, these factors also apply to other branches of the media, whether it is light entertainment or highbrow documentary programmes. Media producers are in a position where they can, and in fact have to, select the content that they believe their viewers, listeners or readers will want.

What other factors might cause bias?

The media is also influenced by political constraints that limit what can and cannot be printed or broadcast, and this can led to various biases. For example, the government operates what is known as the 'D notice' system, which enables it to prevent the disclosure of military and defence-related information. The media are also required to adhere to guidelines imposed by the Press Complaints Commission and the Independent Television Commission, although critics argue that these are lightweight regulatory bodies with relatively little power.

In addition to these factors, sociologists would also argue that the media could be biased by ideological and structural factors. In terms of ideological factors, sociologists would refer to the dominant ideas within a society, and argue that these could lead to systematic bias in what or how particular issues are reflected in a society. For example, the long tradition of the 'page three' topless woman in *The Sun* newspaper reflects the patriarchal values of British society. This example can also be seen as reflecting the structural factors that lead to bias – a key one in this case being the need for profit. Marxist-influenced sociologists would argue that the need to make a profit leads to bias in the media. This is because media editors and owners have to publish and present material that meets the demands of the audience. Moreover, the media also have to be sensitive to the needs of those businesses that buy advertising space. Articles that bring attention to, for example, the dangers of smoking, or the exploitative employment practices of a large multinational corporation, could clearly have a negative effect on a business. Businesses can therefore exert pressure upon the media, since the media depend not just on their audience, but also on advertisers.

The work of the GUMG in the 1970s found evidence of considerable bias in the coverage of industrial relations disputes. In the 1960s and 1970s relations between workers and employers in the UK were characterised by mistrust and conflict, and strikes were common. The political situation, with trade unions seen to be questioning the right of the government to govern, meant that strikes were very newsworthy. In this climate, claims of biased reporting became quite common (on both sides) and so it was an obvious area for sociologists to investigate.

Conclusion

In the light of the evidence considered here it seems indisputable that the media is biased. In theoretical terms, many sociological viewpoints would concur (see the frequently asked questions at the end of this chapter) with the idea that the media is inevitably biased. However, this does not necessarily mean that we have to be completely despairing of the media. Sociological research shows us why we need to view the media more cautiously, and indeed by showing us the techniques media professionals use, it teaches us how to be more critical. Also, criticism from academics has forced media professionals to think more carefully about their editorial decisions.

◆ **What, When and Why?**

The Glasgow University Media Group (GUMG) has been researching the media since the1970s. They found that coverage of industrial relations was routinely biased in various ways. Trade unionists were usually filmed protesting outside factories, and this made them look like mob leaders. Managers, on the other hand, were filmed in their offices, looking calm and professional.

✓ **Top Exam Hint**

In discussing and evaluating to what extent the media is biased you will show a greater understanding of the issue if you can relate it to other concepts and perspectives studied in the topic. Pluralist, Marxist and neo-Marxist perspectives on the media would have very different views on the extent of bias here and whether it should be considered a problem. These different views are the result of the different view of power that each perspective adopts.

For consideration:

1 What effects can bias in the media have and how important are these effects?
2 Is it possible for the media to be unbiased?

Is the media sexist?

THE OTHER WAY
TO YOUR MAN'S HEART
IS DOWN THE M6 AND
OFF AT JUNCTION 4

A recent advertisement for the 2002 Motor Show, which caused much debate. Does it support the view that the media is sexist?

✳ Key Ideas

- Gender
  Remember that sex and gender are two distinct things. Gender, or sexual identity, refers to the way ideas about the sexes are socially constructed and learned. The media is an important source of reinforcing or even creating certain gender roles and stereotypes.

- Masculinity
  Sean Nixon argues that media images helped to create new views of masculinity in the 1980s. Nixon studied the way men's fashions were represented in men's magazines like Loaded, as well as looking at advertising. He argues that media representations did contribute to a changed cultural climate, where it was more acceptable for men to act in ways previously considered feminine, for example, wearing an earring, and using a range of perfumes (aftershave, deodorants, and so on).

What does this mean?

Sexism is discrimination against individuals or groups on the basis of their sex.

Many sociologists have claimed that media representations or images discriminate against one sex or the other by portraying them in a narrow and **stereotypical** manner.

How are men and women portrayed in the media?

There is a great deal of research showing that media representations of men dominate the media and are more positive (but nevertheless still stereotypical) than those of women. Representations of women tend to reflect negative stereotypes.

- Since the 1970s, for instance, various studies (e.g. Dominick and Rauch (1972), Brelt and Cantor (1988), Cumberbatch (1990)) have shown that images of men are predominant in adverts, usually in more authoritative roles or in higher status occupations. The majority of voice-overs in adverts use male voices.

- Studies such as Marjorie Ferguson's *Forever Feminine* (1983) and Dee Meehan's *Ladies of the Evening* (1983) argue that media representations promote and reinforce powerful norms of femininity. Women in the media thus tend to be portrayed in roles submissive to men. They are, for example, sex objects, housewives and mothers; roles that are emotional and passive rather than physical and assertive.

- Feminist sociologists such as Gaye Tuchman (1978) have therefore concluded that women are symbolically annihilated (symbolically destroyed) and marginalised in media representations. Men have tended to be represented in the opposite way to that of women as detailed above, usually being portrayed as strong, independent, resourceful, and authoritative. Some male and female characters may fail to meet the norms, but the obvious implication in such media representations is that these characters are not 'proper' men or women.

Do media representations of gender matter?

To some extent we probably all dislike being stereotyped, but sociologists have been interested in whether negative media representations can have harmful effects on us. For example, feminists such as Andrea Dworkin (1981) have argued that the negative portrayal of women may reinforce male violence and aggression. Susie Orbach, counsellor and author of *Fat is a Feminist Issue* (1986), has argued that the dominant images of 'supermodels' play an important part in causing some young women to develop eating disorders (anorexia and bulimia). This is not just something which affects women; increasingly we may see images of the male body as an object of desire in the media, as research into men's magazines and fashion by Sean Nixon (1996), and Tim Edwards (1997) has shown.

However, not all sociologists would agree that media representations are necessarily harmful. Sociologists who emphasise the ability of people to construct their own identity may suggest that the audience can actively use media representations – positive or negative – to help them do this. In other words, people may reject some representations, and react against them, and accept other representations and perhaps try to emulate them. The sociologist Sherry Turkle (1996) takes this approach in her study of women and computers. The women Turkle studied were able to use the fact that the world of computers appeared unfeminine and closed off to them, to construct a version of femininity that made a virtue of the fact that women were not assumed to be conversant with computer technology. In this version of femininity, women asserted their superiority over the technology-dominated world of computing.

Conclusion

In assessing how important media representations of gender are, we have to take into account sociological ideas about power. Many models of media effects, including some of the ideas discussed here, assume that the audience is a passive consumer of media representations. This may not necessarily be the case. We also need to remember that masculinity and femininity are not fixed categories. They change over time and so do media representations of them.

For consideration:

1 How can women use media representations as a source of identity and meaning?
2 Are men now being represented as objects of sexual desire in the media? If so, is this a good thing? What does it tell us about how masculine identities are changing in contemporary societies?

✓ **Top Exam Hint**

If you have to evaluate the relationship between media representations and gender, remember to link the material in this section with different theories of the media (sections 4, 5, 20, 22) and with the material on how audiences respond to the media (section 14).

● **Synoptic Link**

Remember that gender is an aspect of stratification, so you can draw on material in this section in answering synoptic questions on stratification in the A2 Sociology exam. This section has examined different views about how media representations of gender can influence gender identities and thus how these might reinforce one aspect of social stratification.

4.10 Is the media racist?

What does this mean?

When sociologists make the claim that the media is racist they are making a claim about the way that the media represents ethnic minority groups. Sociologists might also want to claim that the media operates racist employment procedures – just as many other employers may do. But sociologists' main focus of attention has been on the question of whether media representations are racist. However, we are still left with the issue of what is meant by 'racist' media representations. The term '**racism**' is often used rather loosely in everyday language, and many people associate it with deliberate prejudice and discrimination. Sociologists use the term rather differently to refer to systematic stereotyping and bias in the portrayal and representation of members of ethnic minority groups – this is a form of **institutional racism**. Racism in the media may not necessarily be intended to cause offence, but it may nevertheless exist.

How are ethnic minorities represented in the media?

A number of sociological studies over a long period of time indicate that media representations do reflect a biased and stereotyped image of members of ethnic minorities. In the 1970s, Stuart Hall (1978) argued that media representations helped to construct the 'myth of black criminality'; while Hartmann and Husband (1974) found that the media played a key role in reinforcing racist views amongst the media audience.

More recently, studies by Alvarado (1987) and by Van Dijk (1991) have demonstrated that media representations of ethnic minorities are overwhelmingly presented in terms of various negative stereotypes. Van Dijk, for example, conducted an extensive content analysis of newspapers and found that ethnic minorities were presented in terms of a severely limited number of negative stereotypes. Thus, black people were portrayed as criminals, as abnormal or alien, as presenting a threat to 'normal society' (e.g. being thought to be illegal immigrants or terrorists), as dependants (illegal immigrants, victims of famine or natural disasters, incapable of being independent) in need of help or aid, and lastly, were often marginalised through being portrayed as unimportant in comparison to issues affecting the white majority.

Are media representations changing?

These findings may not reflect our own experience of the media. This may be because of our own social position or identity (see section 14), but it may also be because media representations have changed since the 1970s and are continuing to change. For example, you may have seen what are often considered to be more positive stereotypes, such as movie

66 99 Key Definitions

Racism – this is any form of discrimination against a person or a group of people because of their assumed racial or ethnic characteristics. **Institutional racism** refers to the ways in which institutional procedures and practices can systematically (either intentionally or unintentionally) discriminate against ethnic minority groups.

👉 Who is this Person?

Stuart Hall was born and brought up in Jamaica, but came to Britain to study at Cambridge University where he read English. He has commented on his feelings of confusion on growing up in Jamaica and being taught British history and Wordsworth's poetry, and yet finding his own West Indian culture and identity to be neglected. These experiences go some way perhaps, to explaining his sociological interests.

directors like Spike Lee, or actors like Halle Berry and Denzel Washington winning an Oscar. There are also the examples of television programmes like *Goodness Gracious Me*, *The Kumars at Number 42* or *Smart Guy*, and the more assertive black identity presented by rap artists, to support the idea that representations of race are changing. However, Jhally and Lewis (1992) point out that television programmes such as *The Cosby Show* (a popular black sitcom in the late 1980s/early 1990s featuring a successful middle-class black man) are highly unrepresentative of the situation of the black population in the USA, and it might be argued that stereotyping blacks as athletes and musicians still traps them within a limited framework of stereotypes.

Black people are still less likely to be shown in other successful roles, for example, medicine, law or business. One way of explaining these complex media representations comes from Manuel Castells (1997). Castells argues that ethnicity, as well as being a source of oppression, can also be a source of identity and meaning. Thus some black Americans have been able to gain access to the mass media and create new ethnic identities and challenge old identities. However, this does not mean that oppression and discrimination do not exist. Instead Castells argues that we are living in a much more complex situation, since ethnic groups have fragmented on the basis of class and other divisions.

Conclusion

The implication of recent research by sociologists like Manuel Castells is that in evaluating how media representations portray ethnic groups, we have to acknowledge the different social positions (including class, gender and religious positions) that can divide what may seem to be a single ethnic group. Evaluating this argument means thinking carefully about the nature of social stratification. As stratification systems in contemporary societies and attitudes to race and ethnicity are changing, so too are the ways in which the media represent race.

In a landmark win for black actors, Halle Berry and Denzel Washington take home Oscars for best actress and best actor at the 2002 Academy Awards. But why is this still considered a landmark?

✓ Top Exam Hint

If you are evaluating media representations of race, remember that a lot of the studies mentioned here are based on content analysis. This means that they will, of course, reflect the weaknesses of that method. A common criticism of content analysis is that the categories used in analysis lack validity and reliability. The findings of such studies are therefore open to question.

● Synoptic Link

Remember that race and ethnicity are aspects of stratification, so information in this section can be used in synoptic questions about stratification in the A2 exam. Issues about race are also relevant to perceptions of crime and deviance (see sections 16 and 18).

For consideration:

1 Do media representations cause or merely reflect racism?
2 How important are media representations?

Is the media ageist?

What does this mean?

Many people believe that characteristics such as race, gender and age are natural categories. Sociologists, however, are keen to point out that all of these categories are socially constructed. In the case of age, sociologists are interested in examining how age is represented in the media because this can tell us something about the dominant ideas about age in our culture. Studying the media and age also allows us to see how these representations are created, how audiences respond to them, and the social effects that they have.

How is age represented in the media?

Some studies, such as that by Signorelli (1989), have found that there is an under-representation of the very old and the very young in television programmes, but a content analysis by Lambert (1984) found that over a period of two weeks 50 per cent of programmes depicted people over the age of sixty. Significantly though, the people involved tended to be predominantly male and were often 'experts' or in positions of authority, such as that of a news presenter. A more recent content analysis study by Simon Biggs (1993) found that middle-aged and older characters dominated UK soap operas, and in situation comedies the portrayal of older characters was largely negative. A more sophisticated case study of one magazine (Retirement Choice) by Featherstone and Hepworth (1995) found that positive images of older people could be found, but these images emphasised how youthful older people could be. In summary then, representations of old age do tend to portray it as a social problem, and the evidence here provides some justification for describing the media as 'ageist'. However, representations of age can reflect the seniority and high status conferred by the wider society to men, as opposed to women.

At the other end of the spectrum, youth too, tends to be represented as a social problem, in need of firm control, as sociologist Stan Cohen's ground-breaking research indicated (see section 18). However, there are alternative representations available within contemporary culture. As James and Prout (1990) argue, the dominant images of the young in our culture portray them as dependent innocents in need of the protection of caring adults. The media are therefore quick to spot the newsworthiness of stories about the destruction of childhood innocence (for example, by cases of child abuse, abduction, and so on). Above all, though, these representations portray age and the ageing process as something natural and unchangeable, not as a social construction.

66 99 Key Definition

Ageism – this is commonly regarded as discrimination against people on the basis of their age. People could be discriminated against at any stage in the life cycle, though the most common examples occur against the old or the young. Discrimination can include stereotyping or any other form of differential treatment on the sole basis of age.

✳ Key Idea

Social Constructionism

Ageing is a natural process, but sociologists point out that it is also a socially constructed process. By this, sociologists mean that the behaviours accompanying particular age groupings, and the way other members of society regard these groups, are the result of social norms and rules, and thus are not inevitable, naturally created, ways of behaving. This is seen from the fact that different cultures confer differing degrees of status to, for example, the young or the old.

How do audiences interpret representations of age?

Sociological views about how audiences interpret the various representations of age in the media reflect the theoretical models discussed later on in this chapter (see section 14). Many contemporary sociologists take the view that audiences do not automatically agree with the way a social group is represented by the media, and social forces such as class, race and gender, as well as the culture of a particular society, will structure the way in which audiences respond.

Conclusion

Sociologists disagree in their views as to the effects of these media representations of age. Those taking a more structural view, such as Dick Hebdige (1979) for example, would argue that the media reinforces the idea that age differences are natural biological categories, and that they have the effect of justifying (or legitimising) the way our society deals with the young and the old, and the ageing process itself. Those taking a Marxist perspective will see this in the context of the needs of capitalism for a trained, obedient, and efficient workforce. Others, influenced by action theories, or more recently postmodernism, would argue that people can use media representations more creatively, accepting or rejecting particular elements to create their own identity. However, these views can be criticised for exaggerating the amount of freedom people have, and neglecting the influence of factors such as class, race and gender in terms of economic and cultural differences.

For consideration:

1   What factors could limit (or structure) the way audiences respond to media representations of age and how could they do this?
2   Would media representations of age be altered if the media employed more people over the age of sixty, or if children (under sixteen) had a greater influence on programming decisions?

✓ **Top Exam Hint**

It's worth remembering here our previous points about the problems with content analysis. How are categories operationalised and measured (e.g. what counts as 'very old' or 'very young')?

● **Synoptic Link**

The issue of how audiences interpret representations of age and the effects of these representations provides a good demonstration of the structure/action debate in sociology.

▼ **Thinking like a Sociologist**

Three evaluations to use in the exam are:

1   Remember, age is not the only aspect of stratification.
2   If a media representation is portraying a particular stereotype of age, it will also be important to consider how that representation is related to other aspects of stratification, such as class, race or gender.
3   Age is not such a stigma for men, and studies have shown that there is a greater proportion of older men, in comparison to older women, represented in the media.

4.12 How is disability represented in the media?

What does this mean?

Sociologists are interested in the way disability is represented by the mass media for the same reasons that they are interested in the representation of other social differences, such as class, race, gender and age. In examining these differences, sociologists will want to answer several key questions. First, are the disabled involved in media production and what images of disability are created? Second, how frequently is disability portrayed in the media and in what ways? Lastly, sociologists want to know how audiences interpret these representations and what effects they have.

How is disability represented in the media?

The first question above is hard to answer with precision, but it would seem that most media professionals are 'able-bodied'. It is much easier to discover what images of disability are created. Research conducted by sociologists indicates that the media do present stereotypical and stigmatised representations of disabled people. Cumberbatch and Negrine's research (1992) found that the disabled were predominantly seen as figures we should pity. Other research (Longmore 1987), found that the disabled were seen as dependent, maladjusted or even evil. There could however be interesting variations on this theme, for example when the disabled were turned into heroic figures coping courageously with their fate. However, it is also important to note that the disabled do not appear in the media very often. The 1999 Broadcasting Standards Commission survey found that the disabled only appeared in 7 per cent of programmes in their sample. It seems that the disabled are a social group the media would prefer not to publicise; there is a denial of their existence.

How do audiences interpret these representations?

Cumberbatch and Negrine (1992) found that how audiences respond to these representations depends upon their own experience of disability. Those who had some experience of disability were more likely to reject stereotypical or stigmatising representations of disability. This reminds us of some general points about media effects and audience interpretation. Audiences are reflexive, and they can 'read' media messages in alternative ways.

Conclusion

The effects of media representations always have to be seen in the social context in which they are constructed and interpreted. As Cumberbatch and Negrine's study indicates, audiences can reject stereotypical representations of disability. Equally though, those who have no experience of disability (either individually or within their family or friendship groups) may well be confirmed in their view that disability is to be defined as a social problem. Part of the wider social context in which we have to examine disability, then, is in terms of a culture that portrays disability in a negative light.

Sociologist Tom Shakespeare has researched and written a great deal on the sociology of disability, and he argues that contemporary culture is one where the role for disabled people is as what he calls 'dustbins for **disavowal**'. What he means by this is simply that society tries to ignore the fact that disability occurs and, very importantly, tries to avoid the fear and anxiety that disability not surprisingly gives rise to. The sort of approach that Shakespeare takes would be very similar to the cultural effects approach we examined earlier (see section 14). However, we have to evaluate that model of media effects with care, and as we have noted here, audiences are varied and can read media representations in a variety of ways. The effect of media representations of disability can therefore also be varied. Perhaps most important is the finding that disability is largely disavowed by the media.

Dr Tom Shakespeare is Director of Outreach at the Policy, Ethics and Life Sciences Research Institute, Newcastle-upon-Tyne

☞ Who is this Person?

Tom Shakespeare is a sociologist involved in studying disability, health and genetics. He is himself achondroplasic (he is what is commonly called a 'dwarf'). Clearly this may help us understand his interests in disability and encourage us to reflect upon whether sociologists really can be entirely value-free in their choice of research topics.

❝❞ Key Definition

Disavowal – this means that we deny knowledge or responsibility for or about something. In the case of disability, Shakespeare is arguing that society refuses to accept its reality, and that this works as a way of diffusing the anxiety which disability arouses, since we could all become victims of it, either ourselves (e.g. through an accident) or for example, through our own children or other relatives.

For consideration:

1 Do you think that media representations of the disabled would become more positive if greater numbers of disabled people worked in the media?

2 In what ways does the media contribute to the social construction of disability?

4.13 How does the media represent class?

✳ Key Idea

Class Identity

Modernist sociologists claim that people who occupy the same class position will generally have a shared identity of themselves as, for example, working class or middle class. This means that they will have similar norms and values, opinions, and cultural tastes. Recently postmodernists have argued that class is fragmenting (because higher incomes mean that class is less important) and so class identity is in sharp decline.

Did the BBC show bias in its coverage of the 1970s miners' strike?

What does this mean?

Many sociologists interested in the media have been influenced by Marxist approaches to the media. Sociologists from this tradition, such as Stuart Hall or the Glasgow University Media Group (GUMG) for example, have been very interested in examining how the media portrays classes and class relations, and how it transmits ideologies that legitimise class inequality. If it does all these things, then the media is an important means of social control in capitalist societies.

What evidence is there for biased and stereotyped representations of class?

The work of the GUMG suggests that the media present biased and stereotypical representations of class. The GUMG (1976) has shown how the news coverage of industrial relations by the BBC in the 1970s was biased against workers and strikers, and tended to portray the arguments of management in a more favourable light. Workers were all too easily portrayed as rowdy and ill-informed troublemakers. Representations such as these could be conveyed by interviewing managers in neat and tidy offices, whilst workers were filmed huddling around a fire outside the factory gates, trying to keep warm and preventing lorries entering or leaving.

Studies by Glennon and Butsch (1982) and Jhally and Lewis (1992) also support the view that television entertainment programmes tend to feature more middle-class than working-class figures, and that middle-class figures are more likely to be represented positively than working-class characters. Glennon and Butsch, for example, found that in the US only 4 per cent out of 218 family sit-coms were set in a family where a blue-collar (manual) worker was the head of household, whereas such families actually constituted about 36 per cent of the US population at that time. In the US study by Jhally and Lewis it was found that the percentage of working-class characters in television programmes actually fell between 1971 and 1989 (from 4 per cent to 1 per cent). Whether research on British programmes would today yield the same results is unclear. Certainly though, it could be argued that working-class characters in British soap-operas and comedies are represented in a stereotyped way – as either honest but poor or as lovable rogues, but further research is needed to ascertain the empirical accuracy of this hypothesis.

What effects does the representation of class have?

Sociologists influenced by Marxism, such as Stuart Hall and Raymond Williams, would claim that the media has helped to legitimise (justify) class inequalities and has reinforced strong class identities. Positive representations of the middle and upper classes have made them seem to be society's natural leaders, whilst negative representations of the working class portray them as naturally inferior. Hall and Williams see the media as a means of social control. Creating strong class identities leads to a strong 'them and us' feeling and so perpetuates a class hierarchy. Hall has studied the history of the BBC and has argued that it enabled the ruling classes to promote their culture as the dominant culture, and tried to promote a shared national culture, aiming to bring the masses what it considered to be the best in culture in order to 'educate, entertain, and inform'. It even tried to establish the RP (Received Pronunciation) accent as the preferred way of speaking.

Critics of the Marxist approach (pluralists and postmodernists) argue that such views exaggerate the force of social structures and underestimate the freedom people have (agency). Stuart Hall, though, is more influenced by neo-Marxist or Gramscian views (see section 4), and would claim that ruling class cultural domination is never total or complete. In fact it is strengthened by challenges to its authority, since these help to make it appear more negotiated and open than it really is, thus justifying it as a tolerant and liberal regime. This view of media effects can be challenged though, and other sociologists (see section 14) would argue that people (and audiences) are not passive and are much more able to interpret and reject media representations than neo-Marxists assume.

Conclusion

Whilst there have been some very clear examples of biased media representations of class, many sociologists would now recognise that this is a very complex issue.

David Morley's research (1980) (see section 14) offers a particularly useful way of drawing some conclusions on this matter. Morley's *The Nationwide Audience* study makes several important points that are relevant here. First, Morley suggests that the audience negotiates media representations. This means that how audiences interpret or respond to a media representation will depend on their own position in the social structure. Second, Morley notes that social structure does not just mean class, but also race, gender, age and culture. Moreover, these different factors can be mixed in quite complex ways. This means that media representations of class do matter and do have effects, but that they are worked out in many different and complex ways, depending upon the other structural factors influencing the various social groups that go to make up an 'audience'.

For consideration:

1   Does the media continue to transmit representations of social differences in terms of social class, or are postmodernists right to say that identity is now constructed around consumption categories?
2   Do you think that different social classes are more likely to watch particular TV channels? Do the different TV channels appear to target particular social classes and if so, how do they do this?

✓ **Top Exam Hint**

Media representations of class can be important sources of identity but some sociologists argue that people do not accept them unquestioningly. Remember that class is only one element of stratification. We don't all consider class to be the most significant aspect of our identity. For some people other elements, such as race or gender, may be considered more important. This matters, because it means that media representations of class may not be as important as some sociologists imply.

● **Synoptic Link**

If you go on to study Stratification for A2 Sociology, remember that both topics are interrelated and you will need to show you understand this in synoptic questions. This section has shown that some sociologists argue that media representations can play an important role in forming class identities.

✎ **Coursework Suggestion**

Given that many sociologists argue that class has fragmented and the lack of British-based research in the account here, it would be very topical to conduct a content analysis of class identities in the mass media. Are there still strong class stereotypes in the British media?

4.14 How do audiences respond to the mass media?

What does this mean?

A famous radio broadcast of H.G Wells' story, *The War of the Worlds*, in the 1930s led hundreds of American listeners to be panicked into believing that aliens from outer space were invading the earth. Throughout the 20th century, political leaders like Adolf Hitler have been able to use the mass media as a powerful means of propaganda. In more recent times, public debate has focused on the possibility that violence and other criminal behaviour is simply learnt and copied from the media. Are we really so easily led?

What have sociologists said about audience response?

There have been four main models or approaches that sociologists have proposed to explain how audiences are affected by the mass media. The first approach to be developed suggested that the mass media could have a direct and dramatic influence on human behaviour, acting much like an injection of a lethal drug. This led to the approach being termed the '*hypodermic model*'. This model assumes that the audience is helpless to resist the seductive power of the mass media. This approach was used by Albert Bandura (see section 15). It was mainly developed, though, by the so-called 'Frankfurt School' of sociologists.

A slightly more sophisticated approach argued that the influence of the media was not so direct. The '*two-step flow*' theory, developed by Lazarsfeld (1944), claimed that individuals were influenced by a significant figure such as a teacher, a parent, or employer. It was suggested that the media first influenced opinion at these levels, before being fed down the chain as it were, to street level. Later this theory was challenged by the '*uses and gratifications*' model, developed by various sociologists, including Trenaman and McQuail (1961) and Rosegren and Windahl (1972), which suggested that people were in fact much more active in their use of the media. Rather than just believing each and every media message they were fed, people actively used the media for their own purposes. The media could not, therefore, control them as if they were mindless puppets. More recently several theories, which can be collectively called '*cultural effects theory*', suggested that media effects were a background influence – some likened the effect to a dripping tap – and that constant exposure to the media gradually came to have a pervasive influence on behaviour.

☞ **Who are these People?**

The Frankfurt School of sociologists included a number of academics, including Theodore Adorno, Max Horkheimer, and Herbert Marcuse. These academics were all German Jews and they left Germany in the 1930s, fleeing to the USA to escape persecution by the Nazis. All of the Frankfurt School were interested in the way in which mass societies as different as Nazi Germany, the communist Soviet Union and capitalist America, used the mass media as a way, in their view, of indoctrinating a population.

How can we evaluate these different approaches?

To evaluate these theories we can first of all examine the theoretical assumptions that they involve, and then assess what empirical evidence is available or would be needed to confirm them.

- Most of the above theories assume that the audience is passive, and this is a common criticism. The hypodermic model also assumes that the audience is homogeneous and reacts in the same way to media messages. This seems unlikely since we know that 'the audience' is highly differentiated (for example, by class, race, gender, age, religion, nationality, and so on). Surely the diversity of social characteristics means that a range of different reactions is more probable?

- The two-step flow theory does not assume that all of the audience is passive, but it is unclear why only some individuals have the ability to influence others – can't individuals think for themselves? Additionally, it is not at all clear why there should be only two steps to influence – why not three or four, or more? There seems no clear reason why the media cannot exert influence through numerous individuals or social positions.

- In contrast, the pluralist-influenced uses and gratifications model suggests that media audiences are more active than the other models imply, and are able to selectively choose what to watch. However, it neglects differences amongst the audience and also the fact that media organisations determine what choices viewers have.

- Morley's influential research *The Nationwide Audience* (1980), reflecting an approach very similar to the 'cultural effects theory', found that the way an audience responded to media messages depended on social position, e.g. class, race or gender (see section 13). The benefit of this model was that media effects are seen as only being comprehensible by looking at the social situation of the audience. However, it may be that the cultural effects model exaggerates the audience's power and neglects the important limitations to audience choice imposed by limited ownership and control.

Conclusion

In terms of empirical data, a key issue is whether studies based on the models discussed can demonstrate that any effects or changes in behaviour are due to the media and not some other cause, for example, socialisation or the social background of an individual. Examples in other sections will examine this issue in detail. For the moment we only need to make a general methodological point that perhaps sociological research cannot control the many variables influencing human behaviour sufficiently to offer conclusive evidence on this matter.

For consideration:

1 Is there one 'audience' for the mass media?
2 Are media messages intended to influence the behaviour of the audience?

✓ Top Exam Hint

When evaluating these models it's a good idea to apply key sociological concepts like power. The hypodermic and cultural effects models reflect broadly Marxist views, whilst the others reflect a pluralist approach. You can therefore apply the criticisms made of each view (see sections 4 and 5). It's also worth pointing out that the question of whether the audience is active or passive echoes the theoretical debates about structure and action and the problems of free will and determinism (the opposite of free will – all our actions are caused by social structures).

● Synoptic Link

This topic has lots of important links to other topics in sociology. There are important links to theory and method, about whether we should see the audience as passive or active, and how we can study media effects and distinguish them from the effects of socialisation. It also links to crime and deviance, politics and stratification, to name just a few.

✍ Coursework Suggestion

If your coursework uses or proposes the use of content analysis, it's a good idea to point out that a weakness of this method is that it tends to assume that audiences are passive and will be unduly influenced by media content. This section indicates that there are many views about how audiences respond to media representations.

4.15 Can the media cause violence?

What does this mean?

It is probably a common assumption that the saturation of our lives with images of violence must invariably de-sensitize us to violence, and may therefore lead some of us to be more likely to copy what we see in the media. The frequency of moral panics about violence (see section 18) seems to support this view. Also the hypodermic model we examined in section 14 suggested that the media could have direct effects on social behaviour. Sociologists have therefore wanted to find out whether the media really can cause violent behaviour. If the media can be found to be an important cause of violent behaviour, the implications for social policies regulating the media would be clear. We could simply ban the portrayal of violence and expect to see a rapid decline in violent behaviour.

What research has been conducted and what have been the findings?

As indicated, there has been a huge amount of research on this issue from psychologists and sociologists. One of the problems with the research, though, is that it is not conclusive – different researchers reach differing conclusions and the findings are contested. Three key studies usefully summarise this body of research.

The psychologist Albert Bandura carried out laboratory experiments in the early 1960s, and claimed that exposure to aggression and violence in the media would indeed lead to violent behaviour. Bandura explained these findings in terms of modelling and what he called 'social learning theory'. Bandura claimed that our behaviour is learnt in an imitative sort of way, as we learn to model our behaviour on that of others. The media, as a key factor in young children's environment, was also liable to act as an influence, as young children could imitate things they saw in the media.

Another influential piece of research was that conducted in the 1970s by William Belson (1978). He carried out detailed interviews with a large sample of young boys and claimed that his results indicated that exposure to high levels of violence on television led to a higher level of involvement in violent behaviour.

In contrast to these pieces of research, however, the findings of the 1994 PSI (Hagell and Newburn, Policy Studies Institute) research into the influence of media violence were far more ambiguous. This research

In 1993, 10 year-olds Robert Thompson and Jon Venables were caught on CCTV camera and convicted of the abduction and murder of 2 year-old James Bulger. Judge Mr Justice Morland stated that he suspected exposure to violent films to be an explanation for their actions. But, can the effects of violent images on young children be conclusive?

☞ Who is this Person?

William Belson is an American media researcher. He was funded by the American media organisation CBS to conduct his research on violence and television. This raises questions about the relationship between researchers, funders, and the outcome of research. Some would suggest that there may be serious conflicts of interest, and such research may reach conclusions that support the prejudices of the funder.

investigated two sample groups; one consisting of 78 juvenile offenders who were interviewed; the other consisting of the views of 538 children (non-offenders), gathered using a questionnaire. The research found no significant differences in terms of the amount of television watched, and both groups had very similar favourite programmes and videos/films. This research concluded that as young offenders appeared to be watching no more violence than other children, it seemed extremely unlikely that there is a 'direct **causal connection**' between watching violence and behaving violently.

How can we evaluate this research?

Given these contradictory conclusions, we have to evaluate the findings very carefully. Why do some studies show clear evidence of media effects, while others are more ambiguous? To answer this question it is vital to look at how the research was done.

Bandura's research can be criticised for its artificiality. Sociologists often avoid the use of laboratory experiments because they do not allow the observation of participants in a natural setting. This can mean that participants alter their behaviour because they are being watched, a phenomenon very similar to interviewer effect. This means that the research may lack validity.

Belson's research has been criticised because of the way in which he operationalised violence in the media. Belson examined the viewing habits of boys and then rated the programmes for their relative violence. However, Belson used adults to judge which programmes were violent and to what extent, and they may have had very different views to those of the young boys. Belson also used self-reporting to find out how much violent behaviour the boys exhibited, and he then categorised this himself. At each of these steps, validity may have been affected and so we cannot have confidence in Belson's findings and conclusions.

Conclusion

Both of the studies examined above have been based on the hypodermic theory of media effects. However, the criticisms detailed, in conjunction with the findings of the PSI survey, seem to indicate that there are good methodological reasons for doubting that the mass media can have such direct effects.

For consideration:

1   Would levels of violence fall if the media showed less violent behaviour?
2   Would violence decline if the media mounted a major advertising campaign discouraging violence?

6699 Key Definition

Causal connection. A causal connection or relationship exists when one factor can clearly be seen to have caused another.

✓ Top Exam Hint

Make sure you use methodological concepts when evaluating complex debates such as the one discussed here. You need to use terms like 'indicator', 'operationalisation', 'representative' and 'validity'. Show that you understand them and show why they are relevant to the question.

⚇ Thinking like a Sociologist

Three evaluations to use in the exam are:

1   It is important for sociologists to interpret statistical data with great care.
2   In the case of Belson's study, many sociologists would point out that 'correlation does not equal causation'. This means that just because there are high levels of violence in the media, correlating with a high level of violence in society, we cannot assume that one factor has caused the other.
3   We need to remember that there may be other factors at work.

4.16 How does the media represent crime?

What does this mean?

Several sociological studies indicate that the media does not in fact present a true picture of crime. Research by Philip Schlesinger and Howard Tumber (1993), for example, suggested that the BBC programme 'Crimewatch UK' did indeed tend to focus on atypical and violent crime (although the BBC dispute this claim). Research by Williams and Dickinson (1993) found that about 12 per cent of current affairs reporting focused on crime, and that over 60 per cent of the space taken by crime reporting was concerned with cases involving violence. This finding has to be put into context – such crimes constituted only 5 per cent of all crimes recorded by the police at the time of their research. Other crimes appear to be relatively neglected by the media, such as domestic violence, pollution, corporate crime or breaches of health and safety rules in the workplace. All of these can involve injury or death and could be considered just as serious as violent crime.

Why does the media seem to be so obsessed by crime?

Steve Chibnall is one sociologist who has argued that the media are indeed obsessed by certain types of crime. In his study *Law and Order News* (1977) he suggests that the reasons for this are related to news values and the 'newsworthiness' of certain types of events. The media are concerned to get as many readers (or viewers/listeners) as possible, since this means that they gain more income. This in turn means that the media has to provide stories or news that will interest or excite their audience; the news media are therefore always seeking something out of the ordinary or dramatic.

Chibnall claims that newsworthiness involves about five key factors. A good news story must be highly visible and spectacular; it must have sexual or political implications; it must lend itself to graphic presentation (e.g. exciting, dramatic, pictures); it must involve individual pathology (an unusual, abnormal or sick individual); and it must involve some element of deterrence and repression. The last point means that good news stories allow society and journalists to blame and repress those who have broken social rules, and that these stories thus help to serve as reminders to deter others from doing the same. The more a particular event reflects these factors, the more newsworthy it is. Certain types of crime thus become a key source of good stories for the mass media, and this explains the media fascination with a particular type of crime reporting. It is also true that certain types of victim become more newsworthy than others, for example, attractive young women and frail elderly women.

What are the social consequences of the media's representation of crime?

Stuart Hall (1982) has argued that the media gets a lot of information about crime from the '**primary definers**' of crime. The media therefore reinforces dominant views about crime and contributes to the social construction of crime and an agenda-setting process. As Steve Chibnall (1977) points out, the media is always selecting and presenting 'news' about crime in the light of various dominant views, and these will usually reflect the priorities of the institutions responsible for law and order. We cannot treat news reports on crime as simple representations of fact; they are always selected and perceived as more newsworthy than another story. Sociologists are interested in how and why these decisions are made. Sociologists also argue that the media reporting of crime can in fact 'amplify' or increase the amount of crime being committed. The media may also create 'moral panics', which simply mean a high degree of social unrest, about crimes. These issues are discussed in more detail in section 18.

Conclusion

The way that the media represents crime can have far-reaching consequences, influencing both public opinion and social policy. The fear of crime, for example, may be influenced by the nature of the media's crime reporting. Powerful social groups and politicians will shape their views as to what types of crime need urgent action at least partly on the basis of what they learn from the media. Of course, all this begs the question of whether the users of the media actually believe what the media tells them. We also need to remember that institutions and groups can be reflexive, and can use the media for their own purposes, as the use of the media by the police has recently shown.

For consideration:

1   How can the 'primary definers' of crime use the media to promote their own institutional interests?
2   What sort of person is most commonly represented by the media as criminal and how can this be explained?

66 99 Key Definition

Primary definers – this refers to the idea that some institutions have the most influence in defining crime. Hall (1982) sees this power as lying with the criminal justice system – essentially the police, the courts, and the Home Office (the government department which deals with law and order issues).

✳ Key Idea

Reflexive/reflexivity. This term is used by Anthony Giddens (1990) to refer to people's capacity for reflection and action. The idea suggests that far from acting passively, human beings have lots of knowledge about how society works, and they use this knowledge in their everyday lives. In this context, the idea implies that people are sometimes able to use the media for their own purposes. Giddens refers to the idea of 'plastic identities'. By this he just means that our identities are mouldable, and the media is a resource we can use to give us ideas about the specific identity we want to create, by copying other people, fashions or media personalities. This links up to the idea of the 'uses and gratifications' model of media effects (see section 14).

✓ Top Exam Hint

You can use Marxism and pluralism to evaluate the idea that media representations of crime are biased against certain social groups and do not give a valid picture of the nature of crime.

● Synoptic Link

Remember that this aspect of the media is highly relevant to crime and deviance at A2. You will be asked to demonstrate your understanding of the way this topic is related to broader issues in crime and deviance. In this section we have focused particularly on how our perceptions of crime and criminals may be highly influenced by media representations.

How does the media influence politics?

What does this mean?

Sociologists are interested in the ways in which politicians can use the media to **legitimise** their activities, to influence public opinion, and to influence the voting process. All of these issues raise important questions about democratic politics and decision-making. Sociologists want to know whether politics in contemporary societies really are as democratic as is often claimed.

Does the media influence voting behaviour?

Early studies of the media, such as the work of Lazarsfeld (1944), were directed towards the question of how the media could influence voting behaviour. Contemporary sociologists, though, are now generally critical of models such as the two-step flow model or the hypodermic model, and see the media as having a more complex influence on politics. In recent years in the UK, voting has been far more volatile, with voters switching allegiance more readily than in the past.

Recent studies in the UK (Curtice and Semetko, 1994, Ivor Crewe, 1992) have suggested that voters are not easily swayed by media opinion. Crewe's research indeed suggests that voters use information from the media to make their judgements, but they can be critical. Particularly interesting was that in a time of increased volatility, voters would use media information to help inform tactical voting. This seems to be evidence favouring a theory of media effects that acknowledges people's capacity to think and act reflexively.

The media may not determine voting behaviour in a direct way, but one contemporary sociologist thinks that the influence of the media is now greater than ever.

How else does the media influence politics?

Manuel Castells (1997) argues that the influence of the media on contemporary politics is considerable, and he identifies a number of changes leading to the current situation of what he calls 'informational politics'.

Castells argues that electronic media (e.g. television, the Internet) have now become the key source of information in modern society. This means that politicians have to use the media to get the attention of

66 99 Key Definition

Legitimise/Legitimation. To legitimise an action, a state of affairs (e.g. inequality), or a set of rules, means to present reasons why these things are fair. Some sociologists argue that the media legitimises the actions of politicians through its representations.

Manuel Castells, Professor of Sociology at the University of California, Berkeley

☞ Who is this Person?

Manuel Castells is a Spanish sociologist, and he is currently Professor of Sociology at the University of California. He was an outspoken critic of the Spanish dictator Franco (1939–1975), and had to leave Spain to continue his education. Castells started his academic career as a Marxist, and though he has tried to apply Marxist concepts to contemporary society, he has modified his views. His current work focuses on the importance of technological changes in the media, and the way these are creating what he calls a 'network economy' and the 'information age'.

voters. To do this, however, politicians increasingly have to follow the logic of the media. This has several important consequences for political debate and presentation in the media.

First, political issues have to be simplified, and they have to focus on events, personalities and conflict, and have to present action rather than lengthy explanations. In other words, politicians' messages have to match the news values of media organisations (see section 7), if they are to gain coverage. As Castells notes, this is because politicians are competing to gain media space. Most of the other competitors are entertainers of one sort or another, and Castells is arguing that politics can only compete by being portrayed in terms of drama, personalities and conflicts. One result of this is that it is mainly 'bad news' that attracts the attention of the media and of the public.

Second, Castells makes the claim that this new form of informational politics is what has led to a greater focus on political scandal or what has been called 'sleaze' in the UK. Castells even says that this will now be a key political tactic, something that he sees as an inevitable consequence of the way politics has been dramatised and reduced to debate about personalities rather than issues.

Conclusion

It is these factors that have helped bring about the current marketing of politics in our society, and they help to explain the increase in the number of government media advisers ('spin doctors'). Castells does not claim that the media determines public opinion, but he does argue that the logic of the media helps to shape politicians' and political parties' actions. What is new about this, though, is the scope of new media technologies, which enable political parties and governments to respond to changes in public opinion very quickly. All of these, however, restrict and shape political life, and make it rather self-obsessed, with even media statements about politics becoming political events. Society and the media are becoming increasingly reflexive.

For consideration:

1 Will the Internet lead to more political participation by the electorate and political interest groups?
2 Does the new media technology (e.g. Internet, digital TV, and so on) cause political change or are political changes simply harnessing the power of new technology?

Bill Clinton and Kevin Spacey show support for Tony Blair at the 2002 Labour Party conference in Blackpool.

✳ Key Idea

The idea of informational politics suggests that politics is now dominated by the control of flows of information, rather than by substantial differences in ideology. This idea is also used by French postmodernist Lyotard (see section 20), although note that Lyotard has a more sceptical view about the nature of the so-called 'information' than Manuel Castells.

✓ Top Exam Hint

Use the new material here to evaluate Marxist and pluralist accounts of the role of the media. Both Marxist and pluralist views are now dated, and the views of Manuel Castells can be used to provide a more up-to-date assessment of the role of the media in what he calls 'the information age'.

4.18 Can the media create moral panics?

What does this mean?

The sociologist Stan Cohen created the term 'moral panic' in the early 1970s (1973). What he was trying to say was that just as individuals can have panic attacks when some stressful or unusual event shocks them, so too can societies. However, in the case of societies, these panics usually arise over what we can broadly call 'moral issues'. This means issues over which social groups have sharply differing opinions about what is right and what is wrong. Examples of the sort of issues Cohen means would be crime, hooliganism, abortion, AIDS and homosexuality. If you examine any society carefully for a while, you will find that big debates about these and other moral issues arise quite frequently. The effect of a moral panic, though, is that a certain group of people are stigmatised and negatively labelled, and become seen as presenting a threat to society.

How are moral panics created?

Cohen argues that the media play a key role in creating moral panics. Moral panics start when some behaviour or events are identified as a problem. Cohen famously used the example of gang fighting at seaside resorts in the 1960s to illustrate his point. The reporting of these minor disturbances in the local press alerted the police and other public officials to the problem. This led to a sequence of events whereby the police were ready to seek out more examples of this sort of offence, the courts were concerned to deter others from copying the behaviour by giving harsher sentences, and the media reported all this activity in order to maximise sales and readership. Cohen argues that the result was that the deviant activity was in fact amplified (increased), causing what he termed a 'deviance amplification spiral'. The sequence develops because the initial police activity appears to be justified by further outbreaks of trouble. Cohen argues that the initial 'problem' is heavily exaggerated and the group identified as causing the trouble is 'demonised' and scapegoated, and is portrayed as a threat to society.

How useful is this concept?

Although the idea of 'moral panic' has been very influential in sociology, it does need to be evaluated carefully. One criticism is that the idea is too deterministic. It therefore makes deviance amplification seem inevitable. Cohen acknowledges that amplification may not occur, but nevertheless

Professor Stan Cohen is Professor of Sociology at the London School of Economics

☞ Who is this Person?

Stan Cohen came to the UK from South Africa, and worked as a social worker in London, before going on to do research into deviance for a higher degree at the London School of Economics. His view of sociology above all reflects a concern for the underdog, something that is also reflected by his interest in human rights.

✳ Key Idea

The idea of the 'deviance amplification spiral' suggests that far from eradicating perceived social problems, moral panics see those 'problems' increase. The targeting by the media and law and order agencies of a particular problem leads to the identification of further perpetrators, and creates a cycle of action and reaction.

he argues that once a moral panic is underway, it does indeed follow a logic that is determined by what he terms 'recurrent processes of news manufacture', or the inability of the media to put down a good story. However, we may want to consider whether this neglects the fact that many different institutions and groups are involved in creating a moral panic, and that some of these groups have the power to reject media representations. Sociologist Anthony Giddens' idea of reflexivity suggests that as people learn about ideas such as 'moral panics' they can change their behaviour.

Conclusion

Sarah Thornton (1995) has argued that the type of moral panic that Cohen identified is outdated. The concept never really involved a sophisticated view of the audience, implying that they would simply accept media symbolisations (see section 14). Thornton argues that contemporary society is fragmented and very diversified, and so it no longer makes sense to talk as Cohen did of a 'societal reaction'. In contemporary society it is more likely that there will be many different reactions. Some groups labelled as 'folk devils' for example, may, as Thornton argues, fight back with their own alternative symbolisations.

In July 2000, 8 year-old Sarah Payne was abducted and murdered. Her death sparked nationwide outrage, supported by the *News of the World*'s campaign to 'name and shame' sex offenders and implement 'Sarah's

● **Synoptic Link**

Don't forget to use the concept of moral panic if you go on to study crime and deviance at A2 level. Sociologists such as Steve Chibnall argue that 'crime waves' are in fact simply moral panics and do not necessarily reflect real changes in the rate of crime. Just like crime itself, crime waves are social constructions.

For consideration:

1 Does the concept of moral panic assume that there is some degree of consensus about key social values?
2 Do you agree with Thornton's view that some groups now actively seek to be scapegoated as 'deviant', since it gives their sub-culture 'authenticity'? Can sub-cultures use moral panics for their own purposes?

4.19 Does advertising really influence people?

✍️ Coursework Suggestion

Advertising would be a good topic to study for a coursework project. You could usefully relate advertising to changing definitions of gender identities. How does advertising appeal to differing conceptions of either masculinity or femininity? Does it determine gender identities or can people use advertising to create their own sense of gender identity? See also section 9.

● Synoptic Link

Advertising is a pervasive aspect of our lives and it links with many other topics in sociology. Advertising can be related to: families and households; gender and sexuality; how advertising influences how we live and what we see as normal; politics and power (can it shape our political views?); health (are health campaigns effective?).

✔️ Top Exam Hint

Asking questions about advertising and searching for empirical evidence to answer those questions can help us review our theoretical ideas about the role of the media in capitalist society. So don't forget to apply the ideas from previous sections (see particularly 4, 5 and 14) to this section and to any questions on advertising.

What does this mean?

Studying advertising forces us to reconsider some important theoretical questions that have occurred throughout this chapter, such as:

- Are we the passive victims of media messages?

- If advertising is influential, what implication does this have for Marxist and pluralist theories of the media (sections 4, 5, and 6)? Initially it would seem to imply that the Marxist view is more accurate, and thus imply that we are all the victims of powerful capitalist interests.

- If advertising is influential it also has important implications for our evaluation of theories of media effects (section 14).

How do advertisements work?

Advertisements can work in many ways. Earlier in the 20th century, advertisers made assumptions similar to those in the hypodermic model examined previously (see section 14). Now though, advertising can be very sophisticated, and advertisers may aim to tap into the audience's consumerist aspirations (in terms of desire for high status goods), or by appealing to a target audience's perceived social identity and desire for status. Marxist-influenced sociologists would suggest that we have a limited ability to resist these messages, whereas pluralists or postmodernists would emphasise the ability of audiences to select and use those messages most in tune with their own beliefs, values and desired identity. Businesses presumably do believe that advertising works, given the sums of money they are prepared to spend on it. At the very least, they are not willing to risk losing trade by opting out of the advertising market.

What does empirical research tell us about the effects of advertising?

David Buckingham (1993) is one sociologist who has researched this question. He found that children appeared to be quite knowledgeable about advertising. They were able to resist advertising and could be very critical of television adverts. However, criticisms can be made of Buckingham's methods. He used small discussion groups (focus groups). These can be seen as lacking in representativeness, allowing the interviewer to influence responses, thus threatening validity.

Does advertising influence the content of the media?

It has been suggested that advertising does not just influence audiences, but that it can also have important effects on the content of the media. Peter Curran (1996) points out that advertising is a big source of income for many media organisations, and this puts pressure on them to attract a large audience/readership. This in turn pressurises media organisations to adapt their content to suit the mass market, and this may involve 'dumbing down', and avoiding controversial issues (including critical questioning of business practices of companies who also provide the media with lots of advertising income). However, these are not the only outcomes, and it can be very difficult for sociologists to find conclusive evidence that media organisations have been influenced in these ways by advertisers.

Conclusion

Reaching firm conclusions about the effects of advertising is not easy. In the case of advertising's effects on both audiences and media organisations, evidence can be hard to come by, and when it is available it has to be interpreted through competing theoretical perspectives. Perhaps it is less debatable though, to claim that while advertising does not work according to the hypodermic model, it certainly reflects the norms and values, and aspirations, of the culture it is situated in. This means, though, that the effects of advertising will not be simple. Advertising acts upon different social groups in different ways, and whilst people can resist the pressures of advertisements, they may not always do so. So understanding the effects of advertising will always have to involve understanding the nature of power and social stratification.

For consideration:

1 Which sociological concepts help explain why people cannot always effectively resist the pressures of advertisements?
2 What theoretical explanation of media effects best matches the conclusion reached in this section?

Thinking like a Sociologist

Three evaluations to use in the exam are:

1 Remember to mention that when sociologists are evaluating complex research findings and theoretical arguments, they may often draw upon and synthesise differing views.
2 This means that they will reject some aspects of each theory, but draw together a few elements to create a new theory.
3 This new synthesis modifies the views of those theories it is constructed from.

4.20 Is contemporary society dominated by the media?

Jean Baudrillard, French social theorist

☞ Who is this Person?

Jean Baudrillard (born 1929) is a French writer. At the beginning of his academic career he was strongly influenced by Marxism, and wrote on consumerism and consumer society. From this he moved on to study gift giving and other forms of exchange, and this eventually led him to reject Marxist views of the importance of economic factors, and instead to take the view that meanings are created and negotiated through interaction. This led him to the study of signs, symbols, and media.

66 99 Key Definition

Postmodernity – this refers to the idea that we are living in a very different historical period from modernity. A key part of this idea is that society is fragmenting, and differences such as class, race, and gender are no longer socially significant. Identity is instead formed through consumption. The media plays a key role in this new form of society, creating and transmitting the images through which identities can be created.

What does this mean?

The claim that the media dominates contemporary society is one that has been made by postmodernist writers such as Jean-Francois Lyotard (1983) and Jean Baudrillard (1985). They argue that we are living in a new and distinctive period in history, which is dominated by the media. By this they mean that our knowledge of the world comes predominantly from the mass media, and that our identities are formed in terms of images that come from the media. They argue that this makes contemporary society (i.e. now) very different from modern society (i.e. anything from the 18th century onwards).

What is postmodernity?

Writers like Lyotard and Baudrillard argue that we are living in a period of time that they call **postmodernity**. They make a distinction between modern society and postmodern society, arguing that various social, political, economic and cultural changes have occurred. For our current purposes there are three important characteristics of this period that postmodernists identify.

Postmodernists argue that consumption (what we spend our money on) is now more important than class position (what we do to earn our money) and class identity.

Economically there has been a shift to produce goods, services and products (including media, e.g. television programmes, magazines, mobile phones, computers) for small niche markets.

In terms of culture there is a blurring of the boundaries between so-called high culture (this means cultural or artistic forms like classical music or ballet which are mainly watched and enjoyed by elite social groups) and mass culture (the cultural or artistic forms, like television or pop music, used by the mass of people).

The upshot of all this, postmodernists say, is that we are able to construct our own identities in postmodernity, and we are not constrained by structures of class, race and gender, as people were in modern society.

How has the media changed in postmodernity?

Baudrillard claims that we now live in a society that is 'media saturated', meaning that it is now impossible for us to escape the influence of the mass media. Media images have become part of our way of seeing the world. Baudrillard claims that the media creates a view of reality that is distorted, and he terms this 'hyperreality'. Baudrillard is suggesting that the media is constantly trying to produce images that are so accurate and realistic that they are in a sense, 'more real than reality'. Baudrillard argues that they are not at all realistic, but since so much of our knowledge comes from the media, we are no longer in a position to be able to tell the difference. The media presents us with 'simulacra' – artificial images or reproductions (copies) of events.

Lastly, the media has tended to reduce differences between cultures. News and other material and images transmitted by the media have tended to make all cultures more similar to each other. An example of this would be the way we can see Hollywood films or Australian soap operas all over the world. This is very closely related to the idea of globalisation, which is explained in the next section.

Raymond Williams (1990) would add a note of caution to these radical views. Writing in the 1980s, Williams also talked of the way that we live in 'media saturated society'. However, Williams points out that it is a very sweeping generalisation to suggest that it is the media that has changed society. On the contrary, Williams argues that the nature of contemporary television is shaped by contemporary society. In his view, it not that our world is being transformed by television, but it is the rapid social changes we are experiencing which are changing television and the media.

Conclusion

One of the big problems with postmodernity and the views it has about the role of the media in contemporary society is that it is very hard to find evidence to support it. The claims outlined above are all very hard to measure and study empirically. Postmodernism and postmodernity are primarily theoretical ideas, and whilst they may be convincing in some ways, they are very hard to test. Some sociologists are therefore highly sceptical of postmodernist views. Whilst they are provocative, a key weakness is their lack of empirical evidence and rigour.

For consideration:

1   Are postmodernists right to say that we live in a media-saturated world? What evidence is there for this view?
2   What implications would postmodernism have for theories of media effects?

✳ Key Idea

Hyperreality
Hyperreality is the view of reality that we get from the media – the media constructs our idea of what reality is. There is no way to tell whether this view is in fact the 'truth' or not.

✓ Top Exam Hint

When evaluating postmodernist views of the media several key issues ought to be addressed if you are going for a high grade. You need to highlight the issue of whether there is any empirical evidence for postmodernity, and also the theoretical criticisms that can be made of postmodernism (e.g. its relativism).

Has the media created a global culture?

What does this mean?

Postmodernist sociologists have been particularly influential in arguing that the media is reducing cultural differences and that cultural products from Hollywood and Western societies are increasingly available all over the world. Bollywood films can now also be seen worldwide. Postmodernists would say that this means that Asian culture is becoming more and more like a part of Western culture. These supposed trends are examples of what sociologists call **globalisation**. Globalisation can be seen in terms of cultural, economic and political change, but when studying the media we are interested in the cultural aspects of globalisation.

What effects is globalisation supposed to have had on the media and society?

The idea of cultural globalisation implies that the mass media has become a global phenomenon. For example, we can travel around the world and see Western media products everywhere, such as Hollywood films, American TV programmes, and computer games from California. There is now a global market place for films, television programmes and other mass media.

Sociologists who believe in globalisation say that it is having the effect of creating an increasingly global culture. By this they mean that more and more people all over the world share the same beliefs and values, and traditional local cultures are in decline. Media globalisation thus leads to cultural globalisation. Because so much of our knowledge and shared social meanings are now transmitted through the media, the same cultural values and meanings are generated across the globe. This is called 'cultural homogenisation'. An example of this might be how American cultural values are spread across the globe through the selling of television programmes like 'Friends'.

Anthony Giddens is one sociologist who has developed the idea of globalisation (1990). Giddens argues that globalisation has the effect of spreading a cosmopolitan lifestyle and culture, but that it does not necessarily lead to a homogenous culture. This is because there is often resistance to the pressures of globalisation, as people reject what they see as cultural values which threaten their traditional way of life.

Ali G, Sacha Baron Cohen's ethnically blurred comic creation – an example of media cultural globalisation?

66 99 Key Definition

Globalisation – this is the term given to the process whereby there is a decline in the importance of nation-states. Globalisation therefore involves political, economic, cultural and social changes. A key aspect of globalisation is that different societies are becoming increasingly interrelated, so that events in a faraway place may have effects in different parts of the globe, e.g. the decisions of a company in Japan may lead to the closure of a factory in the UK.

66 99 Key Definition

Cultural homogenisation – this concept is linked to globalisation, and refers to the idea that cultural differences will decline, with different societies becoming increasingly similar.

What empirical evidence is there for this idea?

There is evidence both for and against the view that cultural globalisation is occurring. Evidence supporting claims of globalisation comes from the quantitative research showing, for example, that in the 1980s 44 per cent of programmes on European TV had been imported, and that over 40 per cent came from the USA (Varis, 1984). Another researcher calculated that five large Western news agencies were responsible for 80 per cent of the world's news items (Masmoudi, 1979). These examples support the theory because they suggest that the production of media content is heavily biased towards one main source.

Against this evidence, Colin Sparks (1998) has argued that while there has been an expansion of cable and satellite television (for instance in the UK one-third of households now have these services) the audiences of anything that could be termed 'global' media such as satellite television are minute. By and large, most of the population in the UK watch British terrestrial television channels and read the British press. Most of the population do not appear to be interested in using 'global' media.

Conclusion

Sociologists disagree as to whether cultural globalisation has occurred. Cultural globalisation in terms of ownership is at least a growing trend, but it seems clear that there is often resistance to globalisation from local cultures. In an age when the mass media seems to be becoming increasingly globalised, which culture, and whose culture the mass media transmits is, however, becoming an increasingly contested issue.

For consideration:

1 Is cultural globalisation mainly the result of changes in technology?
2 What effects can cultural globalisation have on cultural identities?

● **Synoptic Link**

Globalisation is an issue that relates to a wide range of topics. It can be useful to demonstrate the links between the AQA course themes of socialisation, culture and identity, and power, stratification and social differentiation.

✓ **Top Exam Hint**

You can use the idea of globalisation to update your evaluation of other theories and concepts in the mass media topic. For example, applying the concept of globalisation to the Marxist/pluralist debate puts that debate into a completely new perspective (see section 22 for more tips on this).

How has the media changed and how has it changed us?

What does this mean?

The mass media is the product of modern societies, and by 'modern' we usually mean from around the mid-late 18th century onwards. Sociologists believe that this was an important period of change leading to very different forms of communication from those used by individuals in traditional society. The German philosopher Jurgen Habermas (1989) has argued that the invention of the modern mass media led to the creation of a '**public sphere**' – a separate area for the debate of political and social issues. This meant that public opinion became important in the politics of modern societies. Habermas, though, argues that this has not led to greater democracy, as public opinion is managed and controlled by dominant social groups, and the media becomes a means of cultural transmission for these groups.

How has the media changed?

In recent years there has been great change in the world of the mass media. We have witnessed enormous technical change, including the development of digital, satellite, and cable television, DVDs, the Internet and the World Wide Web. There have also been tremendous changes in the concentration of ownership in the mass media and in the content of the media.

American media writer Marshall McLuhan (1963) has suggested that the type of mass media technology a society has is important; in an age of electronic media the nature of mass media has led to significant developments. For example, media information can now be transmitted much more quickly than previous technologies allowed, and over greater distances. Many sociologists see these changes in the relationship between time and space as important characteristics of globalisation.

How has the media changed us?

Sociologists maintain that these changes in the media have had important social effects, and that in fact they have changed our social world. For example, the boundaries between our public and private lives are now blurred, since the media now intrudes into areas of people's lives which were previously private or closed off to some social groups. There are no

66 99 Key Definition

Public sphere. The idea of the public sphere suggests that public opinion and debate is a phenomenon of modern society and did not exist in the same way in traditional societies, which were much more dominated by elite groups.

☞ Who is this Person?

Jurgen Habermas is a philosopher whose work has been important to sociology. Habermas grew up in Nazi Germany, and in many ways he shared the optimism of a post-war generation seeking a new and democratic way of life. After completing his PhD, he worked for two years as a journalist, and this may have led him to develop his interests in communication and the role of the media in contemporary society, and the possibilities of democracy.

◆ What, When and Why?

Postmodernist views have recently challenged many of our ideas about the media. Thinkers such as Lyotard (1924–1998) and Baudrillard (1929–) have suggested that all of our knowledge of the world comes from the mass media, and indeed that we can no longer tell the difference between reality and the media representation of it. However, one critical comment on this would be that postmodernist views themselves are a response to the chaos caused by the rapid social change we have witnessed in recent years. It may be that it is not the media which has changed us, but that it is ourselves who have changed the media.

longer separate social spaces where the media does not intrude, and privacy is hard to maintain. This is very clear to us from the many examples of how those in public life may fall foul of media scrutiny and lose their jobs. It also affects people's everyday lives, influencing the way that identities are socially constructed, and our perceptions of gender relationships, or class or race, for example. Postmodernists claim that these changes open up a wide range of choice for us in terms of our personal identity.

The Marxist and pluralist perspectives we examined earlier are also still important. Some sociologists argue that the expansion of the mass media, through technologies such as the Internet, provides more space for alternative views. Others take the view that this will only lead to a stronger cultural hegemony and to a new social division between those with access to new technology, and those who don't have this access (**information rich** and **information poor**).

Conclusion

So the media has changed a lot, but as we have seen, the effects of the media are experienced through the influence of social structures, and people do have the capacity to interpret the representations of the world provided by the media. Nevertheless our identities and our self-image as modern individuals are things that are themselves in part the product of the mass media.

❋ Key Idea

Information rich/information poor. This term refers to new types of inequality in contemporary society. Information rich refers to those who have access to information, usually through ownership of their own computer, whilst those who cannot afford such technology are 'information poor'. As computer technology becomes more pervasive, and used for activities such as applying for jobs, and communicating with government agencies, for example, it seems clear that not having access to, or ownership of a computer will put many people at a disadvantage.

● Synoptic Link

The division between information rich and information poor can be related to stratification. This is a new dimension of inequality and it can have important social effects.

For consideration:

1   Does our bombardment by increasing numbers of media signs and symbols mean that we now have a limitless ability to construct our identities in contemporary society?
2   Does the development of the Internet mean that public debate will be more democratic?

4.23 Examination advice

What are the examiners looking for?

The examiners want to see what you know about the sociology of the media and test your understanding by seeing what you can do with that knowledge.

This means that you need to be able to show that you can do the following things with your knowledge:

- Tell the difference between facts, opinions, and value-judgements.

- Use your knowledge and understanding of key methodological concepts (validity, reliability, representativeness, operationalisation) to evaluate sociological studies, empirical evidence and research designs.

- Weigh up competing theoretical arguments and present your own arguments coherently and in a sustained fashion.

What do I need to know?

Make sure that you have covered all the ground in this topic. Go back and look carefully at section 2, but also look at a copy of your exam specification. This will familiarise you with the language and terms used by the exam board.

You need to make sure that you have a thorough knowledge of the following.

- The main theories of the media, theoretical debates, and key concepts, as discussed in this chapter.

- The key studies discussed in this chapter.

- Key methodological and theoretical concepts in sociology in general. Don't forget the AS course themes – socialisation, culture and identity, and social differentiation, power, and stratification. If you use these words (concepts) carefully you can show the examiners that you have a sociological imagination.

How do I remember everything?

Try to use different techniques to make revision easier.

- Mind maps, spider diagrams, checklists (key points, key studies), and mnemonics, are all useful methods.

- Test yourself regularly (in addition to tests set by your teacher) – make your revision active. Tape record some of your lists of key points and listen to them on a personal stereo.

- Get hold of past papers and work through the short answers with a friend. For longer answers, making essay plans is a very good way of thinking through ways of applying your knowledge.

- Lastly, try to make your revision sessions frequent (a bit every day), and sharply focused. Avoid making them too long; about an hour is probably most effective.

Key points to remember

- You need a strong knowledge of key studies, concepts and theories, but you also need to show that you can identify, analyse, interpret and evaluate sociological studies, theories and concepts.

- Remember to use general sociological concepts and theories.

- Make your revision sessions frequent, focused and active.

✓ Top Exam Hint

To show the examiner that you are evaluating, analysing and interpreting sociological material, use these words in your answers, e.g. 'In evaluating the Marxist approach to the media, sociologists need to address the criticism that this theory is economically deterministic'. A good answer would then continue to explain what this means, and whether and why it is an important criticism.

● Synoptic Link

You will not be asked to make synoptic links in the AS exam for the mass media topic. However, if you are taking the A2 exam next year, you can use knowledge from this topic to answer the synoptic questions on either crime and deviance or stratification.

✎ Coursework Suggestion

If you find an exam question which relates to coursework that you have done you can relate this material to the exam question. However, use this sort of material sparingly and with great care – you do not want to give the impression that it's the only thing you can remember about the topic.

4.24 Pushing your grades up higher

What do I need to do to get a good grade?

Students often have a number of mistaken views about the skills required for successful exam performance: some remarkably optimistic, such as the belief that 'you can cram it all in at the last minute', and the more pessimistic 'you've either got it or you haven't'. Both are far from the truth. The following points should convince you that the key to success lies in your own hands.

1 **Time management**
   You must apportion your time in a logical manner. You should never spend more time on a question worth 6 marks than you do on a question worth 8 marks. It is only 2 marks difference, but if you follow this principle through you will come unstuck and will not do as well as you could have done. Generally you can make a rough formula of around 1 minute for each mark, and around 15 minutes reading and planning time for all the question.

2 **Answer all questions**
   This does not mean that you should attempt all questions on the exam paper! It means that you must answer the correct number of questions. This is vital. Even if you are not doing your best work, if you attempt all parts of a question you will collect a few marks and these can make a significant difference. Grade boundaries in most exams are pretty narrow.

3 **Lay out your answers in a clear and logical manner. Write as neatly as you can.**
   The shorter style questions in the AS exam (often, for example, requiring you to 'identify and explain two advantages or disadvantages') require careful presentation of answers if you are to avoid losing marks. Many students seem to be skilled at making the same point twice, or missing out part of the instruction, for example, not bothering to 'explain' both points in the above example. If you present each part of the answer clearly by, for example, leaving a line between each part, it is easier for both yourself and the examiner to see clearly what your points and explanations are.

4 **Demonstrate your sociological knowledge**
   There is no point in waffling on about how 'sociological studies show that . . .', or 'some sociologists argue that . . .'. Be specific. In a sociology exam it is a reasonable expectation that you will be able to show that you know about a range of relevant studies, concepts and

theories. Use the language of sociology and show that you understand what it means.

5   **Use the skills explicitly**
    Both the AQA and OCR specifications place a big emphasis on skills of identification, analysis, interpretation and evaluation. Examiners do not want to see how many studies you have learnt parrot-fashion (though they do expect knowledge of studies). They want to see how much you understand, and this is demonstrated through AO2 skills. Make this explicit by recycling the skill words, e.g. 'it is useful to evaluate this study in terms of its methodology, since positivists would claim it lacks representativeness'. You would then need to develop the point in detail.

6   **Practise planning and writing balanced, logical and coherent arguments**
    Longer questions at AS level require an argued answer in response, not a narrative or description of lots of studies or theories. Get hold of past papers/practice questions, and practice planning out answers, working out how you would evaluate different sociological approaches.

7   **Develop your points in an extended manner**
    Do not assume that readers will understand your point if you make a brief, unelaborated point, e.g. 'Marxism is often criticised for being an economically reductionist theory'. This is the start of some evaluation – it needs to be developed in full.

8   **Express ideas in your own words**
    Avoid learning quotations to use in the exam. Make sure that any notes you make in revision have been put into your own words.

9   **Avoid quoting from the items**
    This is a complete waste of time. The items are there to stimulate your own ideas, not to provide something for you to copy. Just refer to the items, e.g. 'As the extract in Item A indicates . . .'.

Key points to remember

- Manage your time carefully and answer all the questions.

- Develop your command of English and your ability to write a coherent and sustained argument.

- Make sure that you have a good knowledge and understanding of key studies, concepts and theories, and the skills of analysis required to use your knowledge.

Frequently asked questions

Q. Is bias in the media inevitable?

A. Yes. Bias is about power, and as the French thinker Michel Foucault reminds us, it is impossible to escape from power relations. Therefore there will always be bias in the media. However, this shouldn't prevent us from challenging and fighting bias, and it shouldn't prevent us from trying to make the media a truly public forum for debate.

Q. Is more choice of TV channels a good thing?

A. Your answer will depend on which sociological perspective you find most convincing. Those influenced by Marxism will be sceptical that having more channels actually does create more choice, simply providing more of the same and 'dumbing down' standards. Pluralists might take the view that more channels mean more opportunities for minority interest groups to air their views.

Q. Why can't sociologists agree about the effects of the mass media?

A. First, the methodological issues around operationalisation mean that researchers disagree about how and what to measure, and can generate very different results. Second, the structure/action debate shows us that sociologists have very different ideas about how much freedom people have in their lives. Whichever view you think is best, make sure you can support it theoretically and empirically.

Chapter 5

Education

Key issues in the sociology of education

Why are sociologists interested in education?

The sociology of education grabs the attention of all types of sociologists, whatever their theoretical background. For some, education manages to act as a way of socialising people into the norms (e.g. eating food with the correct hand or cutlery) and values (e.g. 'ambition' or 'honesty') that are seen to be important for a particular society. For others it can be seen as a source of conflict particularly when issues surrounding gender, class and ethnicity are put under the sociologists' 'microscope'.

What are the key debates in education?

There are *five* key debates that examiners are keen to explore when setting exam questions.

1 What is the relationship between education and the economy?

2 To what extent has formal education provided equality in educational attainment?

3 To what extent has formal education provided equality of opportunity?

4 Do vocational qualifications share the same status or 'parity of esteem' that other 'academic' (e.g. AS and A2 qualifications) subjects possess?

5 To what extent has 'comprehensive' education been a success?

What are the key ideas and concepts in education?

- To answer the key debates students need to be aware of the views about education from the point of view of: the classical sociologists, functionalists, Marxists, neo-Marxists, Max Weber, postmodernists, symbolic interactionists, interpretive sociologists and feminists. You will learn all about these theories in this chapter.

- You need to know about the connection between the education system and the economy. You also need to be clear about differences between private and state education along with the five major policy changes since 1944: namely, the introduction of the tripartite system, comprehensive systems, new vocationalism, the 1988 Educational Reform Act and 'Curriculum 2000'.

● **Synoptic Link**

Sociologists of education examine how education in its various forms might be a source of 'power' for some groups and individuals and not others. Sociologists can examine why this might be the case and finally explore the effects of that power on different classes, ethnicities and genders.

✓ **Top Exam Hint**

Looking at the five debates mentioned on this spread. Make sure that by the end of this chapter you can clearly write one sentence about each debate using the following theories: functionalism, Marxism, neo-Marxism, Weberianism, postmodernism, symbolic interactionism and feminisms. Make revision even easier by turning these sentences either into a revision table or create cards that you can then use to revise from.

- Finally, you need to be aware of the many processes and concepts that exist when focusing on explanations to do with educational attainment by class, gender and ethnicity and the interplay between the three.

What are the key problems in the sociology of education?

When discussing to what extent research may be reliable, valid or representative (by 'representative' sociologists mean findings that can be use to make generalisations about the group from which the sample has been taken), sociologists have to face the following four specific problems when examining education.

- 'Operationalising' (or 'defining') what we mean by 'education' (e.g. do we count *informal education* such as learning to cook at home or do we only refer to *formal education* i.e. education for which we receive certificates?)

- Measuring any particular aspect relating to its success or failure (e.g. success or failure in relation to other children or other schools or other countries?)

- Government policies determine/affect what happens within education systems. However, governments seek election and then win or lose on voting day. This can mean that policies that take time to develop are instantly 'reversed' when a new party comes into power. This makes the job of the sociologist extremely difficult when evaluating the success of such policies.

- It is not enough to simply look at a particular school or type of school. Schools vary depending on whether they are rural or inner-city; large or small; run by a strong or weak senior management; and if they are single-sexed or mixed. Therefore any research that is carried out needs to be considered in the light of these significant cultural variations. Generalisations for sociologists are always something to be treated carefully.

✎ **Coursework Suggestion**

Carry out two **'focus' groups** with teachers to explore how their feelings change about education the longer they are working within the system. Do this first of all with a group of teachers who have just qualified or who are in the process of training (ask your teacher for help in how to contact them) and then with a group of teachers in your school who have been working for a few years. See how their reactions vary (or not) to some questions you pose to them. Then you can try to come up with reasons for their differences in opinions.

❝❞ **Key Definition**

A **focus group** is a small sample of people gathered together by the researcher. Focus groups are often used as a method of research to initially explore issues of interest to the sociologist. In doing so they can gain valuable information in a way that is not too threatening to the respondents. The aim is to introduce a question or questions that the group can discuss possible answers or solutions to. Sometimes the researcher will then carry out 'follow-up' interviews with one or two of the members of the focus group to explore particular issues raised.

What do we need to know about the sociology of education?

What do we need to know about the sociology of education?

✓ Top Exam Hint

Evaluation in the sociology of education exam means that you question how data was gathered and when (e.g. ethnicity statistics on exam pass rates). You question to what extent the empirical data (what sociologists use as evidence i.e. events that can be observed, measured or tested) can be 'verified' for its accuracy. You analyse the argument to see if it 'holds together' logically (i.e. no wild claims are being made). Finally, you identify to what extent the theory, study or claim is 'comprehensive' i.e. that it can be used to explain other situations in a different culture, time or place.

☞ Who is this Person?

Paul Willis studied English at Cambridge before gaining his doctorate at the famous Centre for Contemporary Cultural Studies in Birmingham. Willis' work is fascinating because as a Marxist he is looking at the big 'macro' issues of class, identity and education but his methods reflect an 'ethnographic' edge normally associated with 'micro' or 'interpretive' methods.

✍ Coursework Suggestion

You can always 'replicate' a study when carrying out sociology coursework. This means that you can choose one of the famous studies carried out (preferably one that is slightly dated, e.g. Paul Willis' 1977 study on working-class 'lads' in which he explored why working-class males chose to 'opt out' of the education system and enter low status jobs when they left school) and see if the findings are still applicable today. This is fun because you can use the sociologists' ideas to formulate your own version of your chosen study, while at the same time discovering new developments following in their footsteps.

What does the specification say about the sociology of education?

The AQA examiners will expect you to know about:

- *Government policies on education* – and their significance on the role, impact and experience of pupils within education systems.
- *The role of education systems* – as seen from the eyes of sociological theory.
- *Educational achievement* – focusing on class, gender, ethnicity and sociological theory.
- *In-school factors* – as explained by the different theories with a focus on teacher/pupil relationships, subcultures, the 'hidden curriculum' and how teaching and learning are organised.
- *Out-of-school factors* – including parental involvement, government policy, material and cultural factors.

How will I be examined in this topic area?

The exam for this unit will be 75 minutes and will be composed of one data response question with two items of information to be read followed by six questions. These questions will test you on your knowledge of the issues raised in the items but also will extend to the full coverage of the material presented in the sociology of education.

As with all of the AQA units you have to show competency or ability in the assessment objectives of AO1 (*knowledge & understanding* and *presentation & communication*) and AO2 (*interpretation & analysis* and *evaluation*). For AO1 you need to show *knowledge* and *understanding* of: the names of sociologists and their case studies; the relevant theories; the key concepts (e.g. 'cultural reproduction'); evidence to support the claims sociologists make; and show a keen awareness of the research methodologies used by sociologists of religion.

For AO2 you need to show how you can actually *interpret and apply* this knowledge when putting forward a particular argument and evaluate continuously throughout any answer you are writing. For example, this might mean that you draw on the ideas of a theory or case study that was carried out thirty years ago and see how it might (or might not!) be relevant to an area of the sociology of education today. You might also identify trends from the past and see to what extent these trends still exist today.

How well does this topic relate to course work?

One of the joys of carrying out sociology coursework on education is that there is no shortage of material, resources or people to either research or ask for help. Nearly everybody has got an opinion on education be it positive or negative. You also have great experience about this topic area (after all, you have spent the last few years in it) and can use part of your time researching while you study.

There are dangers to watch out for, however. Your own values might get in the way of your research. The fact that you are 'in' education may also mean that you take things for granted and therefore overlook something that could be worth investigating (e.g. why are so many senior managers of schools males when the majority of teachers are female?). You may also feel 'I can do this tomorrow' and then leave things to the last minute. Nevertheless this is an ideal topic for coursework and allows you to develop your knowledge gained in the AS year.

How well does this topic help with synopticity?

- If we accept that some of the key ingredients to synopticity include 'class', 'gender', ethnicity', 'power', 'socialisation', 'culture', 'differentiation' and 'locality' *and* that we can use these ingredients to make connections to either crime and deviance or stratification (the synoptic units in A2), then the topic of education is an ideal tool for making these connections.
- The 'power' relationships that exist in school, either with other pupils or teachers, can have enormous implications for how well pupils do in school, the subcultures they join and what position they later hold in society. Education is described as 'secondary socialisation'. That means that after the family ('primary socialisation') sociologists place huge importance on the impact that schools have on our lives. Much research has shown that depending on your class, gender or ethnicity, the socialisation process can determine what strata of society you enter.
- Finally, not all schools are the same. They vary depending on where they are, i.e. the locality of the school may strongly influence the experience that pupils have of the education system. For some, this might mean that truancy is one solution to being confronted by values that seem alien. In some cases truancy can lead to deviancy and/or crime.

Key points to remember

- The sociology of education raises a variety of synoptic possibilities with crime and deviance and stratification.
- This topic makes for an exciting option in coursework because of the availability of resources and your own personal experience.
- Identify, practise and perfect the skills required for AO1 and AO2 described above (the many examples in this chapter will help you do this).

● **Synoptic Link**

Education provides a variety of links to the A2 subject of stratification. By focusing on the way that education is seen by some sociologists to allocate 'roles' to individuals you can examine whether this is a good or bad thing. The gap between middle-class educational achievement and working-class achievement is growing. Gender achievement has also reversed in recent years (i.e. girls are doing better than boys in all levels of education). Enormous problems exist for some members of the ethnic minorities on leaving school (gaining places at university or finding employment).

How can we find out about the sociology of education?

✓ Top Exam Hints

- What do sociologists mean by 'unstructured' interviews? How often is an interview really 'unstructured'? The moment a sociologist is exploring a particular issue in an interview there is automatically some sort of structure. Tell the examiner that most interviews are to a certain extent structured because they reflect the interests and values of the researcher. One of the few examples of truly unstructured interviews would be when the patient is talking to a psychiatrist or counsellor about their problems. This means that in the sociology of education *all* interviews will vary between being semi-structured or structured.

- Gain evaluation marks by drawing to the examiner's attention the fact that the work of Paul Willis *confuses* the debate about whether sociology should be macro or micro. His work certainly has a macro element to it (i.e. he is a Marxist and interested in how 'class' shapes the lives of the pupils he is researching). But his 'interpretive' research methods focus on the *attitudes* of the 'lads' he talks to. Using interviews and observations this is a small, in-depth study that is definitely 'micro' sociology at its best. Mention this when you get to the concluding paragraph of your exam answer.

How have sociologists tried to measure 'education'?

Sociologists can approach education from a macro perspective (i.e. how school pupils are shaped by the processes that they experience both inside and outside the school?). They can also study education from a micro perspective (i.e. examining close up how pupils experience education). Sometimes they combine both macro and micro elements in their research. Either way, this area of sociology provides huge possibilities for the sociology student to show off their knowledge of sociological **methodology**.

Apart from their own particular theoretical interests sociologists choose their methodology as a result of issues that include:

1 *The nature of the research problem* e.g. are you researching documents or people; is the research 'overt' (research that is carried out with the full knowledge of all those involved) or 'covert' (research that is carried out 'under-cover' from those being studied); or is the researcher looking back over time and comparing past with present?

2 *The traditional research strategies, methods and data sources* thought to be appropriate for a particular problem (e.g. looking at school records to assess which pupils are excluded from school).

3 *How available or accessible the data is* that the sociologist requires (e.g. how willing would some schools be to have sociologists roaming around in their midst!)

4 *The resources at the researcher's disposal* (e.g. funding, time, equipment and assistance).

Values also determine how a particular sociologist approaches the sociology of education, i.e. are they a Marxist, feminist or symbolic interactionist? The aim or particular focus of their research will reflect the theoretical interest of the sociologist.

Such values will also determine whether or not the sociologist is gathering quantitative data or qualitative data. This might depend on whether the researcher considers themselves to be positivist (i.e. scientific) or interpretive (i.e. more interested in how the respondent feels about what is being researched) in their approach to the sociology of education.

What methods do sociologists tend to use to study education?

Methods vary depending on what the sociologist is trying to find out. Questionnaires that are highly structured provide useful broad-ranging data although their completion rate is low. They also do not allow pupils to open up, and tell it like it is. Observation is a fabulous method to use in the classroom but is time-consuming and the presence of the researcher can change and/or affect what they are looking at. Interviews allow the researcher to probe and 'fish' out particular trains of thought but children can sometimes not grasp the particular issues the researcher is examining.

Three sociologists who have used a variety of methods to study education:

- Ethnographer Valerie Hey (1997) used a variety of *qualitative* methods when exploring girls' friendships in two London schools. Her methods included participant observation, and analysing girls' notes written to each other in class, and an examination of girls' personal diaries.
- Interactionist David Gillborn (1990) used classroom observation to explore how ethnic differences influenced how teachers perceived their students.
- B. Davies (1989), in exploring gender roles within literature and the perceptions of these stories from young children, spent hundreds of hours over a period of two years reading different types of stories to children to assess their responses.

What problems with definition are encountered in education?

Remember that whatever definition (or 'operationalisation') we use to start our research will then affect what we look for and what we uncover as a result.

To start with the word 'education' is problematic. Do we mean 'informal education', i.e. learning to cook or learning to drive, or 'formal education', i.e. learning sociology! But if we define 'formal' education as something that is 'examinable' do we mean that learning to drive is formal education – see the difficulty? Even the word 'intelligence' is difficult to 'operationalise' because, as you will see in this chapter, the tests used to evaluate intelligence can sometimes reflect the values of the people who wrote the tests rather than assessing the abilities of the person being tested.

What do we mean by 'education'?

What does this mean?

If you stop and ask somebody 'what is education?', the chances are they will mention school books and teachers and noisy playgrounds. And yet if you were to ask that same person what the most useful thing they had ever learnt was, they might reply in a completely different fashion. They would probably mention learning to cook or to drive or learning about a particular hobby. Does this mean that learning to cook is not a type of education? Sociologists make a distinction between 'formal' and 'informal' education.

What is the difference between informal and formal education?

Informal education is exactly the kind of education mentioned above but for which we receive little reward other than the enjoyment taken from the activity itself. You may learn to cook but, unless you have studied cookery in a school or a college, you may not receive any certificates for it. By 'formal' education sociologists refer to different types of schools and learning environments where, in one way or another, pupils will be taught, assessed and accredited with an exam award, certificate or merit.

Sociologists are fascinated by formal education because we spend so much of our time being educated. You will have spent probably twelve years of your life within some sort of formal education institution by the time you read this page. Many sociologists refer to this type of 'socialisation' as secondary socialisation ('primary socialisation' taking place within your family). Education interests sociologists for two reasons.

- There are a variety of ways that education affects the individual.

- There are a number of ways in which education affects society as a whole.

What is state education?

Think about the primary school you went to if you were educated in England. The chances are you are imagining a building of orange bricks and big windows. The building is probably quite old and there are many of them all over the country. The playground gates are probably black and of heavy metal and the entrance to the building has probably got 'boys' or 'girls' above the doorway.

The reason for this is that the 1870 Education Act provided, for the first time, free compulsory education for most children from the ages of five to ten. That is why many primary schools all date from the same period. The school-leaving age was gradually raised (to twelve in 1889, fourteen after the First World War and finally reached sixteen in 1973). State education refers to the free provision of education for all people who live in England. It is paid for by tax-payers, e.g. employees. State education does not include 'independent' schools (sometimes referred to as 'private' or 'public' schools) for which fees are paid in order to study. Sociologists are interested in 'state education' because of what different governments have argued should be taught, and how.

Is there a connection between formal education and the economy?

Many sociologists would argue that there is an extremely strong connection between state education and the economy. This is also quite often the focus of exam questions. This chapter will explore this relationship between state education and the economy when we look at the different theories. By studying the history of education sociologists have shown that major changes within the education system have always come about when there is a fear about how well the British economy is doing compared to other economies. This has enormous implications for what happens in the classroom and why. This chapter will explore these processes.

Conclusion

So when you look at your old primary school again or see one of those old Victorian buildings, you might consider that perhaps it was built not only for the needs of the children inside it, but also to provide educated workers for a country that was facing international competition within a globally competitive business world.

For consideration:

1. How many connections can you make between education and the economy?
2. Do you think formal or informal education is more important? Why?

Victorian primary schools were built from 1870 onwards and introduced free 'state' education for the first time in England and Wales.

66 99 Key Definition

Be careful when talking about 'state' education and using the word 'public'. In America 'public' education means the same as 'state' education here, i.e. it is provided free to residents of the country. The term 'public education' in England has a different meaning and refers to the most famous 'private' or 'independent' fee paying schools e.g. Harrow, Eton and Marlborough. Do not confuse these terms.

◆ What, When and Why?

It is interesting to note that whenever there has been great concern expressed over the economy, major changes within education have soon followed. In the 1870s concern was over Britain's competitive edge with other countries and in 1870 state education started. After the economic crisis created by World War Two came the introduction of a new educational system called 'The Tripartite System'. In the 1970s there was an economic recession and this gave rise to the vocational qualifications of the 1980s.

5.5 What do we mean by 'intelligence'?

What does this mean?

When you hear somebody being referred to as really 'intelligent' what do you actually think? Perhaps they are good at maths, or tests, or have an amazing memory. Perhaps they are extremely good problem solvers or can speak five different languages. They probably have got lots of qualifications and attended a well-known university.

Yet the idea that there is an intelligence that you can measure, test and grade, is actually only one particular theory or view as to the nature of intelligence in general. Unfortunately, not only has this view dominated much of educational thinking throughout most of the 20th century but it is also an idea that has led to a way of sorting children into taking certain subjects at school and, in some cases, then jobs that affect the rest of their lives.

What do we mean by 'IQ'?

An intelligence test is a standardised test where the score is given as an 'intelligence quotient' or 'IQ'. It is a way of numerically measuring somebody's intelligence. Such tests were first constructed in France by Alfred Binet (1857–1911) to assess children's 'educability' in schools. Psychologists and educationalists in the 1920s and 1930s developed these ideas to argue that there were different 'types' of children that could be identified by such tests. As we shall see in this chapter, such tests were used to allocate different types of schooling to these students on the basis of how well they performed in the test.

Such tests can be criticised because they assume that there is only one intelligence and that intelligence can be measured. They are also attacked because the tests are culturally biased, i.e. they reflect the ideas and ways of thinking of the people who wrote them. The following example shows this.

Q. Which item is the odd one out? Tumbler; Acrobat; Flute; Shot
A. Acrobat (the other three are names for different types of glasses)

Many writers argue that the results of such tests favour middle-class children in the UK. These culturally-biased tests discriminate against all those who have English as their second language, or those children whose normal English is very different from the English of those who wrote the tests. In many cases such tests were/are written by middle-class, white males.

✳ Key Idea

The idea that people have innate or born intelligence can be taken to quite racist assumptions. Herrnstein and Murray (1994) argued that there are differences in intelligence between black Americans and white Americans and that this could be shown using IQ testing. They argued that the evidence of black Americans scoring 10–15 points below whites on average proved their case. Critics, however, argue that such tests only go to show that the IQ test is 'culturally biased' in favour of the people who wrote the tests in the first place – namely middle-class whites.

✍ Coursework Suggestion

Explore the effects of IQ testing on individuals by carrying out your own 'focus group' in which you administer an IQ test and then get the group to discuss the difficulties they faced when carrying out the test. Use their opinions to critically assess the explanations about intelligences that you have read about in this section.

Are there other ways of defining intelligence?

There are other ways of defining intelligence although the problem is that most education systems and exam assessments do not recognise alternative ways of conceptualising intelligence.

American psychologist Howard Gardner argues that rather than having an intelligence defined by somebody's 'IQ', humans are better thought of as having nine intelligences:

- *Linguistic* – the ability to learn and develop language or languages.
- *Logical/mathematical* – the ability to be good at mathematical problems.
- *Musical* – the ability to remember a song or piece of music on only one hearing or the ability to pick up a musical instrument and play melodies without instruction.
- *Spatial* – the ability to map read, recall and describe places by picturing them in your mind.
- *Bodily kinaesthetic* – athletes, dancers and other physical performers have the ability to control and move their bodies in ways that others cannot.
- *Naturalist* – the most recent of Gardner's intelligences this refers to the ability to recognise and categorise natural objects like plants, or rocks or animals.
- *Interpersonal* – the ability to read other people's moods, feelings and motivations.
- *Intrapersonal* – the ability to understand one's own moods, feelings and motivations.
- *Existential* – the ability to raise fundamental questions about existence, life, death and the universe.

American psychologist Howard Gardner challenges the idea of a single measurable intelligence

Conclusion

Gardner's ideas of multiple intelligences challenge the idea that one test is enough to classify pupils and students into different types of education. Much more is needed than that. Gardner also argues that many teachers teach in the style that reflects their own sets of intelligences rather than those of the students in the classroom. This means that when children do not do well in subjects this may well be the fault of the teacher rather than the inability of the student.

For consideration:

1   Think of examples to show how you possess each of Gardner's intelligences.
2   To what extent do you think your education meets the needs of each of those intelligences?

5.6 What is the tripartite system?

◆ What, When and Why?

The 1944 Education Act came at a time when Europe was coming to the end of the Second World War. People in those countries had experienced war at first hand and in many cases were disillusioned with the policies and the politicians that had allowed such a war to take place. There was also general enthusiasm to create a new and better society when the war had finished. The education act needs to be seen in this light because of the powerful role education has within society – particularly in relation to the economy. Not only can the level and standard of education affect what status *individuals* may have later on in life, but it also can determine the status of *countries* internationally in terms of their economic success and status.

▮ Thinking like a Sociologist

Three points you can make in the exam are:

1 Remember that any IQ test can be said to be culturally-biased in favour of those who wrote it.
2 The allocation of grammar schools discriminated against girls because in the early years of the system figures were readjusted to make more boys gain places at grammar schools.
3 The schools were unequally funded, i.e. grammar schools gained more money per student than the other two schools.

What does this mean?

The tripartite system of education was set up as a result of the 1944 Education Act. 'Tri' meaning three, it referred to three types of schools that children could attend: the technical school, the secondary modern and the grammar school.

The aim of the 1944 Education Act

The years 1939 to 1945 had witnessed widespread destruction, mass killing and human suffering on an enormous level. Policy makers and the general public in many Western European societies wanted a new and better society to replace the one that had been partially responsible for the Second World War taking place. Education as an institution was seen as one vehicle for change.

The Act aimed to offer an equal chance to develop the talents and abilities of all pupils in England and Wales. This was to be done within a free system of compulsory state education that was to be completely reorganised into primary education (nursery, infant and junior education) to the age of eleven; secondary education from the ages of eleven to fifteen; and then post-compulsory education, i.e. that of free choice that could take children into further and/or higher education at university level. These were exciting and ambitious aims.

A psychometric or IQ test was given to children in their last year of primary school. The test would be used to measure intelligence and was known as the 11-plus exam. It would be used to 'determine' which type of secondary school in the tripartite system these children would attend once they had completed their primary education.

What were the three schools?

- *The grammar school* – accepted what it considered to be academically bright pupils who had done well in the 11-plus exam. Such schools taught a wide range of academic subjects including Latin and in some cases Greek. These schools entered their pupils for public examinations ('O' and 'A' levels) which were needed for any pupil that wished to attend university. Twenty per cent of the population at that time attended these schools.
- *The secondary modern* – accepted most students in the country. Such children would not have performed as well in the 11-plus exam as

those from grammar schools and as a result they would receive a basic education with a more practical emphasis. Up until the 1960s there was very little opportunity for public examinations to be taken in such schools meaning that the opportunity to go to university was effectively ruled out if you went to such a school.

- *Technical schools* – only accepted about 5 per cent of students in the country at that time. Such schools were designed for pupils that excelled in technical subjects and consequently emphasised vocational skills and knowledge.

Criticising the tripartite system

Despite its ambitious and exciting aims there were many problems with the tripartite system of education:

1   The problem with IQ tests, as we have seen, is that they can be culturally-biased in favour of middle-class pupils. That meant that the majority of grammar school pupils came from the middle classes. Far from providing an equal education for all, the tripartite system reflected the existing social divisions in society.

2   **'Parity of esteem'** (the idea that one school should be considered to have the same 'status' as another) did not exist between these three types of school. Parents, teachers and students saw the grammar school as superior to the other types of school. This could mean that some parents, some teachers and some students could see themselves as failures if they were involved in any school that was not a grammar school.

3   Despite the aims of the 1944 Education Act to provide better education for all, the tripartite system did not include those pupils whose parents or guardians *paid* for their education, i.e. independent or private school education. At that time 7 per cent of the population of school children attended such schools.

Conclusion

Far from providing an equal education for all, the existence of both the tripartite system of education and private schools meant that an extremely small percentage of the population were gaining the opportunity to go to university and to have life chances in general that most others could not. 'Most others' in this case tended to be working-class families.

For consideration:

1   Can you see a similarity between the tripartite system of education in the 1940s and 1950s and the system today?
2   Why do you think that many parents argue that grammar schools should not be abolished?

● Synoptic Link

Functionalists argue that societies should be meritocratic, i.e. that those that possess ability to work hard and do well academically need an education system that recognises both these traits. *Marxists* are critical of whether this is in fact the case, arguing that people do not start on a 'level playing field' as functionalists suggest. The tripartite system can, in A2, be used in any discussion you have about stratification and its connection to education.

✳ Key Idea

'Parity of esteem' means that two or more objects have the same status. This phrase comes up again and again in education, for example to refer to whether or not comprehensive schools and grammar schools have had the same status (or 'parity of esteem'). We can use this term here to discuss whether or not vocational qualifications are viewed by the public as having the same status or parity of esteem to A-levels. This phrase must be memorised for any education exam question.

What is the comprehensive system?

Why is it difficult to evaluate the comprehensive system?

What does this mean?

In 1965 the then Labour government, led by Harold Wilson, requested that all local education authorities in the country run secondary education along comprehensive lines. Comprehensive schools were set up to provide *one type* of school for all types of student, inclusive of all types of ability regardless of gender, class or ethnicity. This meant that there was also no requirement for an entrance exam, 11-plus result or interview. Students were placed in **streams** or **sets** based on ability.

Is there or has there ever been a 'comprehensive' system?

When looking at the British education system it is extremely difficult to talk about one particular system lasting over any length of time. There are two main reasons for this:

1   Due to the nature of British politics and what is effectively a two-party system, what one political party works hard to set up, the other party will work equally hard to change, modify or destroy when it gains power. Traditionally the Conservative party has favoured the tripartite system while the 'old' Labour party supported the idea of a fully comprehensive system. Until the Blair government came into power, the Conservative party largely dominated post-war politics in England and Wales. Consequently they worked hard to destroy or attack any idea that comprehensive schools could be a success. Tony Blair's New Labour is encouraging a variety of different types of education and continues to push the idea of parental choice, formerly associated with the Conservative party.

2   The idea of any system is that it works in the same way for a large group of people. However, in the case of comprehensive schools they took their pupils from what are referred to as catchment areas i.e. pupils had to live in the immediate area around the school. That means that it is very difficult to compare, for example, a comprehensive school in inner-city areas to one in the leafy green suburbs. In the first case the majority of students will be from a variety of cultural backgrounds and will probably be mainly working-class, and in the second students will probably be white and there will be a larger percentage of middle-class children.

These two reasons can be used to explain why it is very difficult to evaluate the comprehensive system or any other system of education that has been put in place by each successive government.

Evaluating the success of comprehensive schools

There are a number of difficulties in trying to measure how well comprehensive schools have performed in the past.

- Stop-go policies have meant that no one comprehensive system has been in place long enough to evaluate its success.

- With a small minority of rich children attending private schools it is impossible to know how well comprehensive schools might have performed had these children attended them.

- Measuring the 'performativity' (how well a school performs) of any school depends on what you are actually measuring, i.e. exam results, the ability to take children from very low ability to a significantly higher one, or in fact, the creation of a warm supportive and caring environment.

- Although comprehensive schools were extremely popular, there were always a significant number of grammar schools around to 'attract' high-achieving students. Had the grammar schools not been there, these students would have attended the comprehensive schools and boosted the schools' overall exam pass rates.

Conclusion

The popular complaint, voiced by parents, that comprehensive schools lowered standards for high-achieving students was used by the Conservative party as an excuse to attack and restrict the number of comprehensive schools that existed. However, a study carried out by the National Children's Bureau attacked such an idea. By taking 16,000 pupils all born in the same week of 1958, it explored how children performed in different types of secondary school. It showed (by exploring maths and reading tests) that high-achieving children made the same level of progress regardless of whatever different type of secondary school they attended.

For consideration:

1 To what extent do you think it mattered to teachers or students which type of school they attended?
2 How might the views of teachers about the type of school they work in affect the methods and ways in which they teach their pupils?

✳ Key Idea

Policies that change when one government loses and another one wins are often referred to as 'stop-go policies'. This idea explains why many excellent policies have never really been given a proper chance because when a new government is elected they will probably attempt to change or stop the policies of the previous government. Use this as an evaluative tool when referring to any educational policy that you discuss in the exam.

♟ Thinking like a Sociologist

Three criticisms you can make about comprehensive schools are:

1 Heath (1992) argues that class differences in education have largely remained unchanged since their introduction in the 1960s.
2 The streaming system that many comprehensives use results in social class segregation, i.e. working-class children tend to be labelled and placed in lower streams.
3 Comprehensive schools tend to be single- rather than multi-class institutions. Pupils come from the catchment area where the school is. This might mean a working-class catchment area, e.g. Newham, or a middle-class catchment area, e.g. Kensington.

● Synoptic Link

There are a variety of concepts that would enable you to make links with stratification and education. These concepts include 'locality', 'social control', 'identity' and of course, 'class', 'gender' and 'ethnicity'. Make sure that your folder has got these links highlighted before you start A2. Show your folder to your teachers and get them to check that these synoptic links are correct.

What is 'vocationalism'?

✳ Key Idea

The exam will want you to make a connection between education and the economy. As a result of the British economy not doing well in the 1970s, British politicians changed the traditional way in which people were educated in England and Wales. By encouraging teachers to focus on skills required for the work place, it was hoped that a newly trained work force would increase British business competitiveness. In this way it also placed the emphasis (and blame) on teachers to increase employment (by equipping them with the right skills) rather than on economic policies that could lead to more jobs in the first place.

What does this mean?

Vocational training refers to any type of training that is preparing people for the world of work. In many countries in Europe throughout most of the 20th century, vocationalism was very much part of the school curriculum. However, in England in the 1960s, vocational training was viewed by the government as something that should be tackled in the work place rather than in school. 'New Vocationalism' refers to the change in view by the government that vocational training should also take place in schools and colleges. It emerged in Britain in the late 1970s and is still something that is continuously being developed within schools and colleges across the country today. In January 2003 the government announced that a complete overhaul of education would need to take place for 14–19 year-olds which would have to take into consideration the employment needs of industry.

Why was 'new vocationalism' introduced by the government?

During the 1970s the British economy (as well as many other European economies) went into recession, i.e. its economy became very weak. British politicians were concerned about the rising unemployment that this created and, in particular, the rising youth unemployment. Rather than accepting any responsibility, in 1976, at Ruskin College, Oxford, the then British Prime Minister James Callaghan blamed teachers for the lack of skills that young people possessed. Schools, he argued, should improve vocational training and education to meet the requirements of industry.

What government educational policies and organisations have been inspired by 'new vocationalism'?

*   The Manpower Services Commission became the main agency in developing youth training in the 1970s.

*   In 1978 the Youth Opportunities Programme was introduced to offer young people six months of work experience and 'off the job' training.

*   In 1983 the Youth Training Scheme was introduced to offer school leavers a year of training in a variety of different occupations.

*   In 1986 the National Council for Vocational Qualifications was set up to offer a nationally recognised system of qualifications.

- General National Vocational Qualifications (GNVQs) were quickly introduced as alternative ways for young people to gain qualifications that were work-orientated.

- With Curriculum 2000 came the introduction of Advanced Vocational Certificates of Education which were to replace GNVQs and offer a qualification equivalent to 2 A-levels.

Conclusion

Four critisisms of 'new vocationalism'

1 Professor Dan Finn (1987) argued that it was the poor economic management of the British government that was responsible for unemployment rather than the lack of skills of young people.

2 Philip Cohen (1984) argued that in many vocational training programmes young people were used as cheap labour rather than being trained in the work place to learn new and valuable skills.

3 Paul Stephens (2001) argues that in Britain there has always been a class snobbery between those that are 'trained' and those that are 'educated'. He argues that in many other countries no such snobbery exists. This accounts for why, in the UK, many people see A-levels as being socially more acceptable than the vocational qualifications.

4 Richard Pring (1990) ironically refers to a 'New Tripartism' consisting of those with A-levels, those with BTEC/GNVQs and those who have received some sort of youth training. The qualification can be connected to class, occupation and pay.

For consideration:

1 Is the purpose of education to get a job?
2 Do you think 'parity of esteem' exists between A-levels and vocational qualifications? Justify your answer.

✓ Top Exam Hint

Evaluating any theory or concept in education means that you question how the data was gathered and when. Question to what extent the empirical data (the research data that has been collected) can be 'verified' for its accuracy. Analyse the argument to see if it holds together logically. Identify to what extent the theory, study or claim is 'comprehensive', i.e. that it can be used to explain other situations in a different culture, time or place. Use these points to structure an evaluative paragraph about the writer, theory or concept you are criticising.

What impact did the 1988 Educational Reform Act have?

✓ Top Exam Hint

Tell the examiner that the National Curriculum did not affect all students in the country. It did not affect private schools within the independent sector nor did it affect the variety of specialist schools that existed for children with special education needs. You should also remember that the National Curriculum only affected the English and Welsh education systems. Scotland has continued to have a completely different education system. In AQA sociology you will not be expected to know anything about the Scottish system.

● Synoptic Link

The concept of 'identity' makes a useful synoptic link between education and stratification. David Gillborn (2001) has shown that some teachers make damaging generalisations about class and ethnic identities. With the increase in testing that the ERA has brought about, he shows how pupils from working-class ethnic minority backgrounds may be entered for lower tiered tests. As a result these pupils are stratified into lower paying jobs and career opportunities later on based on the decisions made for them by their teachers.

♟ Thinking like a Sociologist

Three criticisms you can use in the exam are:

1 The Education Reform Act does not cover those children attending private schools.

2 The league tables create 'sink schools', i.e. those schools that people see at the bottom of the tables, a position from which it is very difficult to recover.

3 The information in the league tables does nothing to reward those schools that, although at the lower end of the tables, accept children with special needs, language difficulties or from very low income families. It is these schools that require extra funding.

What does this mean?

The 1988 Educational Reform Act (known as the ERA) was the largest change in educational policy-making since the 1944 Butler Act and reflected the New Right ideas of the Conservative party who led the country at the time. By taking its ideas from the ideas of business, the ERA attempted to increase parental choice and introduce market forces into education, i.e. that by competing with each other, schools would raise standards.

What changes did the ERA introduce?

* State schools were to be inspected in a more thorough fashion than at any time since their creation.

* A 'National Curriculum' of subjects was introduced for all pupils within the state primary and secondary education system and was composed of: maths, science, English, history, geography, technology, music, art, physical education and a modern language (in secondary schools).

* Compulsory testing at Key Stages in these subjects was required at the ages of seven, eleven, fourteen and sixteen within the state sector.

* The ERA also introduced league tables of local education authority schools listed in order of performance based on the national curriculum assessment (exams). Parents, as a result, would have the right to send their children to the school of their choice. Schools, for the first time, were in competition with each other.

* Local Management of Schools (i.e. where schools themselves have the major responsibility in saying how they should be run) replaced the previous system where LEAs (local education authorities) had control over how the schools were run. The new system gave greater power to individual heads of schools.

* Many schools (including a large number of grammar schools) could opt out of local funding. This meant that the complete budget for running the school from the government was given to the headmaster/mistress. Such schools believed that they would have greater freedom in how they might use their resources.

- Private industry was to play a bigger role in English education by the setting up of City Technology Colleges (CTCs). Once again, independent of LEAs these institutions focused on maths, science and technology and were generally located in inner-city areas.

How can you evaluate the success of the ERA?

Parental choice sounds like a wonderful idea and league tables may well show how well some schools are doing but they also hide three processes of social marginalisation (the process whereby some people become 'left out' of mainstream society) outlined below.

1 David Gillborn (2001) argues that in the pressure to be successful in the league tables some teachers and heads of schools may not accept certain types of pupil because of the stereotypical ideas they may have about some pupils' performance. Such prejudice may mean that some students may not be accepted because of their ethnicity, gender or class backgrounds.

2 Parental choice affects how much money a school may receive. Every extra pupil means more money for a school and if a school performs well in the league tables then more parents will want to send their children there. This can have disastrous consequences for some excellent inner-city schools. A school that is slightly selective, or is in a predominantly middle-class area may well perform better than an inner-city school that attracts a greater share of pupils with social problems. It is these schools that need extra money; however, they may well not perform highly in the league tables and, as a result, miss out on much needed cash.

3 While the introduction of a National Curriculum has definitely helped to increase female educational performance (i.e. girls for the first time study the same subjects as boys and therefore have more opportunity to out-perform them than ever before), the key stage tests have been strongly criticised. The tests are tiered according to ability, resulting in teachers having to judge which tier pupils should be entered for. Both post-structuralist Stephen Ball (1999) and interactionist David Gillborn (2001) argue that there is a disproportionate percentage of working-class and ethnic minority pupils in lower tier groups.

● Synoptic Link

'Power' can be used to show how any group (e.g. those based around age, gender, class, ethnicity, sexuality) can lack power over others or be exploited by others because of their status. Use the concept of 'power' and highlight how, as a result of the education system, groups can be stratified within English society (e.g. the power of some teachers to not enter certain students for exams!)

For consideration:

1 Do you think business ideas of competition and market choice can be applied to education?
2 What evidence can you see in your school or college that these ideas exist?

5.10 What is 'Curriculum 2000'?

Curriculum 2000 – increasing the levels of education or the levels of stress?

What does this mean?

The chances are if you are reading this book, that you are a product of Curriculum 2000 – an entirely different way of organising what was once the A-level system of exams. Curriculum 2000, named after the year the policy came into force, has been the biggest reorganisation of post-16 education since the 1950s and has introduced AS and A2-levels (the equivalent to a full A-level) which have replaced the A-level system.

What was the aim of Curriculum 2000?

As a result of the Dearing Report in 1998 it was found that while students in France and Germany experienced thirty hours of 'taught' time, sixth-formers in England studying A-levels were taught for between 15–18 hours a week. European students were also seen to study a much broader range of subjects than English students, who specialised very early on in a narrow range of subjects. In response to the Dearing Report's findings, the aim of Curriculum 2000 was to broaden the curriculum for 16–19 year-olds to include a mixture of arts and sciences, vocational and academic subjects and to increase the skills awareness that industry required in maths, communication and IT.

How can we criticise Curriculum 2000?

- Before Curriculum 2000 teachers and pupils could use a lot of the third term to prepare for any exam that might have been set. Chris Savory (2002) from the Institute of Education argues that the 'two-term' dash that all AS students now face when preparing for the summer AS exams means that there is too much to learn in too little time, particularly for less able students.

- Jacky Lumby (2002) from Leicester University argues that it has created too much work for both staff and students and has reduced the possibility of doing other non-curriculum related subjects that add so much to some pupils' lives, e.g. the Duke of Edinburgh award and work experience.

- While the AS examination has been constructed to be significantly easier than the A2, students taking Advanced Vocational Certificates in Education (AVCEs, i.e. vocational A-levels) have a completely different experience. Their first year exams are pitched at the same level as their second. Therefore no parity of esteem (see section 8) can be seen between the vocational and the academic.

- The introduction of examinations in the Key Skills of numeracy, communication and IT has been also criticised for offering exams that are too difficult for the level they are meant to be testing. They have also added to the exam load of students making England the most exam-orientated country in the world.

- While the aim was to increase student take-up of the arts and sciences, in reality students have been choosing the subjects that reflect their own strengths. In addition to this, although the expectation was for students to take five AS subjects in their first year, hardly any are actually doing this.

Conclusion

It is too soon to explore the effects of this educational policy on working-class and ethnic minority pupils although much research is currently being carried out. For many less-able students, the increased work pressure along with the reduced amount of teaching time available in the year means that certain students are suffering. The final term is now a term of examination rather than teaching.

With a greater share of working-class and ethnic minority students being channelled by teachers into an AVCE route, and, with the current situation where AVCE year one exams are harder than AS exams, it would seem likely that the system will increase rather than narrow the divide between classes and between the majority and ethnic minorities.

In January 2003 New Labour announced that *another* complete overhaul of the education system will be taking place. The changes will almost certainly involve the 14–19 age group and will result in the axing of the AS/A2 system altogether. At the time of writing this, it is too soon to say how this new educational system will look.

For consideration:

1 What benefits can you see from the introduction of Curriculum 2000?
2 To what extent do you think that teachers have had to change the way they teach as a result of the introduction of Curriculum 2000?

✓ **Top Exam Hint**

'Parity of esteem' (see section 8) is an expression that means that something has equal status to something else. You can use this expression to argue that while Curriculum 2000 was meant to help bring parity of esteem between academic A-levels and vocational AVCEs, the unequal way in which the exams have been levelled (see this section) means that no such equality exists. The system works against vocational students and therefore working-class and ethnic minority students.

🍃 **Thinking like a Sociologist**

Three evaluations you can use in the exam are:

1 Curriculum 2000 has only been around for two years and this has not given enough time for sociologists to gather data about its success or failure.
2 If we are talking about its success what are we comparing its success to?
3 By combining the old fashioned A-level with the European idea that students should study more broadly, the government has not really created a new system of education but taken existing ideas from two very different systems – the British and the French/German models.

5.11 What other types of education are there?

✓ Top Exam Hint

Remember that it takes nearly eighteen months to formulate the questions for the exams that you are sitting. The exam questions go back and forth between the chief examiners until the wording is exactly right. This wording is not designed to trick students but rather to allow high-achieving students the opportunities to gain those marks. Look out for the clues in the question. If you see a word like 'system' – ask yourself the question 'is there one?' In other words question the question – always. The chances are you will immediately gain extra evaluation marks.

What does this mean?

When thinking about formal education, it is so easy just to consider different schools within the state educational sector (e.g. grant-maintained schools, grammar and comprehensive schools) and those schools that are in the independent sector (i.e. private schools). However there are a variety of other types of schooling that you need to be aware of when answering questions in the exam.

Is there really an education system?

The sociology student should immediately challenge any question in the exam that refers to an education system by arguing that no one system exists. Do this by pointing out the variety of different 'systems' that are on offer, namely:

- *Primary schools:* schooling for children between the ages of 5–11.
- *Comprehensive schools:* schooling for children of all abilities between the ages of 11–18 (up until the age of 16 if the school has no sixth form).
- *Lower/middle/upper schools:* a different way of organising the age range found in schools. Originally associated with private and grammar schools, many comprehensive schools are splitting the age ranges into these three groupings.
- *Special schools:* Provided by local educational authorities (LEAs) and some voluntary organisations, these schools are for children with special educational needs (e.g. children with Down's Syndrome).
- *Education Otherwise:* With well over 1000 families in England and Wales taking part in this very distinct type of education, EO is where parents educate their children at home. Families who join EO are sent guides in how to provide adequate education for their children. This type of education is on the increase.
- *Pupil Referral Units (PRUs):* These are special institutions set up for disruptive students where their problems can receive special help. Not all local education authorities have these units. A debate exists as to whether such children should be allowed to study in normal schools, be excluded or be allowed to study in PRUs. The majority of pupils in these units tend to be working-class white youths.
- *Grammar schools:* Originally dating back to the 14th century, these schools tend to accept academically bright children. After the 1944 Education Act such schools formed part of the tripartite system of education. Grammar schools are state schools and as such do not charge fees.

- *Independent/fee paying/private schools:* Independent schools (the term generally preferred by private and public schools) are schools that charge fees to the parents/guardians of the pupils who study there. There are approximately 200 of these schools in England and Wales with the majority being boarding schools or having a boarding facility. The best known of these schools (Harrow, Eaton, Marlborough, Westminster, Rugby and Sherborne) are referred to as public schools. These schools have had a tradition of sending many pupils into public office, i.e. pupils have become members of parliament or high-ranking figures within the legal profession. The term public school in the United States has the opposite meaning to that used here. In America public schools are free state schools for the public.
- *Religious schools:* In recent years a variety of religious groups have been forming their own full-time schools, particularly in the Jewish and Islamic communities.

Postmodernists versus Marxists

Many postmodernists argue that **postmodern** society is a pic'n'mix society where diversity and choice have never before existed to the degree that they do today. Looking at the diversity of education listed above and, perhaps, the degree of choice on offer would seem to confirm the opinions that postmodernists share.

However, examining the list of schools above from a Marxist perspective might paint a different picture. The poverty that some working-class families share, along with extremely poor housing conditions, might well account for the high proportion of working-class children to be found in PRUs. Alternatively, how many working-class families could actually afford to have one parent at home, full-time, to provide the education to follow the Education Otherwise package?

Conclusion

As you can see, any question that asks you to assess how successful the educational system has been needs to be instantly unpacked in the exam. It is not enough to talk about the secondary education system without realising that the concept itself is too simplistic. It is also important to realise that the variety of education packages that exist may well represent those from a particular class, gender, ethnicity, region or religion.

For consideration:

1 What do you think about the idea of parents educating their children at home?
2 Why do you think that this type of education is increasing?

What do functionalists say about education?

What does this mean?

Functionalist theory was the dominant sociological theory in the UK and the United States during the 1950s and early 1960s. Functionalists talk about how society creates shared norms and values and therefore tend to highlight the positive functions or contributions that education offers to society. They examine how schools promote a consensual society (i.e. individuals, groups and institutions in general are not in conflict) by *socialising* people in its norms and values.

Education and a 'meritocratic society'

American functionalist Talcott Parsons argued that society was a 'meritocracy', i.e. that the social position you achieved in society as an adult (he called this 'achieved status') was based on your ability. This idea would suggest that the best people get the best jobs. For Parsons the education system acted as a bridge between the ascribed status you received at birth, e.g. your gender or ethnic background, and your achieved status. In this way the education system could be seen to act as a sieve or mechanism for allocating different roles to people in society based on their ability.

Functionalists argue that education performs two functions

1 *An economic function* – in which the education system contributes to economic growth by training its pupils to be a skilled and hardworking future work force.

2 *A socialising function* – in which societies norms and values are transmitted to pupils from one generation to the next.

How do education systems fulfill these two functions?

- *They integrate young people into their roles as loyal adult citizens.* This is done through many subjects in school (e.g. the teaching of citizenship), but also through the '**hidden curriculum**' by teaching students to be obedient in class.

- *They integrate young people into their roles as workers.* By giving students qualifications you reward them for their hard work in the same way that wages are a reward for the labour process (this idea is also called the 'correspondence theory', see section 13).

- *They promote a sense of national identity.* This is done by the teaching of subjects like history, English, and religious education.

- *They transmit the norms and values from one generation to another.* It is not only by teaching the above subjects that such norms and values are transmitted, but also by educating future teachers who in turn will pass on the values they have learnt within the education system.

- *They meet the economic needs of societies by creating a literate, hardworking work force.* This is done through the National Curriculum and the teaching of both A-levels and vocational qualifications. How effective this is would depend on how good the disciplinary system within a particular school or college might be in ensuring its pupils work hard.

- *They select and allocate roles for people based on ability within the classroom.* Closely associated with the functionalist idea of a 'meritocratic' society, this means that education helps to ensure that the most suitably qualified people get the most important and best-paid jobs.

Conclusion

As you can see, functionalists argue that education, as an institution, acts as a secondary form of socialisation, where young people are allocated roles within society depending on their ability in a variety of different ways. Such an idea is strongly criticised by other theorists (e.g. feminists, Marxists and interactionists) who argue that society is not 'meritocratic' and that pupils of different classes, ethnicities and genders face prejudice within a system that is unfair and unjust.

For consideration:

1   What evidence is there to show that functionalists are correct when they believe that the education system is meritocratic?
2   In what ways might Curriculum 2000 have affected the idea that education is meritocratic?

✳ Key Idea

Cultural or social reproduction refers to the functionalists' and Marxists' argument that education is an agency of socialisation. For functionalists this means that it is the job of education to transmit societies' norms and values from one generation to the next. However for Marxists, education is seen as 'culturally reproducing' the class system from one generation to the next.

What do Marxists say about education?

What does this mean?

While functionalism was the fashionable theory of the 1950s and early 1960s, Marxism became the 'in' theory throughout the late 1960s and 1970s. Marxists are highly critical of the role that education plays in people's lives. They completely disagreed with the functionalist idea that society was meritocratic by arguing that education systems automatically work against the interests of the working classes. By providing the rich and powerful with educational qualifications, the working classes could be exploited by those in power above them.

What is the 'myth of education'?

Marxists Bowles and Gintis' 'myth of education' is a complete attack on the functionalist concept of meritocracy. Bowles and Gintis (1976) argued that the meritocratic idea that education offers everybody an equal chance is in fact a myth or story that all of us blindly believe. They believed that education systems worked against the interests of the working classes.

In their 'correspondence theory' they argued that there was a correspondence between social relationships in the classroom and the work place. By this, they meant that the hierarchies, certificates, and discipline systems that can be found in schools are actually very similar to the world of work. In school you are paid in certificates, while in work you are paid in wages.

Education as an agency of social control

Louis Althusser (1971) believed that education as an institution socialised working-class children into accepting their subordinate position to the middle classes. He argued that education socially controls people in two ways.

- It convinces pupils that the capitalist system that we live in is fair and just.
- It prepares people for their later 'exploitation' in the work place.

It does this in three ways:

1 *The hidden curriculum* means that students learn to follow instructions in an unquestioning way (e.g. standing up when teachers come into the class; folding arms; referring to teachers as 'miss' or 'sir'). This is preparing them for their exploitation in the work place when they are older in that they automatically accept the instruction and authority of those above them even if it means that they are 'used' in the process.

2 *'Alienation' of schoolwork* means that many children become bored or 'alienated' with the work teachers set but are rewarded with marks or certificates. Alienation in this sense means that pupils cannot see the

point of much of what they study or indeed do not feel that they have a real say in what they should study. This situation is similar to the world of work where **alienation** becomes something not to be questioned.

3 *Textbooks* that show how western societies might somehow be 'advanced' give the impression to students that capitalism is the only successful economic system. Pupils may well, as a result, start to look down on other, non-capitalist ways of organising the economy, e.g. some Islamic states or parts of China.

Education as 'alienation'

Paul Willis' (1976) work (see also section 2), though now dated throws up fascinating issues for the sociologist of education. He focuses on how working-class children opted out of what they considered to be boring school work, even though many realised that by doing so, they would enter equally boring jobs. Interviewing twelve 'lads' during their last year at school and first year at work highlighted how they rejected the values and attitudes they saw in the school place. They did this by their behaviour to other pupils and teachers but also by 'bunking' off lessons. Willis argued that this showed how, far from being helpless victims within the school, their rebellious attitude was evidence that working-class children could resist the middle-class values that schools encouraged.

Education as a system that reproduces social inequality

Marxists argue that education has a cultural reproduction role. Bourdieu has argued that schools, along with the staff that work in them are generally middle-class institutions. Working-class children simply do not possess the cultural capital (the ideas, tastes, values and lifestyle associated with a particular class) required for success in such establishments. This means that middle-class children will generally do better than working-class children. This makes the school an institution that ensures middle-class dominance from one generation to the next.

Conclusion

While Marxists share many of the ideas of functionalists, e.g. there is a link between education and the work place and the fact that education prepares us for our acceptance of the values of society, Marxists are highly critical of this process. They argue that education socialises children into possessing a false consciousness about the world. This false consciousness fails to see the inequalities of the capitalist society they are being brought up in.

66 99 Key Definition

'Alienation' – this Marxist concept refers to the inability of individuals to relate, or identify with the work that they do. Marx argued that as societies became more and more modernised (i.e. working on production lines) they lost the traditional satisfaction that many areas of work had offered (e.g. carpentry and farming). The meaninglessness of modern day work can produce feelings of frustration, anger and in some cases lead people to acts of crime or deviance.

Working-class boys making the choice to opt out, or victims of the system?

● Synoptic Link

A synoptic link made between education and crime and deviance allows sociologists to explore how schools can 'alienate' some groups, causing them to 'kick back' against the values being taught and create their own subcultures. One reaction to alienation might be truancy. The current debate in the media about truancy shares the concern that disillusionment in school can lead to crime at a later stage. Sociologists explore these synoptic links.

For consideration:

1 What activities are you involved in within education that you consider to be 'alienating' to you?
2 To what extent do you agree with Bowles and Gintis that the school 'corresponds' to the work place?

What do feminists say about education?

What does this mean?

Feminists argue that education helps to enforce 'patriarchy' i.e. the belief that society is structured to meet the needs of males more than females and is, in fact, dominated by males. Feminists take a keen interest in the role that education plays as a 'secondary' form of socialisation. There are however a variety of 'feminisms' that students need to be aware of.

Feminism or feminisms?

Remember that 'feminisms' reflects the idea that there are many different opinions about how patriarchy affects women. In addition to the triple systems theory of Walby (see Key Idea) the key feminist theories are:

Liberal feminists argue that patriarchy will be ended by changes in equal opportunities and educational policies. For example, they would argue that the introduction of the National Curriculum has played a significant role in bringing about equality of education by making sure that both genders study the same subjects in school.

Marxist feminists argue that women's role in society is shaped and determined by the needs of the economy. They blame the capitalist system for allowing women to be forced into a situation where they are socialised into supporting men both in the home and the work place. Education is seen as enforcing these expectations both on men and women.

Black feminists argue that to be black and female is a very different experience to that of being white and female. These very different experiences can be seen in schools and colleges and the way teachers and books treat both groups of students differently.

Radical feminists argue that patriarchy can only end when women are freed from the negative influence (and violence) that men inflict on women – both physically and emotionally. The school classroom and playground are seen as prime sources of such violence.

Post-feminists argue that there is no single meaning to what it means to be a 'woman' but rather that women possess multiple identities. Women can be 'black', 'white', 'gay', 'straight', 'working-class', and so on. They can be any or most of these at the same time. This lack of a single meaning as to what 'female' means confirms the postmodern idea that no single theory or concept can explain anything, including that of gender differences.

How does the 'hidden curriculum' operate?

Heaton and Lawson (1996) argue that feminists point to the hidden curriculum (see key definition, section 12) as a main source of gender socialisation in schools. They argue that it operates in five different ways:

1 *Through books* – Feminists claim that many children's books and school text books portray women as dependent on men. Kelly (1987) argues that women are largely 'invisible' in science texts.
2 *Through students* – Many female students are made to feel uncomfortable in the presence of male students when studying certain subjects. For example Culley (1986), when studying computing, showed how boys liked to 'colonise' the space around computers. In many cases teachers did not intervene leaving many girls to feel excluded from what was wrongly perceived as a male activity.
3 *Teachers' expectations and attitudes* – Although much has changed in recent years Heaton and Lawson argue that many teachers still possess strongly sexist ideas about certain tasks within the classroom, e.g. boys are still asked to move furniture while girls are still asked to clean and wash surfaces (e.g. in the laboratories).
4 *Through a patriarchal curriculum* – despite the introduction of the National Curriculum, many feminists argue that what is taught in schools still creates gender inequalities in education. The way that sport is still taught in many schools tends to focus more on the achievements of boys rather than girls e.g. football and cricket. The choices made by boys and girls in A-levels are still strongly gender-specific in some areas (look around your own sociology class!)
5 *Through a lack of positive role models* – Despite the fact that there are more female teachers in England and Wales than male teachers, more men than women still occupy the senior management levels of schools and colleges. There are also remarkably few black female teachers. Feminists argue that this creates an expectation that positions of power and authority are automatically associated with men more than women.

Conclusion

Education is seen as a major source of gender socialisation by feminists. Different feminisms highlight different aspects of the education system that enforce an ideology that males are somehow naturally in positions of power and authority. The hidden curriculum shows a variety of ways that these processes work. However, you need to remember that despite the many problems that female students face in schools they are, in general, out-performing males in all areas of education.

For consideration:

1 Which branch of feminism do you find the most convincing in its approach to gender socialisation?
2 How might you suggest an alternative approach to education that would challenge many of the criticisms offered by feminists?

Girls and boys in science but who is asked to wash-up afterwards?

5.15 What do interactionists say about education?

What does this mean?

George Herbert Mead's (1934) theory of symbolic interactionalism starts with the idea that we develop who we are, or 'our self' by interacting with other people. By encountering 'significant others' such as parents, teachers, religious leaders and friends we start to see the world from their eyes. It should therefore come as no great surprise that this theory plays a very significant role when examining issues of class, ethnicity and gender in education.

The influence of Howard Becker

The following quote is taken from research carried out by Howard Becker in 1952 on sixty Chicago teachers: 'Said one teacher: "Of course, it's not their fault, they aren't brought up right . . . parents in a neighbourhood like this aren't really interested"'. Such a quote showed how teachers held strong stereotypical ideas of pupils from certain socio-economic backgrounds. His work has strongly influenced the work of David Gillborn, Stephen Ball and many other contemporary sociologists when looking at how teachers label students and the effects this may have on them.

Labelling and the self-fulfilling prophecy

W. I. Thomas (1909) argued that if people defined social situations as real, they were real in their consequences. In what has now become known as the 'self-fulfilling prophecy' he was referring to how people can start to believe, and make possible, situations they would otherwise have thought could not happen. The following three examples show how this happens.

- Interactionists Rosenthal and Jacobson (1968) showed how teachers responded to being told that some of their students were brighter than others. In their experiment, teachers were told that a randomly picked sample of their pupils were actually intellectual 'bloomers'. Despite the fact that this was not true, these pupils, they argued, outperformed others in their class. Rosenthal and Jacobsen used this to show how, when labelled, both those that are labelled and those that do the labelling start to bring about a 'self-fulfilling prophecy', i.e. that subconsciously teachers will start to respond to those students in a very different way. Such accounts can be used to show how teachers who hold stereotypical views about race, class and gender may actually have a major effect on pupils they teach.

> ### ✳ Key Idea
>
> The work of Howard Becker is highly influential in the exploration of labelling and self-fulfilling prophecies within education. Although his work is strongly associated with criminology and deviance, it has been applied to the way that pupils and teachers interact with each other. His work showed how teachers applied labels to students, e.g. 'rebellious'. He argued that teachers constantly reinforced their initial negative judgements in all subsequent interactions with students, resulting in the pupil being 'trapped' in that perception.

- Post-structuralist Stephen Ball's (1981) study, *Beachside Comprehensive*, showed how teacher expectations of some students led to the banding or streaming of certain pupils in a comprehensive school. His work showed how teachers varied their expectations and teaching methodology depending on the band pupils were in.

- Over the last thirteen years, interactionist David Gillborn has continued to be influenced by the work of Howard Becker as he explores the experience of ethnic minority pupils at the hands of some teachers. His work has shown that some teachers 'blame' African-Caribbean students more than white students for poor behaviour even when the behaviour is identical. In what he describes as 'the myth of the black challenge' he shows how teachers perceive certain types of behaviour as 'threatening' and then go on to punish students accordingly. He found that these pupils were disproportionately placed on report, put in detention or excluded compared to other ethnic minorities in schools.

Conclusion

The small-scale nature of interactionalist research has meant that experiences of pupils at the hands of some teachers within the education system would never have become discovered had it not been for this type of research. These experiences show, through the concept of a self-fulfilling prophesy, how pupils themselves along with teachers can affect the educational careers of different genders, ethnicities or classes. There are, however, two criticisms that need to be noted:

1 The small-scale nature of much of interactionalist research can sometimes ignore larger macro dimensions to the classroom experience such as government policy (e.g. the introduction of Curriculum 2000) and funding (greater funding would mean more teachers to fewer students and therefore a more meaningful learning environment for all concerned).

2 Paul Willis' (1976) study on working-class 'lads' has shown how some pupils do not passively accept the labels or expectations that others have for them.

For consideration:

1 To what extent do you think the labelling process is a useful explanation for male underachievement?
2 What other theories can you use, in combination with interactionist theory, when explaining the educational underachievement of pupils?

✓ Top Exam Hints

- When looking at the work of any sociologist remember to use the concepts reliability and validity when talking about micro or interpretive sociological research. Because so much interpretive sociology is about individual, subjective meanings, it is very difficult for the sociologists who practice this to claim their work is reliable; however, they may well wish to describe it as valid. Students will gain high evaluation marks for simply stating this in the exam. Mention these points in your conclusion.

- Both functionalists and Marxists can be criticised for being 'over-deterministic', i.e. that both theories leave little room to show how individuals can themselves affect their own experience within education. Interactionalist theory can be used to show   the individual can indeed respo   own educational   this would   reject or fig   applied to teachers.

236

Blue-collar wo for life – what de today?

Sociolog

5.16 What do postmodernists say about education?

What does this mean?

Postmodernists argue that the period that we are living in now is very different from that of any other time in history. They argue that the 'modern' era of the 18th, 19th and 20th centuries has ended and that education needs to adapt to the enormous changes that are taking place within societies at a global level. They refer to what was once a 'golden age' of certainty and contrast that with today's society that is risk-laden and diverse.

The risks include the dangers of genetically-modified food, chemical warfare and the possibility of global destruction. The diversity includes the variety of languages and the ethnic mix of people who live together in towns and cities; changes in music, fashion and lifestyle; and changing patterns in the way we work. These have huge implications for education systems.

What are some of these changes that have taken place?

1 *A change from 'fordism' to 'postfordism'* – 'Fordism' takes its name from The Ford Motor Company, where cars were mass produced on production lines. Throughout much of the 20th century, 'fordist' methods of production meant that people were trained in a particular skill and then gained jobs that were quite often on a production line or associated with one particular way of working. The expectation was that these were jobs for life. Nowadays, the concept of a job for life no longer exists. 'Postfordism' is the idea that production methods quickly change to meet the needs of consumers/customers whose tastes quickly change from one fashion to the next. This means that any future work force must be trained in schools to be multi-skilled. They must also expect to change jobs throughout their lives.

2 *Societies are become increasingly fragmented and diverse in make up* – traditional institutions like the family and religion have gone through immense changes over the last fifty years. Single parent families make up almost half the families in Britain. Gay couples are becoming accepted in mainstream society. Increasingly the role that religion plays in the formation of schools is rapidly changing to address

...kers in the 1950s with a job
...es somebody's class

the needs of a multi-cultural England. In all cases this means that any attempt to impose a common or national curriculum on all pupils is unlikely to meet the needs of all concerned.

3 A *'collapse of the economy of truth'* – Hebdige (1989) argues that any particular theory or 'expert knowledge' is in fact a 'metanarrative' or big story. Such stories cannot claim to be a 'truthful' portrayal of how the world actually is. What you believed to be true yesterday is likely to be proven untrue today. Knowledge is just a 'social construction,' i.e. something that powerful groups in society say we should know. Evidence of this distrust in expert knowledge can be seen in the way that many people no longer hold the same trust in doctors or priests in the way that they once did.

4 An increase in all types of *'surveillance'* – postmodernists argue that in today's societies we are continuously being 'observed'. They point not only to the increase in CCTVs in operation but also to the increase in record-keeping paperwork and the use of targets so that we can 'monitor' people in schools, jobs and in society in general.

Conclusion

* Moore and Hickox (1994) argue that because of the rapid changes that are taking place in most societies it is impossible to provide a curriculum (national, vocational or otherwise) that can address the challenges that such changes create.

* As a result of the increase in monitoring, record-keeping and target setting that postmodernists argue is a symptom of today's education, pupils suffer because they are increasingly asked to take tests and exams. Thus stress loads increase along with widespread disillusionment about what education really is.

* If there are, as postmodernists argue, no longer right or wrong pieces of knowledge, where does that leave the status of teachers who are supposed to be 'experts' in the classroom? Does this account for why there is a current shortage of teachers in the profession?

For consideration:

1 What evidence can you collect that proves the postmodernist argument that 'experts' are no longer treated with the respect they once were?
2 What certainties can you find that characterise what postmodernists refer to as modernity?

✓ **Top Exam Hint**

Remember that postmodernism is itself a theory that attempts to offer an explanation for what and how education works. Many postmodernists argue that all theories are just stories or 'metanarratives' (the word for big theories that postmodernists use). However, does this not equally make postmodernism a story or theory? Say this in the exam as a way of evaluating postmodernist claims and the examiners will award you for your evaluative skills and knowledge of sociological theory.

● **Synoptic Link**

Apply the ideas presented here synoptically to the A2 subject of stratification. Postmodernists challenge traditional explanations of stratification based on class, gender and ethnicity. They argue that while these old-fashioned concepts belonged to an era where production was what defined an identity (e.g. you were a builder, metal worker, engineer, and so on) and these jobs were invariably linked to your class background, now it is what we consume that defines who we are – therefore these old labels are no longer appropriate.

How does education socialise pupils?

What does this mean?

Most pupils in England spend a minimum of eleven years being formally educated in primary and secondary schools. Whether in the classroom, canteen or playground, a variety of 'interactions' take place that many sociologists argue can affect or socialise our identities.

What does education do to pupils?

The following list identifies some of the ways in which schools might socialise pupils into the adult roles they later take on.

1 *Alienation* – Many Marxists argue that education alienates working-class children (see section 13). The curriculum, textbooks and even the way some teachers talk is far removed from the desires and lifestyles of working-class children. Rising rates of truancy in British schools would be evidence to show this is the case.

2 *Ideological control* – Whether we are talking about patriarchal ideology or capitalist ideology, schools have a variety of ways of making pupils believe society's values should go unquestioned. One example of this process is standing up when teachers come into the class, and calling them 'miss' or 'sir'. In this way pupils learn to 'respect' authority and not challenge those in power regardless of whether or not they are correct.

3 *Labelling* – By allowing teachers and pupils to 'label' each other, many children are placed in an educational 'pathway' that determines their life chances later on (see section 15). One example of this is when some teachers place children in lower sets or streams which, if leading up to GCSEs, can drastically affect their exam results. David Gillborn (1990) has shown how quite often it is members of ethnic minorities that get placed in these lower sets or streams.

4 *Relationships of power* – Pupils are confronted in school by different authority figures from their teacher, to tutor, to year head and all the way up to the headmistress or headmaster. They are also confronted with their own peer groups and the various subcultures that exist within any school. These can leave lasting impressions on children. Some sociologists argue that male underachievement can be traced to the fact that many primary school teachers are female which in turn socialises male pupils into believing that studying is not 'macho'.

5   *Cultural reproduction* – Schools have the capacity to culturally reproduce the dominant culture in the society the school exists in. This can be done through subjects within the National Curriculum (e.g. History where English history is taught from an English perspective) but also through the way that teachers themselves have been educated and then go on to teach new generations of pupils who, one day, will become teachers themselves!

6   *Role allocation* – By placing children in classes and setting them up within a system of tests and certificates, students can be 'sifted' into a role, be it doctor, engineer or road sweeper. Schools also have the ability to 'culturally reproduce' gender roles by persuading male or female pupils to take on specific subjects (although after the introduction of the National Curriculum this has decreased).

7   *The structure of the organisation* – Many feminists would argue that from an early age children are, without realising it, forced to accept that regardless of how many women may be in an organisation, in most cases men dominate the powerful positions in working life. Schools are one very good example of this 'social fact' with most heads and senior management positions being occupied by males.

8   *School sports* – Sociologists argue that sports in schools are one way of socialising pupils into values of competitiveness, discipline, conformity and loyalty. While many functionalists would argue that this is in fact a positive function of the education system, some Marxists would argue that these values help sustain the capitalist system – a system that they are highly critical of.

Conclusion

As you can see, there are a variety of ways that schools, and the teachers who work in them, socialise pupils into particular ways of thinking and acting. Whether you believe that this is a positive or negative process will depend upon which particular theory is used to explain why these processes take place.

✓ Top Exam Hint

Remember to apply the ideas of George Mead's symbolic interactionism when referring to how children are socialised. He argued that the 'play' and 'game' stages of socialisation are crucial to forming a child's sense of self or identity. Both these stages quite often take place in the playgrounds at schools.

● Synoptic Link

Remember that by using the concept of 'socialisation' you can make direct links to the experience that children have in schools and the lives as adults they will be socialised into. As a result, this can be tied to either the second year synoptic subjects of stratification or crime and deviance. In both cases choose case studies that show how teachers, the classroom or the make up of the school directly influences where pupils end up as adults.

What do sociologists mean by 'in-school' and 'out-of-school' factors?

What does this mean?

When examining differences in educational achievement based on class, gender or ethnicity, sociologists focus on what they call 'in-school' and 'out-of-school' factors. In other words, sociologists have to look both within and beyond the immediate environment of the school to explain why students do well or badly within different educational systems.

What are 'in-school factors'?

- *Type of school* – is the school a comprehensive or grammar school?

- *Structure of the school* – is the school made of up of streams or sets or are the classes mixed ability?

- *Leadership of the school* – is the school well managed by the head/principal or senior managers? To what extent are the managers of the school white/black/male/female/working-class/middle-class?

- *Staffing of the school* – to what extent do the staff of the school reflect the cultural make up of its students, i.e. if the school is in a predominantly black or working-class area, how many black or working-class teachers are employed by the school?

- *Funding of the school* – does the school have enough money for resources (e.g. books, desks, rooms, computers, teachers, and so on)?

- *Entry requirements* – does the school accept students with a variety of abilities or does it select on the basis of past exam performance?

- *Labelling* – to what extent do teachers label students and how might that affect which classes and ultimately which exams they may or may not sit?

- *Self-fulfilling prophesies* – as a result of labelling and being placed in a particular set, tier or stream, how might a pupil start to believe the label and then become the label, i.e. 'bright', 'not-so-bright', and so on?

✓ **Top Exam Hint**

When writing a conclusion to any education question on 'ethnicity', remember to point out that issues such as 'class' and 'gender' must be taken into consideration when discussing what it means to come from an ethnic minority or to experience education as an ethnic minority. A good exam answer will recognise that to experience education as working-class and Asian will be very different from that of being middle-class and Asian.

● **Synoptic Link**

The concern expressed within the media about guns can be connected synoptically with both crime and deviance and education. In January 2003 New Labour expressed concern that some pupils who were 'failing' within the education system found status in subcultures outside the school – some of which were gun-carriers. By providing a more inclusive education, the government hopes that this will reduce the numbers of individuals who turn to crime as a result of poor education.

What are 'out-of-school' factors?

- *Poverty* – to what extent are pupils materially deprived of certain essential requirements if they are expected to succeed within the educational system? These requirements might include a room of their own at home to study in, sufficient money for books, a healthy diet, sufficient clothes, and so on.

- *Parental interest* – often (wrongly) associated with middle-class parents, this might refer to taking an interest in homework, attending parents' evenings, encouragement and support for their child's studies in general and making sure that their child regularly attends school.

- *Language differences* – whether because of class or ethnic differences, a culture clash can sometimes exist between the language used at home and outside the school with the language found in text books and used by teachers.

- *Cultural capital* – Neo-Marxist Bourdieu argues that the cultural capital of the middle classes is rewarded by exam success whereas that of the working classes is not. By this he means that the everyday bits of knowledge that many young middle-class children soak up from their parents (e.g. names of classical musicians; names of theatre plays; knowledge of holiday destinations; certain newspapers) is the kind of knowledge that teachers unintentionally reward. Working-class cultural capital is, according to Bourdieu, not rewarded by teachers.

- *Positional theory* – Positional theorist Boudon argues that the difference in class position of both working-class and middle-class pupils impacts on how well both do. A lack of friends, relatives or neighbours coming from professional backgrounds along with less money to invest in education will place restrictions on children from the working classes in considering entering higher status jobs.

Conclusion

Different types of sociologists focus on different factors to explain why some people do better than others at school. In general (although not always) interpretive sociologists look at in-school factors, while in general (but also, not always), structural sociologists focus on out-of-school factors.

To what extent is deviancy a product of the education system?

● Synoptic Link

Education and crime and deviance can once again be linked synoptically through ethnicity by referring to the concern that black males are under-achieving within the education system. David Gillborn's (1990) research shows that in many cases this is as a result of institutional racism within English schools. However, with rising crime rates and the wave of shootings that have been taking place in recent years, the government has been blaming rap music and aspects of black male culture rather than educational policies. Stuart Hall (1979), writing over twenty years ago, emphasised the way that ethnic minorities are almost invariably presented as a 'problem' in the media i.e. they are often blamed for social disorder rather than the government.

For consideration:

1. How might labelling theory be applied to all factors above?
2. How might a 'self-fulfilling prophesy' be associated with all factors above?

What is the relationship between education and class?

◆ What, When and Why?

New Labour was elected in 1997 and continued much of the educational policies that existed under the previous Conservative party's regime. Grammar schools and grant-maintained schools were retained and in March 2000 New Labour announced that grammar schools were 'here to stay'. The 'naming and shaming' of schools that the league tables encouraged has also continued under New Labour. However, with financial assistance being offered for the first time to the long-term unemployed and single parent mothers who wish to continue further education, some things have changed. 'Excellence in Cities' is a £350m programme that has created 'education action zones' targeting under-achievement in schools in major inner-city areas across the country.

✳ Key Idea

The ideas of the New Right have had a great influence in the creation of educational policies over the last twenty years in England and Wales. Using ideas generally associated with the rightwing of the Conservative party, the policy stresses the need for individual freedom, responsibility and very little government involvement in public services (e.g. education systems).

66 99 Key Definition

Basil Bernstein (1990) talks of 'restricted' and 'elaborated' codes. The first is what, he argues, working-class children use and this consists of shortened phrases or 'slang' terms that communicate ideas well in certain circumstances but not in those of formal education. Middle-class children use both restricted and elaborated codes. These are the words that are used by teachers and found in textbooks. He argues that middle-class pupils automatically use these words and therefore perform well in the school system.

What does this mean?

Despite all the different government policies since the 1944 Education Act, students from working-class backgrounds, on average, achieve less within formal education than their middle-class counterparts. Evidence of this can be seen in exam results, lower reading scores in primary schools, higher leaving rates from school at the age of sixteen, and the fact that wherever streaming, setting or tiering takes place, working-class children can be seen to be disproportionately in the lower bands. There are a variety of explanations for this.

Structural explanations for working-class under-achievement

Some sociological explanations argue that it is structures within society that produce inequality within it. Below are a range of structural explanations that can be used to explain working-class under-achievement.

- Sociobiologists and many New Right thinkers argue that IQ tests show that working-class children have lower abilities than their middle-class peers.
- Basil Bernstein (1990) argues that the structure of the language that middle-class children use is the same as the language that teachers expect for exam success. He argues that working-class children's use of **restricted code** does not allow them to perform well in the school system, which is *culturally-biased* in favour of middle-class children.
- Positional theorist Boudon (1974) argues that it is harder for working-class children to aim for university and high status jobs while at the same time easier for middle-class children. When middle class, the expectation from friends, teachers and family is that you must enter a high status profession. Boudon argues the opposite is the case for working-class children
- Bourdieu and Passeron (1977) argue, from a Marxist perspective, that the cultural capital of the middle-classes gives middle-class children an advantage over their working-class peers. By cultural capital they refer to the tastes, knowledge and ideas associated with a particular class. They argue that teachers and middle-class pupils share similar cultural capital and, as a result, teachers reward these pupils with greater educational success than their working-class counterparts.

Micro sociological explanations for working-class under-achievement

These interpretive explanations focus much more on the processes within the classroom and the individual interaction between students and teachers, and students themselves.

- Interactionist Keddie (1971) argued that teachers do not make judgements about students based on their performance but rather on their imagination as to what an 'ideal' student is. Teachers teach in a different way depending on what stream, set or tier students are placed in. This is a clear example of labelling and a self-fulfilling prophesy if the student then goes on to believe that they are bright or stupid, depending on the level they have been placed by the teacher.

- Paul Willis (1977) argues against the deterministic explanations offered above. His research (see section 2) shows how values can be rejected if not relevant to pupils' lives. *The Lads*

Parental explanations for working-class under-achievement

J. W. B. Douglas (1964) has argued that working-class parents are not as interested as those from the middle-classes in their children's educational success. A lack of parental encouragement along with lower levels of general knowledge, vocabulary and access to books was typical of many working-class families. However, it is important to realise that measuring parental interest is highly problematic; for example, a lack of attendance at parents' evenings may actually reflect the need to work nights to support the family rather than a lack of interest in the child's education.

Conclusion

The 'old' sociology of education focused mainly on how class played a major role in determining the educational success of pupils. However, few sociologists today hold this view, preferring to combine gender, ethnicity and class when evaluating the educational success of pupils in schools.

For consideration:

1. To what extent do you accept that these explanations typify the working classes?
2. To what extent is it easy to talk of class without also considering the effects of gender, ethnicity, sexuality and age?

✳ Key Ideas

- Use Boudon, Bernstein and Bourdieu to evaluate the meritocratic idea that functionalists have of a fair society. Functionalists assume that there is a level playing field within the educational system and that education sorts out those with ability from those without and that people are allocated jobs as a result of the certificates they get from school. Boudon's theory argues that this is *not* the case and that the education system automatically works against anybody who is working-class.

- Sociobiologists hold the view that all social behaviour is shaped/determined by your natural instincts which are biologically created. The two most important of these are the desire to survive and reproduce. Sociologists challenge these ideas arguing that culture and the environment are more important than biology.

● Synoptic Link

When you have completed this unit spend one hour labelling any connections with either stratification or crime and deviance. Use post-it notes every time you come to such a connection (e.g. truancy and street crime, Boudon's positional theory and low job status). You can then make a list of the connections with one sentence explaining how they connect either of the second year synoptic subject areas. Keep the list for when you revise for the synoptic component in your exam (make sure you show it to your teacher first).

5.20 What is the relationship between education and gender?

◆ What, When and Why?

By applying a historical perspective, i.e. considering how things might/might not have changed over time, it is possible to identify how education could be linked with stratification. During the 1970s women's status in the workplace was significantly lower than it is today. As Sue Sharpe has shown, female attitudes to education have significantly changed over the last two decades. The introduction of the National Curriculum and the fact that most females now want to stay on in education has meant that women are gaining far better jobs now than during the 1970s.

✳ Key Idea

Feminist sociology has two major concerns regarding education systems. First, what roles do women occupy within educational institutions and second, what role does patriarchy play within the education of women? Many feminists argue that educational institutions legitimise gender inequality (e.g. while many teachers are women, many senior positions in schools and colleges are often held by men). By studying these institutions we can examine to what extent women's role and status is constructed through education and to what extent educational institutions oppress women.

What does this mean?

It is hard to imagine that only in 1948 did Cambridge University accept full membership of women into most of its colleges. Until the 1980s sociologists of education focused on the under-achievement of females within the education system. However, this trend has completely changed over the last twenty-five years with women now out-performing men

Traditional explanations for female under-achievement

- Sue Sharpe (1976) argues that different aspirations for females explained their lower educational achievement. Her study showed that 'love, marriage, husbands and children' were the main priorities for young women.
- Feminist Angela McRobbie (1978) argues that females in the late 1970s were influenced by magazines that highlighted the importance of romance over career.
- G. Griffin (1995) argues that some females leave school early to get out of the 'housework' role they occupy within the family.
- R. Deem (1990) focused on the role of the school curriculum during the late 1970s and early 1980s and how teachers encouraged females to take/not take certain subjects, e.g. Science and Home Economics.

While the above studies are useful to sociology students they cannot explain why females are outperforming males in the classroom today.

So what has changed?

Along with the women's movement in the 1970s, the media played a major role in promoting female individuality and ambition from the 1980s onwards (e.g. Hollywood blockbuster movies at that time, such as *Working Girl*, and more recently, films like *Erin Brockovich*). Other factors include:

- The introduction of the National Curriculum (a product of the 1988 ERA) that for the first time made males and females study the same subjects.
- The introduction of school initiatives in the late 1980s and early 1990s such as GIST (Girls into Science and Technology) and TVEI (the Technical Vocational Educational Initiative) that actively encouraged the role of females within these traditionally male dominated vocational areas.

- Allison Kelly (1985) argued that as a result of an increased awareness of equal opportunities in schools, not only were books more closely monitored for gender-biased language but also teacher training courses were modified to take into consideration the role gender plays within the classroom.
- Changes in the job market that include greater reliability on technology means that male strength is no longer a requirement within many types of manual labour.
- A report by the CBI (the Confederation of British Industry) in the late 1990s argued that if Britain were to remain economically competitive with other countries, Britain's top one hundred companies should be run by female managers. The report argued that they were better team leaders and more able to multi-task.

So why do males under-perform?

- Jane Clark (1996) showed that males were bombarded with images of the macho or anti-authority stereotypes both within and outside the media. This macho cultural stereotype associated with 'laddism' flies in the face of the image of woman as organiser or woman as carer that young males associate with the role of female teachers. This acts as a *dis*incentive for males to be seen to focus on their studies within the school environment.
- New Right theory focuses on the increase in single parent families and higher divorce rates to explain the lack of role models for males. The New Right often blame individuals and families for what they see as a moral decline in the values of society. The increased determination of women to be economically independent is also blamed for recent male under-achievement.
- Mac en Ghaill (1994) argues that many males experience a 'crisis of masculinity' because of the decline in traditional male jobs or professions. This identity crisis, he argues, allows some males to question the need for qualifications when the jobs they would have traditionally gone into no longer exist.

Conclusion

Despite what many commentators argue, after the introduction of tripartite system (brought in after the 1944 Education Act), females actually achieved higher scores than males in the 11-plus exam. However, the government, concerned that more females would gain places in grammar schools than males, instructed their exams to be marked down to even up the scores.

For consideration:

1 Have you observed differences in the way males and females behave in the classroom?
2 Do your teachers react differently to the behaviour of males and females?

5.21 What is the relationship between education and ethnicity?

✓ Top Exam Hints

- When talking about the educational performance of a particular ethnic 'minority', not only must students remember that class and gender are important factors to take into consideration but also differences in language, religious belief and the region where they live. It is not enough to make generalisations about Pakistani or Bengali under-achievement but rather the social circumstances in which some Bengalis may live – whether it is in inner-city London or rural Bedfordshire.

- Remember that racial categorisations such as 'white', 'Asian' and 'Afro-Caribbean' are what are referred to as social constructions, i.e. they have been created by individuals and have become acceptable classifications that most people use. This does not actually mean they are useful. Many statistics categorise Britons, Poles and Americans as 'white' and yet can we really make any generalisations about these groups? Similarly, how useful is 'Asian' when referring to the Chinese, Indians, Pakistanis, Indonesians or Malays, all of whom have distinct cultural differences? Mention this when talking about any racial categorisation or statistical comparison.

✳ Key Idea

Cultural deprivat___ ␣␣␣␣ nts a
group of ␣␣␣␣ ␣␣␣ng-class
␣␣␣␣ to
␣␣␣␣ ␣␣␣hin
␣␣␣␣ to

␣␣␣␣ ␣␣an

245

What does this mean?

It is easy to assume that because Britain is considered to be a multicultural society there must be a relatively meritocratic education system, i.e. one that offers equal chances to all within it. When we look at the performance of Britain's ethnic minorities another picture arises in which huge differences exist between the educational performances of one ethnic minority compared to another. Sociologists explore these differences and, increasingly explore how other social variables such as class and gender help to explain why some ethnic groups seem to perform better than others.

Searching for explanations

- Intelligence cannot, as the Swann Committee (a committee appointed by the government to examine the education of ethnic minorities) showed in the mid-1980s, be a reason for differences in educational attainment between different ethnic groupings. The research showed that other social and economic factors were far more important than any differences in IQ (e.g. levels of poverty, housing conditions and parental involvement).
- Cultural deprivation theory states that many black children are deprived of the values needed for school success. However, this theory can be attacked by referring to how Ken Pryce (1979) showed that many Afro-Caribbean parents send their children to supplementary schools often run on Saturday mornings by the local black community.
- J. W. B. Douglas (1964) has also tried to use *cultural deprivation theory* to explain how the lack of parental involvement by many ethnic minorities explains poor educational attainment. Such evidence is based on lack of parental attendance at parents' evenings. However, this view can be criticised because quite often parents who do not attend parents' evenings are either working or feel intimidated by the formal situation.

Racism

Despite the existence of equal opportunities policies in schools, sufficient evidence exists to show that children from ethnic minorities often experience racism within schools – from teachers as well as other students. Such racism can be seen as:

- *Overt* (e.g. school playground insults)
- *Covert/institutional* (e.g. the 'unseen' ways in which teachers might exclude or unintentionally place students in lower tiers due to stereotypical views)

Most sociologists of education tend to be more interested in covert/institutional racism and its many processes and outcomes.

Confusing evidence

The Commission for Racial Equality carried out a study in 1992 ('Set to Fail') that showed how Asian students of similar ability to whites were less likely to be entered for GCSEs than their white counterparts. This would *seem* to show that ethnicity is indeed a significant factor in explaining educational achievement.

However, Smith and Tomlinson (1989) argued that the class background of pupils was more important than ethnicity in explaining educational attainment. While they argue that ethnic minority groups *were* allocated in general to lower level courses and that many ethnic groups did worse in school tests than white students, they also argued that this was because many ethnic minorities come from working-class backgrounds and that differences in class are therefore more important than differences in ethnic background.

Some factors that explain ethnic under-achievement

1 A study carried out in 1988 by the Commission for Racial Equality showed that at 'Jayleigh' school teacher assessment meant that more white pupils were entered for a greater number of GCSEs than Asian students. More Asians were also placed in lower sets throughout their time in school.
2 Through primary-school classroom observation, Cecile Wright (1992) showed how teachers largely ignored Asian pupils particularly when it came to classroom discussion – wrongly assuming that their levels of English were not good enough.
3 Symbolic interactionist concepts of labelling and a self-fulfilling prophesy show how teachers label some students as 'troublesome'. The frustration of experiencing this process means that some students develop 'attitude' to counteract the expectation that a teacher will pick on them. This becomes a self-fulfilling prophesy.

Conclusion

There is no real clear evidence to show that ethnicity itself is a causal explanation for under-achievement. The class background of students is highly significant along with the labelling processes adopted by some teachers.

For consideration:

1 Ask your school office to give you a breakdown in statistics for exams over the last few years and see if you can identify differences along the lines of ethnic backgrounds.

✳ Key Ideas

- Trevor Jones (1993) found that members of many ethnic minorities were more likely to stay on in education than their white counterparts. His research showed that when looking at specific jobs ethnic minorities were generally better qualified than whites who were doing the same job. Part of the reason for this, he argues, is that ethnic minorities perceive there to be a great deal of racism within the work place and that therefore they will need the qualifications to 'prove' they can do the job that whites do.

- David Gillborn (1995) showed how teachers in secondary schools quite often, wrongly, viewed the behaviour of Afro-Caribbean students as 'threatening'. As a result, disproportionate numbers of these students suffered greater degrees of punishment and exclusion than their white counterparts.

✍ Coursework Suggestion

David Gillborn's research is what is referred to as 'ethnographic' research, i.e. it is based on intensive first hand investigation of small groups over a long period of time. A lot of educational research is carried out in this way. You could carry out your own research into education and ethnicity by shadowing one or two students over a period of months to search for some evidence of institutional racism that Gillborn (1990) writes about. This could be done in break times perhaps once a week and you could ask teachers if you could observe the occasional lesson. Keep a research diary and record your findings. Carry out one interview with both students to increase the depth of your research findings.

5.22 What is 'the marketisation of education'?

What does this mean?

Sociologist Stephen Ball (1994) argues that a major change in the way that schools are managed has emerged over the last twenty years. Influenced by the ideas of the New Right, schools have come to be managed in the same way as businesses. Hargreaves (1989) has referred to this development as a change to 'Kentucky Fried Schooling'. This 'marketisation' of education involves the belief that competition at all levels should provide a higher standard of education in English schools. However, many sociologists argue that this is not the way to run education systems.

How did the ideas of the New Right influence education?

The New Right was primarily associated in the late 1970s and early 1980s with the ideas of Margaret Thatcher, the former Conservative prime minister. Schools were to move away from being run and financed by the local authorities to a more market-style system based on the 'language' of the commercial world of business. The idea was that this market of education would allocate resources where best required. Such thinking had a number of implications for schools.

1 Schools, rather than the local education authorities, were to manage their own budgets.

2 Schools had to provide freedom of choice for the consumer, i.e. the parents of the children they were trying to attract.

3 Schools had to be cost-effective as well as market themselves with an image that would attract new consumers.

4 Schools would compete with each other in the chase for new consumers, i.e. parents. Published league tables would provide parents with the information required for them to make their choices.

5 For each pupil attending a school, that school would gain a specific sum of money from the government, emphasising the importance for schools to recruit new students.

Professor Stephen Ball is concerned about how the 'marketisation' of education affects pupils and teachers.

☞ Who is this Person?

Stephen Ball is a professor of sociology and has worked at the University of Sussex and London University's Institute of Education, amongst others. He is also an author of several books including the famous *Beachside Comprehensive*; *The Micropolitics of the School*; and *Education Reform*. Sometimes described as a Marxist, sometimes described as a post-structuralist, his research ranges from exploring the effects of market forces on education, to families and their experience of children with cancer.

Marketisation of education as a global phenomenon?

The idea that schools should be run along business principles is not unique to England and Wales but is in line with thinking in certain other countries, namely the US, Canada, Australia and New Zealand. However, while it might be tempting to believe that such thinking is part of a global move to produce similar educational systems, this particular way of thinking does *not* exist in most countries in Europe.

Conclusion

The idea that schools should be run along market lines assumes that there is a level playing field, where there is little inequality in society. Therefore if schools compete with each other, costs will be brought down while the standard of education will rise. There are a number of problems with this way of thinking.

- Should we really think about schools in the same way that we think about other businesses? Public services like education and health are dealing with people not consumable goods and therefore perhaps should not be run in the same way that, for example, a supermarket might be run.

- If schools are forced to compete with each other to gain students and financial resources, the danger is that schools will spend money on marketing the school rather than investing in much needed resources for its pupils.

- David Gillborn (2001) has shown that when schools start to compete for places high up in the league tables, then many students get marginalised, i.e. will not be accepted in some of the more high-achieving schools. In many cases this means that disproportionate numbers of working-class and ethnic minority students are to be found in schools lower down the league tables.

- Equality of education cannot be provided under such a system that assumes a level playing field. Middle-class schools in middle-class areas do not face the same problems that working-class schools in predominantly working-class areas face. However, they do gain more money as a result of their higher position in the league tables.

For consideration:

1 What do you think Hargreaves meant by the phrase 'Kentucky Fried Schooling'?
2 How do different schools in Europe finance and run their school systems?

● Synoptic Link

In an attempt to prepare for any synoptic component to a question in the exam go through your subject folder and highlight (this can be done with coloured pens, or labels) any handout, set of notes or photocopy where the topic of education could be connected to the topic of crime and deviance (e.g. 'truancy'). With each example you flag, write a sentence that explains how that particular concept of identity highlights the relationship between the individual and society. Type these up into revision notes and save this for when you start to revise for your exams.

5.23 Examination advice

✓ Top Exam Hint

Now that you have come to the end of the unit, examine your folder. What state is it in? Do you feel that you would like to revise from it? Have you divided it into the various topics looked at in this chapter? Can you *clearly* see your class notes, handouts, homework exercises and marked work returned from your teachers? Have you placed all of these in *separate* transparent wallets or are they all bunched into a handful of such wallets making it difficult to actually know what you have in your folder in the first place? When reading through your folder do you highlight the important bits so that you don't have to 're-read' it all again when you revise at a later stage? Organise your folder and you will find revision so much easier in the weeks leading up to the exam.

● Synoptic Link

The A2 synoptic units of crime and deviance and stratification will examine whether you can make connections between them and other areas of the syllabus. This can be done by referring to methodology and social inequality and connecting these two topics with education. However, there are a variety of other concepts that will enable you to make links with the synoptic module and all other areas of the syllabus. These concepts include 'power', 'locality', 'social control', 'identity' and of course 'class', 'gender' and 'ethnicity'. Make sure that your folder has got these links highlighted before you start year two. Show your folder to your teachers and get them to check that these synoptic links are correct.

How can I best prepare for the exam?

This exam will be 75 minutes and will be composed of a data response question worth 60 marks. The following bullet points should help you in your final stages of preparation for the exam:

- Make sure that you read all the questions at least twice before looking at the items. That way you will automatically pull out from the items exactly what you need for a quality answer.

- Make sure you identify where the item came from (if possible), i.e. from a newspaper or sociological writer. Comment on this to gain extra evaluation marks.

- Make sure you identify when the item was written (where possible) so that you can then comment on whether or not it is a dated source.

- Make sure that you have learnt all the key terms and concepts in this chapter (e.g. alienation, marketisation and labelling).

- Make sure that you show that there is no singularly accepted definition of 'educational system' – memorise the variety of definitions available in this chapter.

- Make sure that you have looked at all the 'top exam hint' boxes in the margins of this chapter and have built them into your exam revision programme.

- Memorise all 'key ideas' and use them in the exam to show your high level of understanding of this subject area.

- Make sure that you fully understand how Paul Willis combines both micro and macro forms of analyses. As a Marxist, Willis focuses on the class injustice of the educational system but shows how his 'lads' create the circumstances in which they fail within the education system.

- Remember that examiners will expect you to be fully conversant with all key educational policies and this means that you must be able to describe them but also show that there are many conflicting views as to whether they have been successful or not.

- Ask your teacher to draw up a list of the key sociological studies you should know for this unit. Make revision cards with all the studies on them and memorise them for the exam.

- Be clear about the problems that this area of sociology poses for methodology (e.g. to what extent is quantitative data useful/not useful when exploring this area).

Key points to remember

- Be absolutely clear about the type of question that you are facing in the exam. Make sure that you ask your teacher to show you as many past exam questions as possible (remember that there aren't that many).

- Remember that this unit provides a fabulous range of synoptic possibilities. Clearly label all your materials in this unit with the synoptic links mentioned in this section.

- Don't forget that the case studies quoted in this chapter (i.e. every time you see the name of a sociologist and the work they carried out) are the key to your success in the exam. Memorise them, being clear about what particular theory they relate to, and use them as evidence in the exam answers you write.

✍ Coursework Suggestion

Use the Internet and email system to contact the heads of different schools in Europe (many European teachers will speak very good English). Carry out interviews to find out the different educational systems that exist. Use your data to evaluate from an international perspective how successful the English system is. Remember that when deciding what questions you are posing you will have to be extremely clear about the definitions you deploy, the sample you use and the theoretical framework that you adopt. You will also need to bear in mind that when evaluating your work you can revisit these issues and discuss them as 'methodological problems.'

5.24 Pushing your grades up higher

1   Remember that many of the broadsheet newspapers (e.g. the *Times*) contain educational supplements. In the weeks leading up to the exam, buy these papers and read the headlines and stories to get a flavour for what is currently happening within government educational policy.

2   Use different named sociologists to back up any argument, theory or concept you are trying to make in the exam.

3   Try to identify either the year or the decade that the research was carried out as this will help you make the point that things may or may not have changed, e.g. female achievement now compared to female under-achievement before the 1980s.

4   When referring to sociologists remember to refer to their theoretical influence, i.e. don't say 'Stephen Ball' but rather post-structuralist 'Stephen Ball'.

5   To gain extra evaluation marks try to mention the methodology of the case study you are referring to in the exam, e.g. 'adopting interpretivist methodology David Gillborn found that . . .'.

6   By referring to whether research was quantitative or qualitative you can link one particular study to another to build up your argument.

7   How do you start your paragraphs? Do you just mention a case study, e.g. 'Sue Sharp argued that . . .'? Much better to start off each paragraph with an evaluative phrase such as '*In agreement with Lees*, Sue Sharp argued . . .' or you could say '*In direct challenge* to the above, Sue Sharp argued . . .'

8   When an exam question asks you to discuss the contribution that a particular sociologist has made to a particular issue, it is important to realise that contributions can be both positive and negative. Remember this, as this will then allow you to fully evaluate the work of the sociologist in question.

9   Always remember to use the concepts of validity, reliability and representativeness when discussing the work of other sociologists. By applying these terms you will show the examiners that you are extremely critical.

10 The 'A' grade student will show that they are in full command of the various theories when discussing a question. Remember that the theories are 'friends' to be called upon when you feel you cannot write any more. Say to yourself 'how might a feminist or a postmodernist analyse this particular issue?'

11 Finally, don't forget that not only are you evaluating the *case studies* you talk about but also the *theories*. Of course you will do this by contrasting one theory with another, e.g. a Marxist approach to the issue with that of a functionalist or feminist approach. However, it is also useful to remember three categories when discussing theory.

- *Empirical adequacy* – i.e. what evidence is there to support the particular theory being discussed?

- *Comprehensiveness* – i.e. can the particular theory be used in all cases under all conditions?

- *Logical coherency* – i.e. does the theory logically hold together? One example where perhaps you might argue that a theory is not logically coherent is postmodernism. It attacks other theories and metanarratives for offering large-scale explanations. You could argue that there is no logical coherency here because surely postmodernism itself is a theory and therefore subject to its own critique.

Key points to remember

1 You must offer evidence in support of whatever argument you are making – without it the examiners will not reward your argument with marks.

2 You must show mastery of the theories when constructing an exam answer.

3 Don't forget to use 'sophisticated' language when criticising the theory, case study or concept. Make sure you start those sentences or paragraphs with those key evaluative phrases (e.g. 'However').

Frequently asked questions

Q. Why are so many sociologists critical of education?

A. The aim of the 1944 Education Act was to attempt to provide equality of education for all pupils within the British educational system. Sociologists over the past few decades have watched with concern how government policies have failed to live up to the aim of an act over half a century old. Many social commentators are critical of standards in education. However, sociologists have noted how the gap between middle- and working-class pupils has widened not narrowed. Gender concerns now focus on failing *male* pupils and/or specific groups of females within ethnic minorities who do considerably worse than their male counterparts.

Q. How many studies/names do I need to know to cope with the exam?

A. If you can, in about fifty words provide information about a named sociologist, her/his theoretical influence, her/his findings, key concepts and an evaluation. By doing this you are producing concise but fabulous revision materials. Type these up and make them into revision cards. Taking the key areas of class, ethnicity and gender it should be possible to produce forty-five studies (fifteen for each sociological variable). In the nine weeks leading up to the exams memorise five cards a week and 'hey presto', the exam is in the bag!

Q. How much of the history of education do I need for the exam?

A. This is a sociology exam rather than one in history; however, you should know when state education first started and the reasons why it was created in the early 1870s. You then need to know about the five big educational policies that have taken place in the second half of the 20th century, namely: the 1944 Education Act; the introduction of comprehensive schools; vocationalism; the effects of the 1988 Educational Reform Act; and the introduction of Curriculum 2000.

Chapter 6

Wealth, poverty and welfare

 CD-ROM 6.1

Key issues in the sociology of wealth, poverty and welfare

● Synoptic Link

Wealth, poverty and welfare needs to be linked to other topics like education and family if you are to gain a proper understanding of those areas. For example, educational underachievement is strongly linked to poverty and multiple deprivations. Single parent families are disproportionately likely to be poor compared to nuclear families.

Why are sociologists interested in wealth, poverty and welfare?

Sociologists are interested in this topic area for several reasons.

*   First, it is because they believe that society is stratified in terms of wealth, and that these patterns of stratification can have significant social effects.

*   Second, the degree of wealth that we have in life also has important implications for our individual prospects of success in life – sociologists refer to these as life chances.

*   Third, sociologists are interested in this topic, because wealth or the lack of it can have important consequences for our sense of identity.

What are the key debates in wealth, poverty and welfare?

There are several key areas of debate in this topic.

*   Whose fault is poverty – is it the responsibility of the poor, or is poverty caused by the capitalist system and the inequality that goes with it?

*   Are the differences in wealth between the richest and the poorest increasing or decreasing?

*   Is the ownership of wealth the most important factor shaping identity, or are consumption patterns now more important?

*   Do differences in wealth lead to the development of distinctive class cultures and identities? This is called the underclass debate.

Debate still continues over whether state benefits should be universal or means tested (i.e. selective, see sections 14 and 16). Universal benefits are those that everyone is entitled to (e.g. the old age pension) and means tested benefits are those that people can only claim providing that they can prove that they do not earn above a certain level. Those earning less than the level decided by the government have to show proof of their income. An example of a means tested benefit would be the grant that local authorities can award for higher education tuition fees. There is also a big debate about what causes social exclusion and what can be done about it.

What are the key ideas and concepts in wealth, poverty and welfare?

Perhaps the single most important idea in this chapter is the view that our definitions of poverty are socially constructed. This view of poverty is called relative poverty, and implies that being poor is not just a matter of having enough to survive, but involves being able to join in the normal and expected activities in a particular culture.

What are the key problems in the sociology of wealth, poverty and welfare?

Like many topics in sociology some of the key concepts discussed here are highly contested. Key problems in the topic therefore centre round defining the very phenomena that we are trying to study, and deciding on the best methods to use to study them. The key issues can be examined in terms of definitions and methods.

1   *Definitions.* What is poverty? Some sociologists and researchers have argued that it has to be defined in terms of social perceptions in any particular society and time or place. Others argue that it can be defined more simply (see section 7). Sociologists also need to define the different types of wealth, and the difference between wealth and income.

2   *Methods and Measurement.* There are some very difficult methodological issues involved in trying to operationalise and measure poverty. These are very important because the answers sociologists reach on this issue shape the questions they ask and thus influence findings and their interpretations of their findings.

✓ **Top Exam Hint**

Poverty is a socially constructed concept. This means that people's understanding of what counts as poverty varies in different times and in different societies. Sociologists do not always agree about what poverty is or how much of it exists. Poverty is therefore a contested (debated) concept.

📄 **Coursework**

This topic offers some interesting opportunities for coursework. You could examine the whole issue of defining poverty by finding out what your peers consider to be essential items needed to survive in today's society. This would allow you to reflect critically on methodological concepts such as the deprivation index.

What do we need to know about wealth, poverty and welfare?

What does the specification say about wealth, poverty and welfare?

The specification lists five main areas that you are expected to know about for the exam, but these can be summarised as three main points.

1   You should know about the different definitions of wealth, poverty and income and the various explanations of the way poverty, wealth and income are spread across different social groups.

2   You should also know about the different explanations of the causes and continued existence of poverty, and have examined the various social policies devised to reduce poverty.

3   Lastly, you should also have studied the various types of welfare provision which have been devised.

How will I be examined in this topic area?

You will have to answer one question on wealth, poverty and welfare, consisting of six parts (a to f). You will be able to score a maximum of 60 marks, awarded as follows: a = 2, b = 4, c = 6, d = 8, e and f = 20 marks each.

There will be two data items at the beginning of the question. This should make you think on your feet and help you bring some originality to your exam work. It should also discourage you from regurgitating material learnt parrot-fashion. The item may be text, or it could be a table of statistics, or some other piece of research data, even a photograph.

You will have 75 minutes to answer all of these questions.

How well does this topic relate to coursework?

There is lots of scope for doing good pieces of coursework in this topic area. A lot of research into poverty and welfare has employed survey research methods. As there are many questions about the validity of this

✓ Top Exam Hint

Check through your exam specification to see how this explains what you need to know and do for your AS level exam. A good exercise is to try and identify which parts of this chapter match up to the different parts of the specification. Some of the sections in this book may be relevant in different parts of the wealth, poverty, and welfare specification.

approach, the topic offers lots of opportunities to be critical and demonstrate your ability to evaluate and think critically. It also offers students the chance to question the commonsense view that inequalities in contemporary society have declined.

How well does this topic help with synopticity?

This topic provides lots of useful **synoptic** insights. As you will find out, the degree of wealth we acquire in our life has a crucial bearing on what sociologists call our 'life chances'. This can also influence our health, our educational attainment, and the likelihood of any one of us becoming a criminal. Also of course, wealth is one of the key factors which differentiates people and it is therefore a vital dimension (but not the only one) of stratification. You might study stratification as a separate topic, but remember issues of 'social differentiation, power and stratification' are also a core theme of your specification. So too are socialisation, culture and identity, and this raises important questions about whether the poor are socialised into a different culture (with different norms and values) from the rest of society (see especially sections 17 and 18).

You should also find that this topic helps shed light on other topics you are studying such as families and households, education, and the media.

In the families and households topic, this topic might help us explain why families in certain social groups (e.g. working-class or single parent families) seem to be most likely to find themselves living in poverty. In education there are strong links between educational attainment and poverty. In respect of the media, sociologists have argued that media representations can often help to stigmatise and marginalise poorer social groups, such as single parent families.

In terms of methodology, the topic helps to highlight a number of the problems of using survey methods (see chapter 2).

Key points to remember:

* Check your specification and get copies of past papers and mark schemes.

* Think about how this topic is related to general sociological topics (such as theory and method, families and households, and education).

* Remember to use the course core themes: 'socialisation, culture and identity', and 'social differentiation, power and stratification'.

66 99 Key Definition

Synoptic/synopticity – means that the different topics you study in sociology are all relevant to each other. You cannot fully understand wealth, poverty, and welfare, for instance, without knowing something about theory and method. Equally, this topic will help you understand stratification more fully. It will also help you understand how poverty can affect the family, and how both of these are relevant to educational under-achievement.

● Synoptic Link

Remember to use the core themes identified by your syllabus. Wealth, poverty and welfare have important implications for a person's socialisation, their culture and their identity. You might want to discuss the disadvantages of having an identity as a 'poor person'. You can also consider how poverty relates to stratification. Where would the poor be in terms of other social strata and how much power do they have?

✎ Coursework Suggestion

A desire to challenge commonsense views about poverty could be a key part of your rationale for researching this topic area.

How can we find out about wealth, poverty, and welfare?

Charles Booth and Seebohm Rowntree reflected the 19th-century belief that it was the duty of the rich to help the poor to improve themselves.

☞ Who are these People?

Charles Booth (1840–1916), a ship-owner and merchant with an interest in social reform, conducted a survey into poverty and living conditions in London in 1886. Seebohm Rowntree (1871–1954) was a member of the family who owned the Rowntree chocolate factory in York. He worked in the family business and had an interest in social reform, conducting studies into poverty and influencing policies on pensions and housing in the 1940s.

How have sociologists tried to measure wealth and poverty?

In the 19th century attempts to measure the extent of poverty in Britain were carried out by social reformers such as Charles Booth and Seebohm Rowntree. Both of these researchers devised a list of what they considered to be the 'essentials' required by a family in order to survive for a week. This included the cost of food, clothing, fuel, heating and rent. Having worked out the cost of these essentials, Booth and Rowntree then calculated how much such items would cost. They then compared the cost of these items with their respondents' income. This enabled them to estimate how much of the wider population was living in poverty.

Wealth has perhaps been of rather less interest to sociologists than poverty, but it has been measured in a variety of ways, which have included measuring income, or estimating the value of land and other property (definitions of wealth are given in section 4).

What methods do sociologists use to study wealth and poverty?

Quantitative methods (of which structured questionnaires and surveys are a good example) have been a commonly used research method in work on wealth and poverty. Early researchers like Charles Booth and Seebohm Rowntree and more recent researchers have used questionnaire surveys. The questionnaire survey has the following characteristics that make it appropriate for investigating this topic area.

- It enables researchers to quantify their results.
- Large samples can be used, gaining a lot of data and aiding representativeness.
- It is quick and relatively cheap to apply.

However, other methods are also useful. More recently, researchers such as Jordan (1989) and Dean and Taylor-Gooby (1990) have used interviews to investigate whether 'the poor' have different values from other social groups, and to gain information about people's perceptions of poverty and wealth. As poverty and wealth are socially defined, these methods add a crucial dimension to sociologists' understanding of poverty and wealth.

What problems with definition are encountered in wealth and poverty?

Both of these concepts are in fact quite hard to measure. For example, if we want to measure how wealthy an individual is, we could use their income as an indicator of wealth. But this might not be accurate enough. There are, for example, several different types of wealth including money, the value of houses or property, shares in companies and land, for example. These factors have to be carefully considered when we come to examine who are the wealthiest individuals and groups in the UK (see section 5).

There are similar problems with defining poverty. When we say people are living in poverty, what exactly do we mean? Do we mean that they haven't got enough money to live on at all, that they are literally starving, or do we just mean that they haven't got as much as everyone else? Whichever of these we choose, we would need to define exactly what we mean and this is not at all easy (see section 7). We also have to bear in mind that not everyone actually agrees about how these terms should be defined.

So there are big problems with defining both of these terms, and for sociologists that means there are problems of measurement. The definitions of both wealth and poverty can be contested (debated). Sociologists' research findings can therefore be challenged on the grounds of their definition and **operationalisation** of poverty and wealth, and there are debates about what counts as poverty and what counts as wealth. This, of course, also means that there are disagreements about the extent of poverty and the distribution of wealth.

Key points to remember:

*   It is not easy to decide how to define either poverty or wealth. Both of these terms are highly debated, and sociologists (and others) may be unclear about the exact level of income at which poverty or wealth starts.
*   Disagreements about how poverty and wealth should be defined usually lead to further disagreements about how they should be measured. This (and the point above) helps to explain why sociologists and other researchers may differ in their estimates of how many people live in poverty.
*   A lot of research into poverty in Britain has been based on social survey methodology. This is a quantitative method and it produces quantitative data, such as graphs and charts, which is very useful in studying poverty. However, critics argue that this sort of data can give a distorted or partial picture of society. Attitudes and values about poverty are also important.

❝❞ Key Definition

Operationalisation – is the term used by sociologists to describe the way an abstract concept like poverty is defined so that we can measure it. Sociologists might, for example, agree with Townsend (1979) that any household with an income more than 150 per cent of benefit levels is in poverty, or they might define and measure it in a different way.

● Synoptic Link

This topic is useful for answering synoptic questions about methodology. The survey method used in studying poverty has been criticised for neglecting the individual choices people make. Surveys can produce a distorted picture by suggesting, for example, that people lacking a certain type of food are in poverty. In fact, the truth is not that they cannot afford it, but that they have chosen not to buy it.

✓ Top Exam Hint

How sociologists find out about wealth and poverty is just as important as what they find. This is because the type of data shapes the results collected. Quantitative data provides lots of charts and graphs for example, but interpretivist sociologists often question the validity of this sort of evidence. An interpretivist approach suggests that sociologists need to examine what people mean by poverty.

How do sociologists define wealth and income?

66 99 Key Definition

Wealth – there is no agreed definition of wealth, but it could be broadly described as the total value of resources and possessions owned by a person. John Scott (1999) points out that wealth has to be seen in relative terms. Those who have wealth have resources that allow them to enjoy benefits and advantages that others (the less wealthy) do not have. Sociologist John Scott has had a particular interest in class throughout his career, particularly the upper classes and wealth. His work is influenced by both Marx and Weber.

What does this mean?

We have seen that sociologists can have different ideas about what **wealth** and income mean, and that this in turn can lead to very different research findings. In everyday language, we often don't bother to distinguish between wealth and income. However, for the purposes of sociological research it is important to be aware of the differences between the two, and to understand what we mean by the term 'wealthy' and to consider how we would define the category of 'the wealthy'. The reasons why these issues are important will be examined in more detail later on. First, we need to examine how sociologists have defined wealth. Sociological definitions of wealth indicate that it consists of different things.

- Wealth is a general term, and refers to the value of the assets or property that a person owns. Usually it is expressed in terms of a cash value – the amount of money a person would have if all their property were sold. Wealth could include, then, the value of a house, land, money in the bank, the ownership of shares, as well as cars, furniture and other goods that a person has for their own use.

These forms of wealth are often broken down into various sub-categories:

- *Productive property*: this refers to things that can generate an income, such as shares, the ownership of companies, or property or land that is rented out.
- *Consumption property*: this refers to goods bought for personal use, but which can be sold to raise cash, e.g. cars, home, furniture, and so on.

Another way of categorising wealth is in terms of marketable and non-marketable wealth:

- *Marketable wealth* refers to any goods or objects that can be sold to raise cash.
- *Non-marketable wealth* refers to salaries, incomes, or pension schemes.

Lastly, there is the term 'income'. Income refers to money received on a regular basis. The most common form of income is a salary or wage received in return for paid work: this would be called 'earned income'. However, regular interest on a savings account would also be an example of income, but this would be called 'unearned income'.

Why do these differences matter?

There are two main reasons why these definitions are important, one empirical, and the other theoretical.

1   Empirical (observed) issues are concerned with methods. The issue with wealth is that if we want to examine wealth accurately, we need to be rigorous in defining it. This is because the way we define wealth will shape the way the statistical data is portrayed. Sociologists want their knowledge of wealth to be valid.

2   In terms of theory, these different definitions are also important, and form the subject of debate between different theoretical perspectives. Marxists, in particular, argue that the most important form of wealth is productive wealth. This is because Marxists argue that ownership of the means of production forms the basis of class formation and is the source of class conflict. Differences in wealth in terms of consumer goods are therefore not so important. What is more important is the structural relationship between the ruling class and their ownership of the source of all wealth: the means of production.

Measuring wealth – how much is a lot?

One more point needs to be made is about how we define wealth. When some people are judged to be wealthier than others, the judgement will always be made in terms of the standards of a particular time and place (and society). It can therefore be difficult for researchers to decide and agree upon a point at which a person can be considered to be wealthy (see section 5).

Conclusion

How sociologists define wealth is a complex matter and has important consequences for the picture they provide of social inequalities. It's also important to remember that wealth is a relative concept; a person or group can only be judged to be wealthy in relation to other groups. Wealth, then, like poverty (as will be explained later), is a relative concept.

✳ Key Idea

Life chances – this term was used by Max Weber to describe the advantages and disadvantages that a person from a particular class might typically expect. Life chances include chances of educational success, financial rewards, chances for upward social mobility, and relative chances of having good or bad health.

✓ Top Exam Hint

Remember to point out that wealth is a tricky concept, and can be defined in various ways. It's useful to remember Scott's point, that wealth is best understood in relative terms. Also remember that wealth and income are not the same thing.

For consideration:

1   What do you think is the most advantageous sort of wealth to have?
2   As there are now millionaires being created every week through the Lottery and television game shows, does this mean that as a society we are becoming wealthier?

Who has the most wealth?

What does this mean?

Defining wealth can be a complex process, but this has not prevented sociologists from trying to find out who has the most wealth. Sociologists want to know not simply which individuals have the most wealth, but whether and why it is concentrated amongst particular social groups.

This is important because if wealth is predominantly the possession of certain social groups it means that they can prevent other social groups from having access to wealth. This process is termed 'social closure'. It is also important because the possession of wealth frequently allows those with wealth to have power. If the distribution of wealth and power are highly skewed towards certain social groups, it will mean that other social groups have less power and wealth.

How much wealth do you need to be wealthy?

According to UK government statistics in 1994 (ONS 1998), the top 1 per cent of the population owned wealth worth over £500,000, and held 40 per cent of their wealth in shares. Perhaps then, this figure would do to mark the boundary between the 'wealthy' and the 'normal'?

This is a tricky point, but as John Scott (1999) has noted, it is impossible to draw with complete accuracy a line above which an individual is wealthy, and below which they are simply 'rich' or 'fairly well-off'. This reminds us again that wealth is a relative concept, and that what counts as wealth changes over time, and is socially constructed.

Who has the most wealth?

Finding out how wealth is distributed in British society provides an excellent example of why sociological research is necessary. A common perception is that inequalities in wealth in contemporary Britain have declined, and that there is more equality. However, empirical research indicates that this is not so, and in fact inequalities of wealth have increased over the last decade or so. The following statistics give some indication of the extent of inequality over the last decade.

*   According to government statistics (ONS 1998), 53 per cent of the financial wealth in the UK was owned by 5 per cent of the population in 1994.

✳ Key Idea

The idea of 'social closure' means that social groups can control entry into their own ranks. Exclusion from one sort of reward can lead to exclusion from other rewards. For example, wealthy social elites can prevent other groups gaining access to top private schools (e.g. by charging expensive fees, interviewing). It can then be very difficult for an individual to gain a top-level job, since they will not have been to the 'right' college.

● Synoptic Link

Being wealthy provides many advantages. In the study of crime and deviance, for example, sociologists have found that the crimes of the wealthy are under-reported and that the wealthy often escape the attentions of the law.

- In the same year, the wealthiest 1 per cent of the population owned 19 per cent of all marketable wealth and the top 10 per cent owned 51 per cent.

- The least wealthy 50 per cent of the population own 10 per cent of the UK's wealth.

So who are the wealthy?

Marxist sociologist John Westergaard (1976, 1995) argues that the wealthy in British society form a ruling class consisting of between 5 and 10 per cent of the population. For Westergaard, these people are the owners of the means of production.

However, others claim that the upper classes have fragmented (split into smaller groups). John Scott (1999), for example, takes a more Weberian view of class (he therefore identifies a more fragmented class structure), and argues that there is a capitalist class in Britain, but that this constitutes about 0.1 per cent of the population, and consists of four types of capitalist. Some sociologists have even argued that there is a transnational capitalist class, consisting of the executives of transnational corporations. Transnational corporations are companies that have branches in many different countries.

Conclusion

Sociologists may not always agree about exactly where to draw a line between the wealthy and the rest of us, but it is clear that considerable inequalities exist in British society. Equally, whilst sociologists disagree as to the precise composition of the wealthy, elite groups can be identified. As we have seen though, sociologists disagree as to the best way of explaining the existence and social role of such groups. The next section will explore this issue in more detail.

For consideration:

1 Does the ownership of wealth always give its owner power?
2 Do the very rich in Britain form a ruling class?

✳ Key Idea

Scott identifies four types of capitalist:

1 **Entrepreneurial capitalists**, who run and own shares in large enterprises.
2 **Rentier capitalists**, who have investments in several businesses.
3 **Executive capitalists** who do not own businesses, but are top executives.
4 **Finance capitalists**, who are directors and top executives in banks and specialist financial businesses.

✓ Top Exam Hint

In evaluating the idea that wealth and power are inevitably linked, it's a good idea to use contemporary views on stratification. These increasingly accept that it is important to understand how class, race and gender are interrelated.

6.6 How do sociologists explain inequalities in wealth and income?

Key Idea

Meritocracy. Functionalists claim that industrial societies offer everyone an equal opportunity to succeed and gain the best jobs. This is called meritocracy. This idea implies that wealth is distributed fairly. Functionalists argue that inequalities of reward (pay) are needed in order to motivate people to compete and work to gain the highest paying jobs.

Key Definitions

Functionalists argue that inequalities in income and wealth reflect the skill and effort required for particular jobs.

Marxists argue that inequalities in income and wealth are the result of the class structure and the inequalities in power which it inevitably creates.

Weberians argue that inequalities in income and wealth are the result of the use of exclusion strategies by workers acting collectively to protect their own interests.

Synoptic Link

Functionalists see the education system as a key mechanism for creating social mobility and meritocratic role allocation. This means that industrial societies are indeed stratified, but stratification occurs on a meritocratic (fair) basis because a person's occupational role is decided by how well they do in what functionalists see as an entirely fair and open education system.

What does this mean?

Sociologists have identified regular patterns of inequalities of wealth (see section 5) and there are also marked inequalities in income. There are also clear differences in income between different social classes, as different occupations receive different rewards. In addition, there are marked differences in income and wealth on the basis of gender and race. Sociologists may draw on several theoretical approaches in order to explain these patterns of difference.

How do functionalists explain inequalities in wealth and income?

Functionalists such as Davis and Moore (1967) and Melvin Tumin (1967) argue that differences in wealth and income reflect the need to offer higher incentives to those undertaking the most demanding occupations. Differences therefore reflect the supply and demand for different jobs and assume that there is a meritocratic (see key idea) allocation of jobs. Meritocratic allocation means that people are appointed to jobs on the basis of their merit (how good they are) and there is open competition for all jobs. This view is virtually identical to the view of the New Right (see section 17), and other sociologists such as Peter Saunders are in general agreement with it.

How do Marxists explain inequalities in wealth and income?

Sociologists working in or influenced by the Marxist tradition, such as John Westergaard (1976, 1995), or more contemporary Marxist influenced theorists like David Harvey (1990), would be highly critical of the functionalist approach. They would argue that meritocracy is a myth, and that the higher incomes paid to professionals and managers simply reflect the power of the capitalists to pay higher wages to those who are key workers. This also has the effect of dividing the working classes (all those who do not own the means of production), preventing them from realising that they all have a common interest in seeing the end of capitalist exploitation. This means that they are weaker as a social or political force, because they do not campaign together against their employers.

In terms of wealth, whilst capitalism does lead to large differences in consumption property, the most important form of property (see section 5), productive property, remains firmly in the hands of the capitalists, and this is still true today. In fact, there is now a greater concentration of productive wealth than there was in the 19th century when Marx was writing.

How do Weberians explain inequalities in wealth and income?

Weber provided a more complex approach to inequalities in wealth and income than Marx. Weber saw inequalities in income and wealth as resulting from several factors, of which the ownership of the means of production is just one. Weber, however, also argued that the ability of groups of workers to exclude others from doing their job was also important.

Social groups can use various strategies and resources to help them achieve this. Weber agrees with Marx that one good way to achieve this is to be a capitalist (own the means of production) so that other people have to work for you.

However, other strategies can be used to exclude people who are competing for the same work. The following example illustrates one form of exclusion. Highly skilled professionals can achieve a significantly higher income than manual workers. Weber does not follow the functionalists and say that this is because the skilled professional really is more skilled and more deserving than the manual worker. On the contrary, Weber takes the view that the professional is able to achieve a higher income and gain more wealth, because of the limited supply of people qualified to apply for professional jobs.

Professionals and workers can create shortages of people qualified to do a job by forming trade unions or professional groups. These can then operate to exclude certain categories of people. This can occur on the basis of status, for example, gender or race, age, or religion. If workers do this, they limit the supply of labour for their occupation, and thus their income (and wealth) will rise since available labour is in short supply.

Conclusion

Sociologists, then, have a number of ways of explaining inequality. The different explanations also lead to different explanations of the causes of poverty and to different views about the working and effectiveness of the welfare state. You will have to evaluate these views carefully in order to discover which theory you think is most accurate. In doing this, a good starting point is to think about which theory has the most accurate view of power.

Richard Branson, founder of Virgin – a good example of the Marxist view of productive wealth?

✓ Top Exam Hint

When you are evaluating these competing explanations of inequality, it's a good idea to use a key concept like power to start to reflect on the accuracy of the different views. Functionalists, for example, seem to assume that we all have an equal amount of power and that we all have a chance to achieve wealth. Other theories would be more critical of this assumption.

For consideration:

1 Which of the following is most important in determining a person's wealth: class, race or gender?
2 Functionalists claim that without high rewards for the best jobs, people would not want to do them. Do you agree with this idea?

6.7 What is poverty?

What does this mean?

You might think that it is a waste of time trying to define poverty since it is so obvious what it is. People who take this viewpoint though very often define poverty in broad terms as 'not having enough to live' or 'being in a situation of starvation with no money to buy food'.

Some sociologists have taken a view similar to this, but nowadays there are probably more who disagree with this viewpoint. In fact, defining poverty is quite difficult. This is because even if we agree with the view above that poverty is 'not having enough', how we define 'enough' will depend on the expected standards or norms in our society.

Even if we are talking about something basic like food, it doesn't take long for people to start arguing about how much is 'enough', given that people eat and need varying amounts depending upon age, health, sex and so on. If we expand the question to consider other needs, like shelter and clothing, matters get even more complicated. So poverty is actually very complex – it can mean different things to different people, and for sociologists this raises difficult questions about how to define and measure it.

How do sociologists define poverty?

There are two main definitions of poverty – absolute poverty and relative poverty.

- **Absolute poverty** is the idea that there are minimum standards of income or food needed to keep a person alive. This is sometimes called subsistence poverty. Subsistence means that a person has enough food and other resources to continue to exist, or in other words, to remain alive. Using this definition, a person is only considered to be in poverty if they cannot subsist, i.e. do not have enough food or money to survive.

- **Relative poverty** is a different idea of poverty. This view suggests that a person is in poverty if they have less than the normally accepted minimum standard in their society. For example, in contemporary British society, it is now the 'norm' to have accommodation with electricity, hot and cold water, an indoor toilet and a bath or shower. A relative definition of poverty would suggest that these are essentials and those without them live in poverty.

Sociologists can use either of these definitions to produce a 'poverty line'. This is a way of defining the level of income at which poverty starts: above the line one is out of poverty, below the line one is in poverty. This

◆ **What, When and Why?**

Charles Booth conducted his survey on poverty between 1886 and 1903 and found around 31 per cent of the population in poverty. Seebohm Rowntree conducted three surveys of poverty in York in 1899, 1936 and 1950. He found respectively 33 per cent, 18 per cent and 1.5 per cent of the population living in poverty. Townsend's research in the late 1960s estimated that 22.9 per cent of the population lived in poverty.

Have levels of poverty decreased in Britain since the 19th and early 20th century?

66 99 Key Definitions

Absolute poverty means that a person doesn't even have enough to sustain their life. If they have enough to do this, then they aren't in poverty.

Relative poverty means that a person doesn't have enough to be able to do the things that most people in their society would expect to be able to do.

sounds straightforward, but the problem is that it is not easy to decide where this line should be drawn.

Why is it so difficult to measure poverty?

- First, one reason (which we have already identified above) is because not everyone agrees on what would count as a minimum standard, whichever definition is being used.

- A second problem is that living standards can change as a result of both increases in wealth and changes in attitude and fashion.

- Third, it is difficult for researchers to make objective judgements about what things count as essentials.

Lastly, it can be difficult for researchers to see the difference between a person who lacks an 'essential' item because they cannot afford it, and someone who has simply made a choice to do without on grounds of personal taste. In the 1960s, for instance, researcher Peter Townsend (1979) thought that having a roast dinner at least once a week was a norm. More recently, researchers Mack and Lansley (1985) have argued that this is no longer the case, since more people eat a vegetarian diet or have cut back on meat for health reasons. Mack and Lansley's ground-breaking work in the 1980s attempted to create a more sensitive way of measuring poverty by taking people's individual choices into account.

Conclusion

The idea of absolute poverty is useful to the extent that it provides a fairly easy solution to poverty: provide all with the means of subsistence. However, it can be hard to reach consensus as to what the 'essentials' are, and this definition neglects the way standards of living are socially constructed.

Relative poverty, whilst it recognises that poverty is socially constructed, still relies on the value-judgements of researchers as to what is 'necessary', and it seems to imply that poverty can never be eradicated as long as inequality persists. Which of these views sociologists think is more adequate will ultimately depend on their own values.

For consideration:

1 Is it possible to eradicate poverty?
2 Is it possible to measure poverty objectively?

✔ Top Exam Hint

When you are evaluating different studies of poverty make sure that you discuss the methods used by the various researchers, showing how these shape researchers' views of the extent of poverty. Remember to use key methodological terms like validity, reliability, representativeness and operationalisation.

Does poverty still exist?

What does this mean?

As we found in the previous section defining poverty is not simple, and the two definitions of poverty lead to different views about whether poverty still exists.

- Those who view poverty in absolute terms are most likely to argue that poverty is a thing of the past in the UK, and can now only be found in undeveloped countries, when, for example, there is a famine.

- Those viewing poverty as relative are likely to argue that British society still has high levels of poverty, despite the fact that there is a social security system that acts as a safety net for those at the bottom of the social ladder. We also need to consider, though, whether poverty is just an issue of material wealth (e.g. possessions owned), or whether it has other characteristics. Poverty may still be with us, but in a new form, and some sociologists have used the term '**social exclusion**' to express this idea.

Peter Townsend's studies into poverty challenged the idea that poverty had been eradicated in the 1960s.

☞ Who is this Person?

Peter Townsend studied Philosophy and Anthropology at Oxford University (1946–48) and went on to work as a researcher and university lecturer at various British universities. He has always had a concern with poverty and disadvantage. He was a founder member of the Campaign Against Child Poverty in the 1960s, and has served on several Labour Party committees to advise on welfare policy.

The re-discovery of poverty

Some of the problems in using an absolute definition of poverty can be seen from the findings gathered by Seebohm Rowntree's surveys. Rowntree conducted three surveys of poverty in York between 1899 and 1950. Rowntree found that the extent of poverty identified in his surveys progressively declined. In 1899 he estimated 33 per cent of the population lived in poverty. By 1936 this had fallen to 18 per cent, and in 1950 poverty seemed all but eradicated, with Rowntree estimating only 1.5 per cent of the population living in poverty.

This research helped to confirm the popular belief in late-1950s Britain that poverty was a thing of the past. However, sociologist Peter Townsend was one of the researchers who rejected this optimistic claim. Using a relative definition of poverty, he conducted research in the late 1960s and claimed that the real extent of poverty was considerable with an estimated 22.9 per cent of the population living in poverty.

Why did Townsend find an increase in poverty?

Townsend was able to identify an increase in poverty because of the way in which he defined and operationalised poverty.

- Townsend rejected the idea that poverty is absolute and argued instead that poverty has to be seen as relative. However, Townsend argued that poverty was not just about income. Instead he defined poverty in a non-material sense, and saw it as also involving an inability to participate in the lifestyles considered normal in a particular society. This means that if a person cannot afford to do things considered 'normal' today, for instance, having a birthday party, going on holiday, or having friends around for a meal, then that person may be in poverty.

- Townsend devised an index of relative deprivation to identify those in poverty according to this definition. He devised a list of twelve key essentials and used this to calculate how many of his sample were living in poverty.

- Since his sample was representative, Townsend was able to estimate the number of people living in poverty in the whole country. He calculated that the level below which he considered a person fell into poverty (the poverty line) was an income of 150 per cent above the government benefit levels at the time. As we can tell from this last point, the idea that poverty still exists and the exact level of poverty are matters of debate.

❉ Key Idea

The idea of the 'poverty line' is that there is a certain income below which a person (or a household) will fall into poverty. The problem with this idea is that different researchers, and those responsible for welfare policy (the government), rarely agree on where this line should be drawn.

✓ Top Exam Hint

In evaluating arguments about whether poverty still exists, it is vital to refer to and explain the differences between the different definitions of poverty.

Conclusion

The re-discovery of poverty by sociologists in the 1960s illustrates the importance of defining concepts with care. It is also an example of the way concepts in sociology are contested. The importance of the relative concept of poverty is that it establishes that our views, definitions and measures of poverty are socially constructed. Townsend's work also shows us that poverty is not just a matter of having enough to subsist – it is also important to be able to partake in what goes for a 'normal' existence in the society in question. But if poverty does still exist it is very important for sociologists to examine what causes it, and this is the subject of the next section.

For consideration:

1   If poverty is relative, is it impossible to eradicate it?
2   Do you agree that poverty should be considered to be about more than just a lack of 'material wealth'?

What causes poverty?

◆ What, When and Why?

Sociological ideas about poverty seem to move in cycles as the cultural view of some 1960s researchers gave way to a more materialist approach in the 1970s (a time of economic difficulty). Cultural views, as exemplified by those such as Charles Murray (see also section 17), returned to dominance in the 1980s and 1990s, and to some extent still are dominant. The 1980s and 1990s were periods of affluence for some individuals and privileged groups in societies. However, there have also been considerable social problems for politicians to tackle, such as high unemployment, high levels of crime, and increasing strain on parts of the welfare state such as the health service and the education system. Some sociologists might suggest that in times of affluence it is easy for poverty to be portrayed as an individual problem, or something caused by anti-social groups, rather than as the result of a structural flaw in society.

❝❞ Key Definition

Fatalism – is the idea that your life is decided by fate. There is nothing you can do which will change things and the outcome of any action is predetermined. Contrast this view with the idea of 'agency', which sociologists like Anthony Giddens discuss. Giddens says that people have agency, which means the capacity to act and transform their lives.

✳ Key Idea

'Welfare dependency' is the idea that people come to be dependent on welfare handouts, and lose the ability to be independent.

What does this mean?

Sociologists are interested in explaining what factors cause poverty and they pose two key questions to help them do this.

1   Is poverty the result of cultural differences, such as values or beliefs, between the poor and the rest of society? For example, are the poor less hardworking than other social groups?

2   Alternatively, is poverty better explained by so-called material explanations? These see poverty as the result of the economic situation of the poor and in terms of their structural position in society and claim that values and beliefs are not important – the poor have much the same values and beliefs as the rich.

Is poverty caused by cultural differences?

The anthropologist Oscar Lewis presented the idea that poverty was caused by the cultural norms and values of the poor. Lewis conducted a study in Latin America (1961) and argued that the poor develop a fatalistic approach to life. This forms into a set of values and is transmitted from generation to generation. **Fatalism** is the idea that your life is pre-determined and there is nothing that you can do to change the course of your life. Poverty thus becomes a state that once fallen into is hard to escape, and it is transmitted – almost like a disease – from generation to generation.

This theory may seem outdated and inappropriate to western societies, but its key ideas live on. In the late 1980s American sociologist Charles Murray (1989) argued that poverty in the USA and the UK was caused by an over-generous benefit system. Murray argued that because benefits were too generous and easily obtained, the poor had no incentive to work. They developed a different set of cultural values; Murray also identified a fatalistic and passive approach to life. Fatalism means that a person believes that their life is a matter of 'fate' that they can do nothing to change, e.g. 'I was born to fail'. To be 'passive' is the opposite of 'active', so again it means that people tend to accept the conditions of their life and do not attempt to challenge or change things, and have no determination to succeed. Murray called this set of attitudes '**welfare dependency**'. Murray's approach is one of the clearest examples of the New Right's view of wealth, poverty and welfare.

Criticisms of this approach focus on the lack of empirical evidence for any substantial difference in norms and values between the poor and other social groups (see section 17 for details). This theory also seems to involve finding the ultimate 'blame' for poverty to lie with the poor themselves. It neglects so-called 'material' explanations of poverty, and fails to address the initial reasons why an individual falls into poverty in the first place.

Is poverty caused by material factors?

An alternative view is that the attitudes of the poor are in fact caused by their economic situation, and not the other way round.

- Two of the first people to put forward this view, American researchers Hannerz (1969) and Liebow (1967) argued that whilst the poor did have slightly different value-systems and sets of behaviour, these were on the whole not significant cultural differences and were responses to the situation poor people found themselves in.

- Other sociologists have taken this view further. British researchers such as Coates and Silburn (1970) argued that the poor found themselves in a cycle of deprivation. This meant that once in poverty, people would find it very difficult to get out of that situation, and would regularly slip into and out of poverty. This was due to structural factors beyond the control of individuals, such as structural unemployment or low wages.

- More recently, researchers such as Field (1989) and Townsend (1979) have identified several groups of disadvantaged at the bottom of the stratification system who are more likely to fall into poverty and find it hard to escape it. Key groups here are the elderly, single parents and the long-term unemployed.

These material explanations all suggest that to some extent poverty follows a cycle. The cycle can be broken, for example by having periods of employment; however, if only low-paid work can be found, many mishaps beyond the control of the individual can throw a person back into poverty, e.g. unemployment, low wages.

Conclusion

Evidence for the idea that poverty is the result of cultural differences is hard to find, despite the interpretations and claims of Lewis and Murray. The evidence discussed later in section 17 seems to suggest strong support for the material explanation. Cultural differences between the rich and the poor seem to be limited, and where they do arise they can be more accurately seen as the result of situational constraints.

✓ Top Exam Hint

When you are evaluating these different explanations, remember that cultural explanations carry the danger that researchers may impose their own values upon their interpretation of the people they are researching. Of course this does not mean that those adopting the material explanation are any less biased.

For consideration:

1 To what extent can stratification be seen as the cause of poverty?
2 What factors lead to the creation of a 'poverty trap'?

6.10 Why does poverty continue today?

What does this mean?

As we saw in the previous section, sociologists have several ways of trying to explain the causes of poverty. When they try to explain why poverty continues to be a feature of society, however, they have to use more general sociological perspectives in order to explain why inequalities of wealth and income are a persistent feature of capitalist societies. The three key theories are Marxism, functionalism, and Weberian theory. These explanations all focus on explaining poverty in terms of the structure of society.

How does Marxism explain the continued existence of poverty?

Marxists, such as J.C. Kinkaid (1973), would explain the persistence of inequality as simply an inevitable consequence of capitalism. According to this view, whilst capitalism creates two classes (bourgeoisie and proletariat), it also divides (and so controls) the working class. It does this by creating a particularly disadvantaged group amongst the working class who are regularly unemployed. This unskilled (and poor) group amongst the working class is necessary in order to create wealth for capitalists for several reasons.

- They divide the working class and create **a reserve army of labour** which helps keep wages low.
- If wage levels are kept low then benefit levels too can be kept to a minimum.

Inequality is therefore a necessary condition for the continuation and reproduction of capitalism.

How does functionalism explain the continued existence of poverty?

Functionalists, such as Davis and Moore (1967), also see inequality in structural terms. When functionalists say that inequality has to be seen in structural terms, they mean that it is an inevitable feature of industrial society. Inequality reflects the supply and demand of skills. Those skills that are in short supply and are highly sought after in society will inevitably be able to attract higher wages, whilst those jobs requiring a lower degree of skill are easier to gain and therefore the large number of people with those skills (e.g. driving) cannot expect to gain particularly high wages.

✳ Key Idea

Reserve army of labour – Marxists suggest that the unemployed are 'reserve' workers. The fact that they exist, acting as a reserve workforce, means that they enable capitalists to offer lower wages to their current workforce. They also divide the working class, since those in work will be resentful of people who could take their jobs. This means that the working class do not recognise their common interests and fail to unite against the capitalists.

Functionalists and Marxists, then, both take a structural view of poverty, but they have very different views of the way society is structured. Functionalists do not see inequality as leading to conflict or being an aspect of social control. On the contrary, inequality is functional for society because without higher wages for the most important jobs there would be no incentive for people to work hard to gain those jobs.

The unequal distribution of wealth is therefore seen by functionalists to be inevitable and functional. Functionalists would say that the worst excesses of poverty no longer exist (they are using an absolute definition of poverty here) and indeed it is the wealthy that are able to give more generously to charities and pay higher taxes in order to give more back to the poor.

How does Weberian theory explain the continued existence of poverty?

According to Max Weber (1948), inequalities are not an inevitable result of class position.

- They are formed by the supply and demand for labour in economic markets. However, the supply and demand for labour is strongly influenced by factors such as race, gender, age, skill levels and the existence of a trade union or professional organisation. What this means is that some groups are poorer than others because they lack power and cannot force other social groups to increase their level of reward.
- This means that Weberians agree with Marxists that inequalities are an inevitable part of capitalism. However, for Weberians this does not mean that poverty itself is inevitable.
- Those who draw on Weberian theory, such as Peter Townsend (1979), argue that inequalities can be reduced through **progressive taxation** and relative poverty can be eradicated. What is required is the political will, or the political power, to create policies that will achieve this.

Conclusion

The ideas of Karl Marx, 1818–1883, and Max Weber, 1864–1920 are still highly relevant to our understanding of poverty and inequality today, although they have to be modified to take into account the way society has changed since the time that Marx and Weber were alive. The main theoretical perspectives all agree that inequality is a key feature of modern industrial capitalist societies. However, they disagree on how inequality is best explained and whether it is a feature that can be eradicated or even if it is needed or not.

66 99 Key Definition

Progressive taxation – means that the more people earn, the more tax they should pay.

✓ Top Exam Hint

When you are trying to evaluate these different explanations for the persistence of poverty, it's worth using the key concepts and core themes of power and stratification. Do the poor have the power to radically improve their circumstances themselves?

For consideration:

1   Can a reserve army of labour act as a form of social control?
2   What sort of taxation policies would be needed to eradicate poverty and how would they work?

What is poverty like between the sexes?

What does this mean?

So far we have thought about poverty mainly in terms of its relationship to social class. This means that the poor are those at the bottom of the class system, and the reason why they are poor is explained in terms of the inequalities that exist between the different class positions. However, from the late 1960s onwards, feminist sociologists began to challenge the idea that class was the most important aspect of stratification and started to focus on the importance of gender divisions. Feminism reminds us that poverty should not just be seen in terms of class. This means that sociologists need to consider whether poverty can have a different impact on people on the basis of their gender.

Are women more likely to be victims of poverty?

Women are more likely than men to find themselves in poverty because of discrimination, inequality, and the demands of their roles as housewives and mothers. This is mainly because of women's structural position in society. There are various reasons for this.

- More women are heads of single parent families than men. This often puts women in a situation where they are dependent upon benefits and cannot gain employment because of childcare responsibilities.

- Women are more likely to be in part-time or low paid employment. This has consequences for their pensions in later life, and also means that they do not get many welfare benefits that are dependent upon the worker being in full-time employment. Also, low pay is of course one of the main causes of poverty (Glendinning and Millar, 1994).

- A demographic factor is that women live longer than men. They are more likely to end up living on their own and the longer they live, the more any private savings will dwindle, leaving them to survive on the basic state pension.

How do sociologists explain the relationship between gender and poverty?

Feminists call the set of assumptions, values, norms and cultural rules which lead to this state of affairs, patriarchy. Feminists argue that we live

◆ What, When and Why?

Feminism became prominent in sociology in the 1960s and 1970s. This happened because more women were going into higher education and having academic careers. These women were critical of a lot of academic sociology, seeing it as male-dominated and out-of-date.

✳ Key Idea

Feminist Harriet Bradley argues that sociologists have to focus on the way different aspects of stratification interact together. Therefore while gender is an important factor in determining an individual's chances of falling into poverty, other aspects also have to be considered. For example, middle-class women, though they still earn less than their male counterparts, are much less at risk of poverty than working-class women. Use this insight for evaluation.

in a patriarchal society. Patriarchy, then, refers to a system of male dominance.

Feminists such as Williams (1993) have pointed out how welfare legislation, even going back before the 1940s, was built on sexist assumptions about a 'woman's place'. The Beveridge Report was no exception. In writing his report, Beveridge (a civil servant in the 1940s – see section 14) reflected the dominant views of his time. He assumed that once the war was over, married women would return to their chief role as mothers and housewives. Many of the benefits offered by the welfare state were only open to those who paid National Insurance contributions (a form of tax), and only those with a full-time job made these payments. This meant that most married women did not pay National Insurance, and so were not eligible for welfare benefits such as unemployment benefit.

Feminists have therefore argued that the welfare state has done much to uphold patriarchy and its institutions, including the nuclear family. This had implications for women's position in terms of wealth and poverty. For example, the state gave men an incentive to be married, with the married man's tax allowance, which existed up until 1990. The idea that men should receive higher pay than women was also legitimised by the state's welfare policies. This can be seen by the fact that Beveridge's plan also assumed that women's place at home would be financed by employers who would pay men what was termed 'a family wage'. This simply meant that the man's wage should be sufficient to pay for the needs of a family.

Conclusion

Some feminists (e.g. Bryson 1992) point out that women have gained from the welfare state, since child benefits go to women, and because women live longer they receive more benefits than men. Others such as Pateman are more ambiguous, noting that the welfare state helped to keep women subordinate to men. Other feminists such as Arber and Ginn (1991, 1995) have documented the 'feminisation of poverty'. It remains the case that women are still more at risk of falling into poverty than men.

For consideration:

1 What do sociologists mean when they say that poverty is being feminised? Do you think this is really happening?
2 Is gender more or less important than class as an indicator of poverty? Why?

Has the welfare state helped to uphold the post-war patriarchal view of women?

● Synoptic Link

Remember to consider why so many welfare services aimed at the family are highly gendered (structured or patterned on the basis of gender). This could be very useful to bear in mind when you are evaluating the role of the welfare state and who benefits most from welfare.

✓ Top Exam Hint

Use feminist theories as a way of criticising other sociological theories for their male bias. Feminists call such theories 'malestream', as a play on the idea of the 'mainstream'. In particular, feminists are critical of Marxists for talking only about class and not gender.

6.12 How are age and poverty linked?

What does this mean?

This means that there are very strong relationships between poverty and age and if you are under the age of sixteen or over sixty-five, you are more likely to be in poverty than others outside those age groups. These patterns are the result of social structures. For example, as Peter Townsend (1981) has argued in the case of old age, the institution of retirement forces people over a certain age into **structural dependency**. This means that they become dependent upon the state (and in some cases their occupational pension scheme) to provide for their subsistence needs. There are then clear links between age and poverty, and sociologists aim to explain why this is so.

How is age linked to poverty?

Recent research has shown that certain age groups are more at risk of falling into poverty than others. However, in recent history there have been some changes.

- Oppenheim (1996) notes that in the 1990s the number of old people in poverty declined but the number of children in poverty increased. Oppenheim suggests that this is explained by the increase in single parent families. Single parent families headed by women frequently fall into poverty. This is perhaps because women find it hard to gain work whilst simultaneously caring for their children.

- Government statistics indicate that in 1999/2000 around 19 per cent of those in poverty were pensioners, and according to 1998/9 figures around 1.3 million pensioners receive only the basic state pension (DSS 2001).

- There are currently around 5 million children living in poverty in the UK. About 2 million of these children live in a household where no adult is in employment, and the other 3 million live in households where the income is less than half of the national average (Howarth 1999).

- We live in a time of considerable social change, and recent research by Bardasi and Jenkins (2002) indicates that early retirement (which is becoming increasingly common) is leading to a sharp increase in the likelihood that men in some clerical and craft occupations are more likely to experience poverty in later life.

66 99 Key Definition

Structural dependency
Dependency is a state of depending on others to look after you. By structural dependency, Townsend simply means that this state is built into the rules of society. This is because we have laws which state when a person can begin to work and when they have to retire. These rules therefore force individuals, whatever their own wishes, to be dependent on other people at certain times in their life.

☞ Who are these People?

Elena Bardasi and Stephen Jenkins are researchers at the Institute for Social and Economic Research at the University of Essex. They used the British Household Panel Survey to conduct their research. They say that the implications of their research for policy are that there should be a concentration of effort in developing policies to prevent early retirement.

Why is age linked with poverty?

It was Rowntree who was one of the first to point to the relationship between poverty and the lifecycle. Rowntree found that families drifted into and out of poverty, being more at risk of poverty when bringing up young children, rising out of poverty as children matured, and being likely to fall into it again as the adults aged and retired.

More recently, sociologists like Peter Townsend (1981) and Alan Walker (1981) have developed what is known as the 'political economy' approach or dependency theory. This view claims that the young and the old are more at risk of poverty due to their position in the division of labour (work) and so is a little influenced by Marxist ideas, though neither of these researchers can accurately be described as Marxists. They do however recognise that low income and position in the labour market are key factors in causing poverty, and that these factors vary with age.

Johnson (1989) is critical of this approach, arguing that it exaggerates the influence of retirement, and neglects the fact that retirement can be a period of affluence and consumption, free of the demands of work. However, this view ignores the strong empirical (from research) evidence discussed above which indicates that many, though not all, older people and children are more at risk of poverty than other social groups.

Conclusion

Age is clearly strongly related to poverty. However, despite the problems of the dependency burden, age is not a source of great social conflict. As Arber and Ginn argue, this is because other types of stratification have an impact on and cut across age divisions. As we have seen here, not all old people, or all young people, are in poverty. Age is therefore a factor that can contribute to poverty but has to be understood in the context of wider stratifying structures, such as class, race and gender.

For consideration:

1   What are the welfare implications of an ageing population?
2   What policy recommendations would you make to a government minister to reduce or solve the problems of an ageing population?

6.13 How are class, ethnicity and poverty linked?

66 99 Key Definition

Ethnicity – refers to the shared cultural characteristics and identity of a group, which could be a religious or a nationally-based group. It is often used as an alternative to the term 'race'.

☞ Who is this Person?

Sociologist Harriet Bradley has been strongly influenced by feminism and has a particular interest in stratification. She is one sociologist who has argued that sociologists now have to focus on understanding how different aspects of stratification (class, race, gender) work as a system.

✳ Key Idea

Poverty and inequality are related but are not the same. Poverty can be defined in either absolute or relative terms. Relative poverty is not the same as inequality. As indicated previously, relative poverty can be defined in several ways, but it is always a standard of living considerably below the average. Inequality simply means a difference between, for example, two income levels and does not entail poverty.

What does this mean?

As we have seen, many sociologists would agree that the causes of poverty are linked to the effects of stratification. Throughout the 1960s, though, sociologists tended to focus on class at the expense of other forms of stratification, such as ethnicity and gender. More recently researchers such as Harriet Bradley (1996) have argued that we need to examine how different aspects of stratification work together and form a system. In this section we will examine class and **ethnicity**, and consider the important question of whether one of these forms of stratification is more important than the other.

How is class related to poverty?

Class does not actually cause poverty. However, if you are in the lowest social class, you will have a much greater chance of falling into poverty than a person from a higher socio-economic position. This is because poverty is caused by factors such as unemployment and low wages and these factors are strongly associated with lower socio-economic classes. However, it would be wrong to say that a person's lower social class caused their poverty because not all people in the same social class will be in poverty. Social class systems create inequality but not necessarily poverty. This is basically a Weberian influenced view of the relationship between class and poverty. Sociologists like Peter Townsend (1973) and John Scott (1994) would take this approach.

Marxist sociologists would disagree with this view to some extent. They would argue that capitalism creates a two-class system, and that the working class are inevitably impoverished by the nature of their relationship with the bourgeoisie. Over time this does indeed impoverish the working class, a process that Marxists call 'emiseration'. One of the criticisms of this view, though, is that this has not happened. It can be argued that inequalities remain considerable and indeed have increased in recent years. However, because the standard of living continues to increase, the working class are not impoverished. They simply have less than those at the top of the system.

How is ethnicity related to poverty?

Ethnicity is also closely linked to poverty and the stark facts are that some ethnic minorities have higher chances of being unemployed or in low paid work and therefore are more highly represented amongst the poor.

- Scott and Fulcher (1999) note that two-thirds of Pakistani and Bangladeshi families are in the bottom fifth of the income distribution in Britain.

- Asian women are disproportionately likely to be in low-paid 'home work' (work carried out in their own home).

- Ethnic minorities are disproportionately likely to be unemployed, although recorded unemployment levels vary amongst different ethnic minority groups. In 2000 the government Labour Force Survey found unemployment levels of 5 per cent for whites, 8 per cent for Asian Indians and 17 per cent for Pakistanis and Bangladeshis.

- There is also a mass of evidence showing inequalities in health (including high infant mortality rates), and poor housing conditions amongst some ethnic minorities.

Are ethnic minorities caught in a cycle of deprivation?

These patterns can be explained using the general theoretical approaches and perspectives we have examined previously. However, some of the sociological perspectives are more useful than others. Critics argue that Marxism tends to explain ethnic inequality in terms of class position, when in fact it has to be seen as a distinctive form of inequality. This means that ethnic minorities are discriminated against precisely because they are from a minority group, not simply because they are working-class. They are in effect being 'doubly' discriminated against.

For this reason some sociologists would argue that the Weberian approach is more sensitive to these issues of stratification, since it acknowledges status differences.

Conclusion

The examination of class and ethnicity tells us more about how poverty is related to the stratification system. It is not possible to say that either class or ethnicity is more important than the other. Both are important aspects of stratification and they both influence a person's (whether they are white or black) likelihood of falling into poverty. It is for this reason that sociologists such as Bradley argue that we have to examine how these stratification systems, of class and ethnicity, operate to create a complex web of risk and opportunity.

◆ **What, When and Why?**

In the 1960s and 1970s many sociologists focused on class inequalities and saw poverty as being caused by the operation of the class structure. This meant that ethnicity and racism were not seen as the cause of inequality and poverty. Sociologists are now more aware of the ways that these two aspects of stratification are distinct, yet interact to create powerful effects.

● **Synoptic Link**

Remember to link the welfare state to other aspects of society such as education. Education is also a highly stratified welfare service in Britain, with wealthy elite groups opting out of the state education system on a large scale, with the exception for the time being of state-funded higher education.

For consideration:

1 Why is the disadvantage and high risk of poverty faced by some ethnic minorities not shared by all ethnic minority groups?

2 What is the difference between poverty and inequality?

What has the state done to reduce poverty?

Sir William Beveridge

☞ Who is this Person?

Sir William Beveridge (1879–1963) was a civil servant. During the Second World War, he was put in charge of a commission which was formed in order to look into ways of creating a more equal society and eradicating poverty. It also tackled other social problems, such as poor health, housing and levels of basic education. The assumptions and institutions created after 1945 continue to shape welfare policy.

What does this mean?

The state is the set of institutions that govern a society. The state includes the government, the civil service and government departments such as the Department for Social Security. The state can play a great role in reducing poverty by creating social policies.

A social policy is a plan or a set of ideas that policy makers (the government and government ministers) will have about an issue that they are responsible for, such as poverty. Throughout the 20th century British governments introduced a range of policies that were intended to reduce poverty. One of the main ways in which the state tried to reduce poverty in the 20th century was through the creation of the '**welfare state**'.

What is the welfare state?

The welfare state is the set of policies and institutions created largely as a result of the recommendations of civil servant Sir William Beveridge in 1942. Beveridge was asked to outline some policies that would eradicate poverty and inequality in Britain. At the time Britain was at war. The government took the view that investigating and announcing plans to eradicate poverty would be good for war-time morale and would help unify the population.

- Beveridge identified five 'evils': idleness (unemployment); want (poverty); squalor (housing); disease (health); and ignorance (education). As you can see, these related to several key areas of social policy, not just poverty.

- In order to solve these problems, Beveridge suggested the creation of a system of universal and means-tested benefits. The 'Beveridge Plan', as Sir William's report came to be known, led to the creation of a range of policies including: old age pensions for all; free state education up to the age of sixteen; a free health system (the National Health Service created in 1948); an extensive council house building programme; and even other benefits like free school milk.

What has the state done more recently to reduce poverty?

The welfare state legislation of the late 1940s still survives in contemporary Britain, although the way in which the welfare state works has changed and the institution itself has come under increasing pressure and criticism as a result of rapid social change. This has led to changes in the social policies that aim to deal with poverty. Arguably all of the more recent policies have tried to force people away from relying upon the state. Two main approaches can be identified.

- Individualisation – this is an approach that has been identified by various sociologists, including Clarke et al (2000). Individualisation means that social policies are aimed at making people feel that they are individuals and ought to take the main responsibility for ensuring their own welfare. This is reflected in policies such as the Child Support Agency and the Working Families Tax Credit scheme.

- Secondly, there has been more of a shift towards means-tested benefits. Various schemes have been created to test individuals' eligibility for benefits. Unemployment benefit, for example, is now rigorously monitored and claimants have to attend job training schemes.

Conclusion

Sociologists can agree that the role of the state in providing welfare services has been extremely important. However, they differ in their explanations of why the state has taken such a strong role. Those influenced by conflict or Marxist theories tend to see welfare services as a means of social control. Those more influenced by functionalist theories tend to see the provision of welfare services as reflecting social consensus that the state needs to provide minimum levels of support in order to create social integration.

For consideration:

1 Why has the welfare state failed to eradicate poverty?
2 What changes need to be made to the welfare state in order to eradicate poverty?

6.15 How do sociologists explain the welfare state?

What does this mean?

Sociologists have not been content to assume that the welfare state came about just because someone thought it was a good idea. For sociologists the tremendous social changes, which saw welfare systems introduced in all industrial and capitalist states in the 20th century, means that there must have been a common cause. Many sociologists therefore argue that the welfare state must perform certain necessary functions for industrial, capitalist societies and attempt to explain its existence in this way. Other sociologists argue against this view.

How do sociologists explain the welfare state?

Two of the main theories which try to explain how and why the welfare state was developed come from the functionalist and Marxist perspectives.

- Functionalists such as Durkheim and Parsons believed that industrial societies inevitably would become increasingly complex. What they meant by 'complex' was that these societies would no longer be run on a small-scale basis. It could not be assumed that small-scale and informal networks of friends and neighbours would provide for welfare needs, as happens to some extent in traditional society. For functionalists the large scale of industrial society leads to social disorganisation and to inequalities which individuals may find hard to overcome without the benefit of close family networks. The welfare state is therefore seen as developing in response to the creation of these new needs. In line with functionalist theory, these needs would be recognised by all groups in society (there would be a consensus).
- Marxists also take a 'functional' approach to the creation of the welfare state, but for them it is not the outcome of consensus but of class conflict. Marxists argue that capitalists developed the welfare state because they realised that if the state did not provide a safety net of minimum conditions, then the working class would protest and eventually this political conflict would lead to unrest or revolution. Marxists such as Mishra (1984) and Westergaard (1976) therefore see the welfare state as a device created by the capitalist class to preserve capitalism. The welfare state means that capitalism continues to thrive, whilst the thing that causes inequalities and poverty – capitalism – remains stronger than ever.

● **Synoptic Link**

Apply your wider knowledge and understanding of social theories to this issue. Marxists have argued that the welfare state can be an excellent means of exerting social control on the working classes. Use this point for evaluation.

- However, another important view is the social democratic approach. This is a political theory rather than a sociological theory. Social democratic theory sees society as made up of lots of competing groups with unequal power and resources. The welfare state is the outcome of political struggles between these groups. Social democratic explanations of the welfare state would argue that it was a compromise between two powerful groups in society: employers and workers. Those who call themselves social democrats think that the state should provide minimum standards. The state should act as a referee and ensure that there is fair play for all.

Which explanation is the best?

Any answer to this question really depends on your view of power and which of the above theories you think gives the most accurate view of society.

- Functionalism is often criticised for its view that society is characterised by consensus. Critics would point out the fierce political resistance to the welfare state from many interest groups, e.g. employers groups such as the Confederation of British Industry (CBI), and trade unions in the 20th century who tried to prevent women and ethnic minorities receiving equal rights at work.
- Marxism can be criticised for its bias against the welfare state, which many Marxists have seen as a cynical device, intended to prevent working-class criticism of capitalism. This ignores the improvements that welfare benefits have made, and also the fact that many working-class leaders and organisations helped to create the welfare state.
- The social democratic approach can be criticised for believing that the state can act as a neutral and unbiased referee. As Marxists and conflict theorists argue, powerful interest groups always dominate the state.

Conclusion

Sociologists do not give a single, simple answer to the problem of explaining why the welfare state was created. This is because they all have different views about the nature and structure of society. However, many sociologists will take ideas from different theories in order to create their own answer to this question, just as you will do in evaluating these views. The different views are therefore helpful because they provide you with a set of ideas to use for your own analysis.

◆ What, When and Why?

All of the explanations of the welfare state given here could seem a bit dated. This is because most of them were developed in the 1960s and there has been rapid social change since then. Both Marxists and functionalists have tended to see the welfare state as performing certain essential functions for capitalism or industrial society respectively. Contemporary sociologists are generally more sceptical of large-scale theories like this, and tend to see the welfare state's origin and current role simply as the outcome of political bargaining between competing groups with differing resources and power.

✓ Top Exam Hint

When evaluating competing views on the role of the welfare state use the core concept of power. This is one of the fundamental differences between the different theories. Show why you think that a particular view of power is more convincing than others, and how this helps to provide a more accurate understanding of the welfare state.

For consideration:

1 Do you think that it is possible for the welfare state to act as a referee and protect the welfare and rights of the poorest sections of society?
2 Does the welfare state reproduce capitalism?

Does the welfare state help to maintain the class system?

What does this mean?

A key idea that comes from Marxism is that the welfare state has an important influence in maintaining the class system. This may seem a little strange, given that the welfare state aims to reduce, in however small a way, inequalities between different classes. However, the welfare state could maintain the class system by, for example, only giving benefits to certain people. This might have the effect of marking these individuals out, and it might also link up to ideas discussed previously about the cycle of poverty. Perhaps the welfare state simply acts as a sort of 'sticking plaster' and does not really change the fundamental structure of society? A number of sociologists, despite being critical of Marxist thought, have felt that this idea is important.

How can the welfare state maintain the class system?

This basic Marxist idea has been developed in more sophisticated ways by contemporary sociologists; particularly important are Bob Jessop (1990), a British sociologist, and Gosta Esping-Anderson (1990), a Danish sociologist.

Bob Jessop has argued that the welfare state was ideally suited to the needs of a **Fordist** economy. The welfare state meant that wealth was redistributed to the working classes, without really threatening the need of the capitalist system for class inequality. The redistribution of wealth through the welfare system meant that the working class was strengthened both economically and politically. Working-class consumerism thrived. Jessop says that in fact, contrary to Marx's idea of class polarisation (an increase in inequalities between the two main classes), this was a good thing for capitalism. This is because increased consumerism (more spending) by the working class maintained the capitalist economy. At the same time of course, inequalities between the different classes remained considerable. According to this view then, Jessop claims that the welfare state did indeed play a vital role in maintaining capitalism.

Do all welfare systems work in the same way?

Esping-Anderson argues that welfare systems have to be seen in the context of the society in which they are devised. Esping-Anderson notes important differences in welfare systems in different countries. He identifies three main type of welfare system: conservative, liberal, and social democratic welfare regimes.

✳ Key Idea

Fordism is the system of mass production used in industrial capitalist societies, named after Henry Ford, the car manufacturer who invented the modern production line. However, sociologists say that from the mid-1970s capitalist societies moved towards post-Fordism, which involves more specialised production for niche markets. This has led to higher levels of unemployment and therefore has increased the cost of providing welfare.

Gosta Esping-Anderson's study of welfare systems, *The Three Worlds of Welfare Capitalism* (1990), has been one of the most influential views developed in sociology. He shows that welfare systems reflect stratification within the society they are developed in, and usually reinforce these inequalities or else produce new inequalities.

1 Conservative welfare works on the basis that people only get out of the system what they have paid into it. Status differences and inequalities are preserved.
2 Liberal welfare systems argue that incentives to work must not be reduced. Liberal systems are not particularly generous, and this means that inequalities are not markedly reduced.
3 Social democratic welfare provision promotes equality by focusing on universal benefits. Universal benefits are given to all, regardless of their wealth or income.

The British system combines elements of all three of these broad types. Esping-Anderson argues that many welfare systems preserve inequalities or else they end up creating new inequalities. This can happen in two main ways.

- Where benefits are means-tested, it is highly likely that status differences between benefit recipients and the rest of the population will be reinforced. This can be seen in the way children who receive free school dinners are easily identified and stigmatised by their peers.
- The other way is through universal benefits or '**decommodification**'. Although this may sound surprising, Esping-Anderson explains it becomes clear if one takes into account the importance of the stratification system. He argues that universal benefits work most effectively where there is a high degree of equality. Where this is absent, and all members of society receive a universal benefit, the affluence of the comfortably-off middle-classes is simply boosted by their earned income. In the UK, all families can claim child benefit. For the middle-class family claiming this benefit, the money is just an extra.

Conclusion

Jessop and Esping-Anderson both suggest that the welfare state, and different types of welfare state in other countries, do help to maintain class and status differences. Esping-Anderson's analysis though goes further, since he argues that welfare systems are structures that create new forms of stratification. Only in the most generous form of welfare state, the social democratic form, are benefits universalised to an extent that equality is maximised. When welfare benefits are available as a matter of right to all citizens, there is then no stigma in claiming benefits. This means that status divisions between those who do and those who do not claim benefits become less likely. However, this system depends on high levels of taxation and high levels of employment for people to be able to pay their tax and thus pay for the services that citizens can claim.

For consideration:

1 Is it possible to have some form of welfare state that would not create new forms of stratification?
2 How would society have to change in order for the welfare state to become unnecessary?

Is there a welfare (dependency) culture?

What does this mean?

The idea of a 'dependency culture' was first thought of by American sociologist Charles Murray in the 1980s, although he drew on a set of ideas about poverty and welfare that go back a long way. By dependency culture, Murray meant that those living on welfare benefits came to be dependent upon the welfare agencies (the local benefits office, the social work department and, ultimately, the government) and lost the ability to be independent and responsible. Murray argued that this led to the development of an urban **underclass**. Murray's solution was that the state should severely curtail its benefit system and, wherever possible, benefits should only be provided if claimants did some form of work in return.

How does a dependency culture develop?

Researchers like Charles Murray (1989) and David Marsland (1989), who has also written about dependency culture, are usually identified as New Right thinkers. The New Right was very important in the 1980s, and their ideas are still an important influence on welfare policy. The New Right was a group of writers, academics and politicians. They argued that the welfare state was itself the cause of much poverty and disadvantage. This was because, as indicated above, by paying out benefits to those who were not working, the welfare state removed the incentive to work. This in turn led to the creation of a distinctive set of cultural values.

What evidence is there for a dependency culture?

Various research has been conducted to examine whether there is any evidence for a distinctive dependency culture amongst welfare benefit claimants.

- Heath (1992) found no evidence for this view, and in fact found that benefit claimants appeared to keener to work than those in employment.

- Hartley Dean and Peter Taylor-Gooby (1992) conducted detailed research with a sample of 85 claimants using informal interviews. The respondents they interviewed were keen to escape their situation. It was found that in fact claimants lacked a detailed knowledge of the benefits system. They were more likely to be

66 99 Key Definition

Underclass – this term refers to a group at the bottom of the stratification system. Researchers like Murray see it as consisting of various groups, such as pensioners, the long-term unemployed, single parent mothers, the disabled and those unwilling to work. Some critics say that this definition makes the concept unhelpful, because all these different types of people are in poverty for very different reasons.

Charles Murray is one of the most well-known advocates of New Right ideas about the underclass and welfare dependency.

☞ Who is this Person?

Charles Murray is an American writer and researcher. He is usually associated with a New Right perspective. He became well-known in the 1980s in Britain and the USA following the publication of his controversial pamphlet on the underclass (1989). He has worked as an advisor to various think tanks and occasionally to the US Government.

eligible for more benefits than they claimed, than they were to be committing benefit fraud.

- Lydia Morris in her book *The Dangerous Classes* (1994) shows that the practice of making the poorest members of society a scapegoat has a long history. Morris argues that the views of the New Right, and their identification of a welfare-dependent underclass, fall into this category; it is therefore a myth, not reality.

Conclusion

In evaluating the views of the New Right it is helpful to consider what sort of explanation of poverty is being provided. The idea of a dependency culture fits in well with individualistic theories of poverty and the idea of a culture of poverty that we examined earlier (see section 9). Like the earlier cultural theories, it identifies the causes of poverty in individual inadequacy. This means that poverty is blamed on individuals, who are considered to have got into poverty because of their own inability, stupidity, lack of discipline or idleness.

However, sociologists such as Dean and Taylor-Gooby, Morris, or Heath, would reject the idea that there is a dependency culture and an under-class, and these sociologists can provide empirical evidence that seems to indicate that the idea of a dependency culture is highly questionable. Ultimately though, how this evidence is interpreted will depend upon the values and theoretical orientation of the sociologists.

For consideration:

1 Do you think that the idea of an underclass is sociologically useful or accurate?
2 How does living on welfare benefits influence the identities that are available to people? Are cultural or material factors of greater importance in shaping these identities?

Should paraplegics such as Stephen Hawking be blamed for potentially being reliant on welfare?

6.18 How are the poor excluded from society?

66 99 Key Definition

Social exclusion – this term refers to the way that individuals or social groups are prevented from full participation in their society. It encompasses social, political and economic activities.

What does this mean?

In recent years sociologists and policy makers have started to use the term '**social exclusion**'. This term refers to inequalities in a broader sense than simply being the notion of poverty. It also refers to the idea that poverty is not just an economic phenomenon.

- Social exclusion therefore refers to the way that some groups in society are excluded from activities and opportunities that the majority are able to partake in. Examples of social exclusion would include the way that being poor excludes people from education and employment opportunities, from the chance of applying for housing, and from participating in politics and decision-making.

- Equally, social exclusion can mean that some social groups are more likely to be the victims of crime.

- Social exclusion is a complex idea, since those at the top of the social hierarchy can also be excluded, in their case by their wealth. Examples of this are the way that the rich are able to exclude themselves from social institutions by using private services such as health, education or even living in separate and guarded residential areas.

How are the poor excluded from society?

Some of the ways in which the poor can be excluded have been briefly indicated above, but these need further explanation. The poor can be excluded from employment opportunities because applying for jobs often involves expense, for example for travel or interview clothes. Additionally, those who do not have access to a computer or a telephone cannot easily look for jobs. For the homeless, lack of an address makes it difficult to even apply for welfare benefits. Another example of social exclusion occurs in education where non-attendance rates and educational failure rates are high amongst particular socio-economic groups and some ethnic minority groups.

As we have mentioned though, social exclusion is not just an economic phenomenon. One of the important aspects of the idea of social exclusion is that it indicates how exclusion in one area can have further consequences. In this way, social exclusion can be seen as having some similarity to the idea of multiple deprivation.

What theoretical perspective does the idea of social exclusion come from?

The concept of social exclusion has its origins in the work of Emile Durkheim. The French sociologist Emile Durkheim (1858–1917) was one of the main founders of functionalism. Durkheim noted that a lack of shared norms ('anomie') led to a lack of social integration, and this could cause instability. More recently, various sociologists including Anthony Giddens and Amitai Etzioni have taken up the idea. Giddens is associated with the 'Third Way', a set of ideas which advocate an approach to welfare that emphasises individual responsibilities as well as rights, and advocates a greater role for welfare pluralism (many forms of welfare – state services and privately provided services, e.g. privately owned homes for the elderly, or private health care). Etzioni is the founder of 'communitarianism' and recommends that social policies need to be aimed at recreating community networks in order to create more opportunities for self-help.

Conclusion

Social exclusion is a popular concept in contemporary social policy. Sociologists from many different perspectives could undoubtedly agree that the poor are excluded from a whole range of activities that the majority of society partakes in.

However, sociologists who are more influenced by Marxist, conflict or feminist theory treat the concept critically. They would argue that the main causes of 'exclusion' are indeed economic, and so to focus on policies which will attempt to 're-integrate' the poor or the excluded into the mainstream, without making any allowance for economic inequalities, will be bound to end in failure. It can also be argued that policies aiming to eradicate social exclusion are likely to become rather authoritarian and intolerant of cultural differences. After all, conflict theorists would point out that trying to integrate a society through shared values and culture does not rule out the possibility of conflict, since the cultural values will be those of the dominant group. Functionalists, of course, take the view that societies can be integrated by a shared culture.

Therefore, how keen sociologists are to use the concept of social exclusion will depend upon which sociological perspective they find most convincing.

For consideration:

1 Are the rich socially excluded from society?
2 Is a truly socially inclusive society possible? What would it mean?

◆ **What, When and Why?**

The idea of 'communitarianism' is associated with the work of American sociologist Amitai Etzioni (1995), and was very influential throughout the 1990s. Sociologist Amitai Etzioni has become highly involved in political debate in the USA, arguing that social problems can be solved by his concept of 'communitarianism'. Communitarianism is the belief that modern society (particularly modern American society) can only be preserved and further developed by returning to the certainties of the older values of community and family.

✓ **Top Exam Hint**

Use the comments here about the Durkheimian origins of social exclusion in your evaluation of the concept. Durkheim is a functionalist, so his view of a socially integrated society assumes that consensus is achievable. A criticism of this view and of social exclusion, therefore, is that it masks differences in power between different social groups. There may be considerable disagreement about the values that society should be integrated around. This can also mean disagreement about which groups and values should be included in the consensus.

6.19 Who benefits from the welfare state?

What does this mean?

The welfare state was supposed to lead to a redistribution of wealth. However, as we have seen, some sociologists are critical of the idea that the welfare state simply benefits those it is intended to help – that is, the poorer sections of society. Research has indicated that it is not always the poor who in fact do benefit most from the welfare state. Some sociologists have suggested that those who benefit the most from the welfare state are the professionals working in and running it.

Why do the wealthy and the middle classes benefit from the welfare state?

One of the key reasons why the wealthy benefit more from the welfare state is due to the way the tax system works. A study by Giles and Johnson at the Institute for Fiscal Studies (1994) found that the tax burden for the poor between 1985 and 1995 increased whilst that of the rich declined. During this period the poor were paying £3 per week more and the rich were paying £31 per week less in tax than they had been in 1985. All of this means that it is the poor who in fact pay more, proportionally speaking, for the welfare benefits that the state provides.

Research by other academics supports this conclusion. Julian Le Grand (1982, 1987) argues that the middle class take advantage of cheap or free state-funded further and higher education, and make good use of the NHS. Although the working class have benefited more than the wealthy from council housing, Le Grand points out that even this has been largely negated by the effect of the tax advantages given to homeowners by governments. Le Grand also uses the idea of the inverse care law as further evidence that the poorest sections of the population receive the worst levels of welfare support.

Recent research still supports these conclusions. Le Grand's findings are confirmed by Hay (1996) and Lowe (1993), who pointed out that taxation remained less progressive. Progressive taxation means that the more a person earns the more tax they pay. Le Grand also argues that the poor pay more tax than the rich, because of indirect taxation and exemptions. Indirect taxation refers to taxes that can occur through spending on goods such as cigarettes and alcohol. Tax exemptions are ways of legally avoiding tax, by, for example, claiming back money spent on petrol if it was for business travel.

✳ Key Idea

The idea of the inverse care law (or inverse prevention) comes from the sociology of health and illness, but is also relevant to welfare. Professor Julian Le Grand, for example, argues that it is the middle classes and the wealthy that benefit most from the welfare state. The poor pay more for the cost of welfare and gain least.

Economist and social policy analyst, Julian Le Grand

How do welfare professionals benefit from the welfare state?

Some sociologists have pointed out that there is another way in which the middle classes can benefit from the welfare state.

- Arthur Gould (1993) is one of several researchers who have pointed out that it is the middle classes who primarily benefit from the employment opportunities offered by the welfare state. This sort of view is broadly compatible with a Marxist approach. It may seem very cynical, but sociologists who find it useful would point to its accuracy. It is the middle classes who dominate the jobs hierarchy in the welfare state. This enables the social and political domination of the working class by the middle classes. Certainly the welfare state may aim to help and reduce suffering, but Marxist-influenced sociologists are surely right to point to the continued existence of, and increases in, inequality between different social groups?

- French thinker Michel Foucault (1979) makes a different point. Foucault was a critic of Marxism. He took the view that the welfare state does indeed represent the interests of the professionals who created it and who work in it. However, for Foucault, this is not caused by capitalism; it is just the way that knowledge and power work. Knowledge becomes a form of power. Foucault argued that in modern society those who create the systems of expert knowledge that we become dependent upon often control our lives.

Conclusion

The research discussed indicates that the welfare state, whilst it may indeed be a good thing, disproportionately provides help to those who perhaps have less need than the poorest. However, this is not simply a result of economic factors. Middle-class professionals are adept at 'working the system'. Whether it is applying for grants for higher education, or knowing how best to get through the bureaucratic hurdles to receive NHS treatment more quickly, it is the middle classes who tend to have the skills and knowledge needed. The welfare state continues to change (for example, with students having to pay more for higher education), but it is the wealthier sections of society who benefit most from its continued existence.

For consideration:

1   Do you believe and trust the advice of welfare experts such as health service managers or doctors?
2   What, if anything, is wrong with the British welfare state?

● **Synoptic Link**

Link this topic to education and family and households. The wealthy gain the benefits of free state higher education and monopolise top positions in the running of the welfare state (medicine, the civil service, politics). Middle-class families have high take-up rates of child benefit allowance, a universal benefit.

✓ **Top Exam Hint**

Apply your knowledge of the different perspectives to this topic in order to evaluate it thoroughly. Marxist, functionalist, social democratic, feminist and New Right perspectives are all relevant. Describe how these theories would give different answers to the question of who benefits from the welfare state. Evaluate the views and give the reasons why one or some theories are better than others.

6.20 What other forms of welfare provision exist apart from the state?

What does this mean?

The state does not have a monopoly on the provision of welfare services. This means that there are other organisations that provide welfare. Sociologists refer to this range of provision as '**welfare pluralism**' or as a 'mixed economy' of welfare provision. Sociologists are interested in this type of welfare because it has an influence on the services that are provided by the state, and it also reveals key assumptions in our society about who should take responsibility for welfare provision.

❝❞ Key Definition

Welfare pluralism – this term describes the mixture of private or voluntary sector and state welfare provision. Since the 1980s there has been a decline in the degree of state monopolisation of welfare services, and an increasing diversity of provision.

◆ What, When and Why?

The Conservative governments in power from 1979 to 1997, strongly influenced by the ideas of the New Right, wanted to reduce welfare expenditure. They promoted the privatisation of welfare services and introduced 'community care' schemes. This has resulted in an increase in private nursing homes and a decrease in state facilities for the care of the mentally ill, many of whom now have to stay at home or become homeless.

What other provision exists?

There are three key forms of welfare provision apart from the state. These are the private sector, the voluntary sector and informal care.

*   The 'private sector' refers to privately-owned companies that are run in order to make a profit. Examples would include private nursing homes, private schools, private pension schemes and privately-run medical insurance schemes.
*   The term 'voluntary sector' is used to refer to non-profit making organisations (often charities) that provide care of various types. Examples would include the NSPCC (National Society for the Prevention of Cruelty to Children), Shelter (the organisation for the homeless), Barnardo's and CPAG (Child Poverty Action Group). Voluntary sector organisations often depend heavily on the help of volunteers, but they usually have a small number of salaried staff.
*   'Informal care' means care given by family, friends, relatives or neighbours.

How important is non-state welfare provision?

Non-state organisations that provide welfare are important for several reasons.

1   They are important politically, because they can act as pressure groups and campaign on particular issues. In this way they can sometimes persuade governments to change policy, and they can act as a 'voice' for groups who are too weak or disorganised to otherwise mount effective political campaigns.

2   They are also important ideologically. The existence of non-state welfare organisations helps to legitimise the idea that welfare is a private, individual matter. This has several consequences. First, it reinforces the idea that the recipients of welfare are unfortunate and inept individuals. Second, it indicates that responsibility for welfare is not primarily seen as a collective responsibility, nor one for which the state must take sole responsibility. Both points mean that the existence of charitable organisations tends to reinforce the idea that responsibility for staying out of poverty and so on, lies with individuals and families, and that it can be adequately dealt with through voluntary means. This means that poverty and disadvantage are individualised.

3   The existence of non-state welfare provision can also remove pressure from the state to take action to tackle welfare issues. If vital services are being provided adequately by other organisations, then the government can save money and effort and focus its energies on other problems. Again, this can have the effect of individualising social problems.

Conclusion

We have seen that there is a range of non-state providers of welfare services. The existence of these providers has fuelled debates about the merits of state welfare provision and about whether benefits should be universal or selective. It is therefore helpful to consider the advantages and disadvantages of non-state welfare provision.

*   *Advantages.* Welfare organisations such as the charities mentioned can develop a tremendous amount of expertise. They may also be more trusted by their users because the government does not run them. They are often cheaper than state services. This can be due to their use of volunteers. Supporters would say it is because they are run more like businesses and are more efficient.

*   *Disadvantages.* Voluntary welfare provision is not guaranteed, unlike state welfare. There can therefore be considerable unevenness in welfare provision from the voluntary sector. Charities lack financial resources and this limits what they can do. Private welfare services (e.g. medical care, insurance, education) are not free, so if you cannot afford them, they are not available to you. This can mean that those who need them most cannot use them.

✓ Top Exam Hint

Use the Marxist and feminist perspectives to evaluate the usefulness of voluntary sector provision. Marxists would argue that this just means that capitalists get free welfare provision. Feminists would agree, but point out that contemporary society is patriarchal as well as capitalist. Use the New Right perspective to show the counter-argument, even if you disagree with it. Evaluate the New Right counter-argument by analysing the accuracy of its assumptions about the power of individuals in the free market.

For consideration:

1   Discuss the arguments for and against the complete privatisation of all welfare provision.
2   What are the advantages and disadvantages of a mixed system of welfare provision (welfare pluralism)?

What is poverty like around the globe?

What does this mean?

Poverty is not something that only occurs in Britain. It is found in other societies, both in the richer and the poorer nations, though clearly what counts as poverty in an African society may be rather different to what is considered to be poverty in the UK. Sociologists are interested in discovering whether there are any connections between the causes of poverty in different societies and in trying to explain these relationships. One of the main ideas that sociologists now use to examine relationships between different societies is globalisation.

What is globalisation?

Globalisation refers to the idea that the different places, nations and societies in the world have become increasingly interconnected. Sociologists like David Harvey (1990) and Anthony Giddens (1990) talk about the transformation of time and space. By this, they mean that the time it takes to communicate and travel across the globe has been vastly reduced by modern technology. This also means that space (or distance) is no longer so important as a barrier to human activity.

How can globalisation cause poverty?

Globalisation has had several implications in terms of wealth, poverty, and welfare.

- Globalisation has led to the formation of TNCs (transnational corporations). These companies manufacture in several countries, and they move around, opening and closing factories wherever it is most economically advantageous for them to do so. This means that workers in Britain may find themselves unemployed because a TNC based in America or Japan decides to close down a factory in the UK. The company can get the work done more cheaply in a factory sited in another country. This is what Giddens means by the transformation of time and space. Distant events can have an impact in places far across the globe.
- Globalisation has led to increased flows of migrants. This creates welfare problems for nations receiving migrants, as well as for the countries which migrants leave, which may experience, for example, labour shortages. In Britain, the flow of migrants has led to moral panics (for an explanation of this term, see the chapter 4, section 18) about 'alleged asylum seekers', and political problems over the policing of immigration.

✳ Key Idea

As you can see, there are several aspects to globalisation. However, basically it just means that the world is increasingly connected. This means that there are now lots of social and economic relationships between people in different parts of the world. Try to use Giddens phrase, 'the transformation of space and time', when you are discussing this, but use the quotation marks and be sure to explain what it means in your own words.

- As sociologist Lydia Morris has identified (1993), migration has also raised considerable problems for the welfare state. Some have suggested that migrants constitute a new welfare-dependent underclass. Morris suggests that the British state is changing as a result of membership of the European Union (EU) and this is challenging traditional notions of citizenship. Citizenship means that a person is entitled to all the benefits of membership of a state. As migration increases, member states of the EU have to tackle the issue of whether they will be able to restrict citizenship rights to their own nationals. Again we can see how access to welfare rights and the risk of poverty reflect stratification processes in society.

These points all indicate that globalisation can be seen as a factor in causing poverty through contributing to unemployment, as well as through the influence of migration on labour markets and welfare systems.

Conclusion

Many sociologists would agree that globalisation is indeed a key factor in creating poverty.

However, Anthony Giddens has argued that sociologists should be more cautious on this issue, and should not be too quick to reach this conclusion. Giddens acknowledges that big differences in income exist between say, the USA and the Philippines. He agrees that this can mean that jobs are 'shipped overseas' to take advantage of cheaper labour. However, Giddens says that things do not always work as simply as this example implies. He claims that in industries where international trade is most significant, labour costs are not always as different as one might expect. Giddens concludes that technological changes are more important, since they increase the demand for skilled workers (who gain higher wages), and decrease the demand for lower paid, less skilled workers.

Whether or not we agree with Giddens that globalisation is a direct cause of poverty, it seems clear that globalisation does at least have an important influence on poverty. Globalisation does this by structuring labour markets that have a big impact on people's opportunities for work and for their risk of falling into poverty.

For consideration:

1 Is globalisation leading to an increase in poverty?
2 Some people have suggest that global government would be the solution to increasing global poverty. Do you agree? What might be some of the problems in achieving global government?

◆ **What, When and Why?**

Sociologists looking at British society now have to be much more aware of social changes in other societies beyond Britain's own national boundaries. Social change and globalisation have changed society and forced sociologists to consider poverty and welfare in new ways. Use these points for evaluation perhaps, for example, to criticise some of the research from the 1980s, such as Mack and Lansley.

● **Synoptic Link**

As Lydia Morris's work indicates, globalisation is very closely linked to stratification, and both have important implications for wealth, poverty, and welfare. Sociologists are now more sensitive to the fact that poverty and wealth are not simply the result of processes within particular countries; they are also increasingly influenced by the relationships between different countries.

✓ **Top Exam Hint**

Show that you are aware of current social trends by using the ideas in this section in the long questions (e and f) in your exam. You can use this material to analyse why poverty persists and how it is distributed between different social groups.

6.22 What is poverty like today?

What does this mean?

In recent years there have been considerable changes in welfare policies, but poverty still remains a characteristic of British society. As we have seen, there are competing definitions of poverty, and different ways of measuring it. It should therefore not be too surprising to find that sociologists have very different ideas as to whether poverty can ever be, or indeed, has been, eradicated. So, in considering whether poverty can be eradicated, we need to take another look at sociological explanations of poverty.

What do different sociological perspectives have to say about this?

There are many different perspectives but we will look at the four that are currently most important today in shaping debates about wealth, poverty and welfare. These are: the Marxist approach, the social democratic approach, the New Right, and what is called the 'Third Way'. Only Marxism is a sociological perspective. The others are more political approaches, but they do overlap with the sociological explanations examined in sections 9 and 10.

- The Marxist approach sees poverty as an inevitable characteristic of capitalism. Marxist solutions to poverty argue that it can only be abolished when capitalism is abolished. Critics of Marxism would point out that the only way to abolish capitalism seems to be through using force, and that communist societies have led to repressive and authoritarian governments.

- Politicians who believed in the social democratic approach were responsible for creating the welfare state in the 1940s. They believed that the state could act as a referee and intervene to help the poor and weak. Critics would argue that the welfare state has not fully succeeded in doing this. It has been biased in terms of class, race and gender. It has been bureaucratic and perhaps most beneficial to its employees rather than its clients.

- The New Right have argued that it is perhaps the welfare state itself that has been the cause of much poverty. New Right thinkers have argued that the welfare state has created a dependency culture, which undermines the incentive to work, and that the taxation required

✴ Key Idea

The 'Third Way' has been highly influential in recent years. It is a very good example of the way in which sociological ideas can influence social policy. Use Marxist, Weberian or feminist perspectives to critically evaluate it. Arguably it underestimates the strength of the structural forces that lead to poverty.

to pay for welfare takes money away from entrepreneurs and prevents them from creating employment opportunities for the poor. The best solution to poverty is the free market and global capitalism. Critics argue that the free market simply leads to more inequalities, since employers and markets prefer low wages and poverty is a good way of keeping wages low.

- More recently, sociologist Anthony Giddens (1999) has been instrumental in creating a set of ideas referred to as the 'Third Way'. These ideas have had a big influence on government welfare policy under New Labour since 1997. The Third Way agrees with the New Right that the welfare state created dependency. It advocates policies that stress rights and responsibilities; for example, claimants of unemployment benefit have to show that they are seeking work, join 'job clubs' and receive compulsory training. Critics argue that the Third Way has the problems of both the New Right and the social democratic approach.

Sociologist Anthony Giddens is the creator of the idea of the Third Way.

Conclusion

One answer to this question would be to say that it depends on how poverty is defined and what sociological perspective is taken. As we have seen above, there are several answers available.

A more direct answer is that yes, poverty – even relative poverty – can be eradicated. However, to do this requires **radical progressive and redistributive taxation policies**, and probably full employment. There would still be differences (inequalities) in wealth and income, but the differences between the richest and the poorest could be vastly reduced. Having said this, the political difficulties in achieving these policies are tremendous. One sociological explanation of this is to say that it is because our society is stratified in many ways. This creates a lot of conflicts and tensions, and makes the prospect of creating political consensus on this issue very difficult.

66 99 Key Definition

Progressive and redistributive taxation policies are those that take more from the richer members of society in order to provide more welfare services to the less well-off. Basically this means that the more you earn, the more tax you pay.

✓ Top Exam Hint

Explaining poverty involves key sociological concepts such as power, structure and action, and stratification. Make sure that you always use these concepts when you evaluate any sociological attempt to explain poverty. Work through each of these issues one at a time.

For consideration:

1 What criticisms might various types of sociologist make of Third Way policies on wealth, poverty and welfare?
2 What sort of polices would be needed to eradicate poverty? What problems would these solutions face?

6.23 Examination advice

✓ Top Exam Hint

Show the examiner that you are evaluating, analysing and interpreting sociological material critically by using evaluative sentences in your answers, e.g. 'In interpreting studies of poverty, sociologists need to critically examine the way researchers operationalise the concept of poverty.' A good answer would then continue to explain what this means, and whether and why it is an important criticism.

What are the examiners looking for?

The examiners want you to show that you can do more than just regurgitate a list of studies and theories that you have learnt parrot-fashion. They want you to show them that you have a good understanding of sociological theories, concepts and studies, and that you know how to apply them to this topic area.

This means that you need to be able to show that you can do the following things with your knowledge.

- Give good, relevant, reasoned and well-argued answers to the set questions. Do not try to learn answers to practice or past questions and simply re-write these in the exam.

- Apply your knowledge appropriately. If a question asks you to explain why poverty still exists, do not, for example, spend most of your time writing about the different definitions of poverty.

- Applying your knowledge in this way will usually mean that you have to explain to the reader (examiner) why your points are relevant and how they answer the question.

- Use your knowledge and understanding of key methodological concepts (validity, reliability, representativeness, operationalisation) to evaluate sociological studies, empirical evidence and research designs. Methodological issues are very important in this topic as you will have seen.

- Make sure that you can weigh up competing theoretical arguments in this area. This means that you need to work out which theory you think is the most convincing. Make sure that you can support your views with reasons and evidence.

What do I need to know?

- Make sure that you have covered all the ground in this topic. Go back and look carefully at section 2, but also look at a copy of your exam specification. This will familiarise you with the language and terms used by the exam board.

- Make sure that you know the main theories of wealth, poverty and welfare, e.g. Marxist, functionalist, social democratic and Weberian approaches.

- Remember to point out that poverty is a contested concept. This means that sociologists do not agree on how it is defined or measured.

- Remember to make it clear that the contested nature of poverty is important because it shapes researchers' views about how much poverty there is and what can be done about it (policies).

- Make sure that you have thoroughly learnt and understood the difference between absolute and relative poverty.

- Don't forget to refer to and use the AS course themes – socialisation, culture and identity, and social differentiation, power and stratification – where relevant. For example, socialisation can be seen as important as a cause of poverty by some theories. The concept of power can be used to explain why some groups of people are most at risk of poverty and why poverty has not been eradicated. If you use these words (concepts) carefully, you can show the examiners that you have a sociological imagination.

Key points to remember

- You need a really strong knowledge of key studies, concepts and theories, but you also need to show that you can identify, analyse, interpret and evaluate your knowledge. Learn at least three or four strengths and weaknesses for each of the main theoretical approaches to wealth, poverty and welfare.

- Remember to use general sociological concepts like power and theories like Marxism and functionalism. These can help you sharpen up your evaluative skills.

- Don't 'fall asleep' in your revision sessions! Ask yourself lots of questions and make your revision sessions frequent, focused and active.

✍ Coursework Suggestion

If you find an exam question which relates to coursework that you have done you can use this material to answer the exam question. However, use this sort of material sparingly and with great care – you do not want to give the impression that it's the only thing you can remember about the topic.

● Synoptic Link

You will not be asked to make synoptic links in the AS exam for the Wealth, poverty and welfare topic. However, if you are taking the A2 exam next year, you can use knowledge from this topic to answer the synoptic questions on either Crime and deviance or Stratification. Go over your notes for this topic early in the second year and note down those studies that can be used synoptically.

6.24 Pushing your grades up higher

What do I need to do to get a good grade?

We may all have different ideas about what exactly a 'good grade' is depending on our expectations and our particular abilities, but this section is relevant to everyone, because it tells you how to improve the quality of your work in sociology, regardless of any particular grade you may be aiming for or that has been predicted for you.

In AS sociology there are two main skills you are trying to develop.

- The first of these is your ability to develop a good knowledge and understanding of sociological theories, concepts and studies (AO1).
- The second is your ability to use this knowledge selectively and critically to create well-reasoned and well-argued answers to the questions set by the examiners (AO2).

In order to do this you need to develop a strong knowledge and understanding of sociology and that means more than just learning off by heart what we have provided in this book. It also means that you have to write fluently and construct a logical and coherent argument. The points below will give you the most important tips you need to help you to do this.

1   Relate what you have learnt to real life by reading broadsheet newspapers like the *Guardian*, or by watching the TV news. You can also compare coverage between broadsheet papers and tabloids like the *Sun*. Look out for articles and news on social policy and welfare. Are the politicians increasing or decreasing welfare benefits? What arguments do they use? Do their ideas reflect any particular theory of poverty?

2   Show that you are aware of social change. Refer briefly to the time period that the research was carried out in and if it was over ten years ago, point out that society has changed now. Try to say how and why, and what implications this can have for wealth, poverty and welfare. For example, if the standard of living has improved, what counts as poverty may have changed.

3   Name the key studies and sociologists relevant to your argument. You can also show greater knowledge by identifying a sociologist's theoretical orientation, e.g. 'Weberian-influenced sociologist, Peter Townsend, has devised the concept of 'relative poverty' and argues that . . .'.

4   Remember, in longer questions (worth 20 marks) you are trying to construct a logical and coherent argument. It is important to remind yourself and the reader of the exact steps in your argument, why you are taking these steps and what evidence you have to lead you to take this view. Therefore, give the reader 'signposts', words or phrases

that will show them the direction you are going in, e.g. 'However, other researchers, such as Weberian-influenced sociologist Peter Townsend, argue that poverty has to be seen as a relative concept. By this, Townsend means that . . . '.

5 Remember that an argument has to have balance. Do not just explain and discuss the view that you think is the best one. Highlight its strengths in contrast to alternative theories and concepts, and say why it is preferable and what is wrong with the alternative viewpoints. Do not just dismiss alternative views. Give good reasons, based on either theoretical weaknesses, or a lack of empirical (research) evidence, to show why they are inadequate.

6 You can make your evaluation even more sophisticated by pointing out the weaknesses in a view that you do find useful and are generally in agreement with. Suggest how these weaknesses can be overcome and you will gain further marks for evaluation, e.g. 'Marxist approaches to poverty can seem rather simplistic as they neglect differences in wealth (e.g. managers or lawyers in contrast to factory workers). For this reason, many Marxist-influenced sociologists have found it helpful to borrow insights from Weber'.

7 Show that you have a more sophisticated understanding of sociology by avoiding inaccurately labelling sociologists. You can do this by pointing out how a sociologist is influenced by a particular perspective, e.g. 'Weberian-influenced sociologist, Peter Townsend'. This indicates that you are aware that sociologists use theories and concepts more creatively than some textbooks might suggest. Real sociologists do as suggested in point 6 above: that is, they use theories creatively, making their own synthesis (mix of ideas) in order to construct an argument that they find convincing.

8 Never forget to apply your knowledge and understanding of methodological concepts such as validity, reliability, representativeness and operationalisation to issues in wealth, poverty, and welfare. These are vital because they shape your view of these phenomena.

9 Do not leave evaluation to the end of your long answers (for answers worth 20 marks). You should be evaluating ideas, concepts, findings and theories all the way through your answer by 'signposting', making criticisms of ideas and then drawing all of these together and showing the answer that your argument leads to in your conclusion.

Key points to remember

- Get a deeper understanding and insight into sociological theories by relating them to real life through your own reading of high quality newspapers and current affairs journals.
- Always remember to use the methodological concepts to evaluate (where they are relevant) in this topic.
- Review your written work and try to see how you can incorporate 'signposts' in order to construct a logical and coherent argument. Ask your teacher for further advice if you need help in doing this.

Frequently asked questions

Q. Does sociologists' preoccupation with wealth and poverty simply reflect their own left-wing bias?

A. Yes, in some cases it does, but not all sociologists are 'left wing'. To neglect questions of wealth and poverty would also represent a bias on the part of sociologists. Neglecting this topic would imply that issues of wealth and poverty are self-evident (obvious) and require no further explanation. This assumption would prevent sociologists from asking searching questions about the topic, and prevent us from challenging assumptions and beliefs common in our society.

Q. Surely inequality is on the decrease in modern-day society?

A. Unfortunately not. Gordon Marshall (a sociologist who has been strongly influenced by the Weberian approach) explains this well. Marshall says we should imagine society and our standard of living as being like a moving escalator. Although we have all moved up in recent years, there is still a top, a middle and a bottom section, and the distance between the top and the bottom has increased, not decreased, in recent years.

Q. Doesn't the idea of relative poverty go against common sense?

A. Yes, it upsets common sense views of the world by challenging them with evidence and argument. Relative poverty doesn't mean that if everyone has three Ferraris, then I am poor because I only have one. It shows that a person's wealth or poverty does depend on socially-constructed views of what counts as 'enough'.

Bibliography

Abbott, P. and Wallace, C. (1997) *An Introduction to Sociology: feminist perspectives* (2nd ed), London: Routledge.

Abercrombie, N. and Warde, A. (eds) (1994) *Family, Household and the Life Course*, Lancaster: Framework.

Acker, S. (1994) *General Education*, Milton Keynes: Open University press.

Ackroyd, S. and Huges, J. (1983) *Data Collection in Context*, Harlow: London.

Althusser, L. (1965) *For Marx*, Hamondsworth: Penguin.

Althusser, L. (1971) *Lenin and Philosophy and Other Essays*, London: New Left Books.

Althusser, L. (1971) 'Ideology and Ideological State Apparatuses' in *Lenin and Philosophy and Other Essays*, London: New Left Books

Althusser, L. (1984) *Essays on Ideology*, London: Verso.

Alvarado, M. et al (1987) *Learning the Media*, London: Macmillan.

Amos, V. and Parmar, P. (1984) 'Challenging Imperial Feminism', *Feminist Review*, no. 17.

Anderson, M. (1971) *Family Structure in Nineteenth Century Lancashire*, Cambridge: Cambridge University Press.

Apple, M. (1995) *Education and Power* (2nd ed), London: Routledge.

Arber, S. and Ginn, J. (1991) *Gender and Later Life*, London: Sage.

Archard, D. (1993) *Children: Rights and Childhood*, London: Routledge.

Archer, M. (1994) *The Social Origins of Educational Systems*, London: Sage.

Aries, P. (1973) *Centuries of Childhood*, Harmondsworth: Penguin.

Arnot, M. and Weiner, G. (1989) *Gender and the Politics of Schooling*, Milton Keynes: Open University Press.

Aronowitz, S. and Giroux, H.A. (1986) *Education Under Siege: The Conservative, Liberal and Radical Debate over Schooling*, London: Routledge and Kegan Paul.

Aronowitz, S. and Giroux, H. (1991) *Postmodern Education Politics, Culture and Social Criticism*, Minneapolis: University of Minnesota Press.

Ashton, D. and Green, F. (1996) *Education, Training and the Global Economy*, London: Edward Elgar.

Askew, L. (1988) *Boy's Don't Cry: Boys and Sexism in Education*, Milton Keynes: OUP.

Ball, S. (1981) *Beachside Comprehensive: A Case-Study in Secondary Education*, Cambridge: Cambridge University Press.

Ball, S. (1990) *Politics and Policy Making in Education*, London: Routledge.

Ball, S. (ed.) (1990) *Foucault and Education and Power: Discipline and Knowledge*, London: Routledge.

Ball, S. (1994) *Education Reform: A Critical and Poststructuralist Approach*, Buckingham: The Open University.

Ballard, R. (1982) 'South Asian Families' in R. N. Rapoport et al. (eds) *Families in Britain*, London: Routledge and Kegan Paul.

Bangow, (CVS Media) *Out of School Advice Leaflet* (1994) Cardiff, HTV Wales: Culverhouse Cross.

Bardasi, E. and Jenkins, S.P. (2002) *Income in Later Life*, published for the Joseph Rowntree Foundation by The Policy Press.

Barrett, M. and McIntosh, M. (1982) *The Anti-Social Family*, London: Verso.

Barker, E. (1984) *The Making of a Moonie: Choice or Brainwashing*, Oxford: Blackwell.

Barrow, J. (1982) 'West Indian Families: an insider's perspective' in R. N. Rapoport et al. (eds) *Families in Britain*. London: Rouledge and Kegan Paul.

Barthes, R. (1973) *Mythologies*, London: Paladin.

Bash, L. and Green, A. (eds.) (1995) *Youth, Education and Work- World Yearbook of Education 1995*, London: Kogan Page.

Baudrillard, J. (1983) *Simulations*, New York: Semiotext(e).

Baudrillard, J. (1988) *Selected Writings* (Edited by M. Poster), Cambridge: Polity Press.

Baudrillard, J. (1990) *Fatal Strategies*, New York: Semiotext(e).

Baudrillard, J. (1995) *The Gulf War Did Not Take Place*, Sydney: Power Publications.

Bauman, Z, (1990) *Thinking Sociologically*, Oxford: Blackwell.

Beck, U. and Beck-Gernsheim, E. (1995) *The Normal Chaos of Love*, Cambridge: Polity Press.

Becker, H.S. (1951) *Role and Career Problems of the Chicago Public School Teacher* (Doctoral Thesis) University of Chicago.

Becker, H. S. (1971) 'Social class variations in the teacher-pupil relationship' in B. R. Cosin et al. (eds) *School and Society*, London: Routledge and Kegan Paul.

Beechey, V. (1986) 'Familial Ideology' in V. Beechey and J. Donald (eds) *Subjectivity and Social Relations*, Milton Keynes: Open University Press.

Belson, W. (1978) *Television Violence and the Adolescent Boy*, Farnborough: Saxon House.

Berger, P. L. (1963) *Invitation to Sociology: A Humanistic Perspective*, Harmondsworth: Penguin Books.

Berger, B. and Berger, P. L. (1983) *The War Over the Family*, London: Hutchinson.

Berger, P. and Luckmann, T. (1967) *The Social Construction of Reality*, New York: Doubleday.

Bernstein, B. (1971) *Class, Codes and Control*, vol. 1, London: RKP.

Biggs, S. (1993) *Understanding Ageism*, Milton Keynes: Open University Press.

Blackledge, D. and Hunt, B. (1989) 'Sociological Interpretations of Education'

in P. Lodge and T. Blackstone (1982) *Educational Policy and Educational Inequality*, Oxford: Robertson.

Blair, M. and Holland, J. with Sheldon, S. (eds.) (1995) *Identity and Diversity: Gender and the Experience of Education*, Milton Keynes: Open University Press).

Bocock, R. (1993) *Consumption*, London: Routledge.

Boh, K. (1989) 'European Family Life Patterns - a Reappraisal' in K. Boh et al. (eds) *Changing Patterns of European Family Life*, London: Routledge.

Bourdieu, P. and Passeron, J.C. (1977) *Reproduction in Education, Society and Culture,* London: Sage.

Bourdieu, P. (1984) *Distinctions: A Social Critique of the Judgement of Taste,*
Havard University Press.

Bowles, S. and Gintis, H. (1976) *Schooling in Capitalist America*, London: Routledge and Kegan Paul, New York: Basic Books.

Boyd, W. L., and Gibulka, J.G. (1989), *Private Schools and Public Policy: International Perspectives*, London: Falmer Press.

Bradley, H. (1996) *Fractured Identities: Changing Patterns of Inequality*, Cambridge: Polity Press.

Bretl and Cantor (1988) 'The Portrayal of Men and Women in US Television Commercials', *Sex Roles*, 18, 9/10, pp. 565-609.

Brown, P. and Lauder, H. (eds.) (1992) *Education for Economic Survival: From Fordism to Post-Fordism?*, London: Routledge.

Browne, K. (1992) *An Introduction to Sociology*, Cambridge: Polity Press.

Brownmiller, S. (1976) *Against Our Will: Men, Women and Rape*, Harmondsworth: Penguin.

Buckingham, D. (1993) *Children Talking Television*, Lewes: Taylor and Francis.

Burgess, R. (1985) *Education, Schools and Schooling*, London: Macmillan.

Byrne, D.S., Williams, B. and Fletcher, B. (1975) *The Poverty of Education*, London: Robertson.

Carnoy, M. and Levin, H. (1985) *Schooling and Work in the Democratic State*, Stanford: Stanford University Press.

Carnoy, M., Cardoso, F. H., Castells, M., and Cohen, S. (1993). *The New Global Economy in the Information Age*, Pennsylvania: Pennsylvania State University Press.

Castells, M. (1997) *The Power of Identity*, Oxford: Blackwell.

Centre for Contemporary Cultural Studies (1982) *The Empire Strikes Back: Race and Racism in 70s Britain*, London: CCCS/Hutchison.

Chester, R. (1985) 'The Rise of the Neo-Conventional Family', *New Society*, 9 May.

Chibnall, S. (1977) *Law and Order News: An Analysis of Crime Reporting in the British Press*, London: Tavistock.

Chitty, C. (1989) *Towards a New Education System: The Victory of the New Right?* London: Falmer Press.

Cicourel, A. and Kitsuse, J. (1963) *The Educational Decision Makers*, Indianapolis: Bobs Merill.

Clarke, J. and Newman, J. (1997) *The Managerial State*, London: Sage.

Clune, W. and Witte, J. (1990) 'The Theory of Choice' and 'The Practice of Choice' in *Choice and Control in America Education*, vol 1, vol 2, London: Falmer Press.

Coard, B. (1971) *How the West Indian Child is Made Educationally Subnormal in the British School System*, London: New Beacon.

Coates, K. and Silburn, R. (1970) *Poverty: The Forgotten Englishmen*, Harmondsworth: Penguin.

Cockett, M. and Tripp, J. (1994) *The Exeter Family Study: Family Breakdown and its Impact on Children*, Exeter: University of Exeter Press.

Coffield, F. and Williamson, B. (1997) *Transformation of Higher Education*, Milton Keynes: Open University Press.

Cohen, S. (1980) *Folk Devils and Moral Panics: The Creation of the Mods and Rockers*, Oxford: Basil Blackwell.

Cohen, S. (1973) *Folk Devils and Moral Panics*, London: Paladin.

Cole, M. (ed). (1989) *The Social Contexts of Schooling* London: Falmer.

Coleman, J.S. and Hobber, T. (1987) *Public and Private High schools*, New York: Basic Books.

Collins, R. (1977) *The Credential Society: An Historical Sociology of Education and Stratification*, New York: Academic Press.

Comte, A. (1951*) System of Positive Polity*, London: Longmans Green.

Comte, A. (1853) *The Postive Philosophy of Auguste Comte* (translated by Harriet Martineau), 2 vols, London: Chapman.

Craib, I. (1984*) Modern Social Theory: From Parsons to Habermas*, London: Harvester Wheatsheaf.

Craib, I. (1992) *Modern Social Theory* (2nd ed) Hemel Hempstead, London: Harvester Wheatsheaf.

Crewe, I. (1992) 'Why did Labour lose (yet again)?', *Politics Review*.

Cumberbatch, G. and Negrine, R. (1992) *Images of Disability on Television*, London: Routledge.

Cumberbatch, G. et al. (1990) *Television Advertising and Sex Role Stereotyping*, London: Broadcasting Standards Council.

Curran, P. (1996) 'Rethinking Mass Communications' in J. Curran, D. Morley, and V. Walkerdine (eds) *Cultural Studies and Communications*, London: Arnold.

Curtice, J. and Semetko, H. (1994) 'Does it matter what the papers say?' in A. Heath, R. Jowell and J. Curtice (eds) *Labours Last Chance? The 1992 Election and Beyond*, Aldershot: Dartmouth.

Dale, R. (1989) *The State and Education Policy*, Milton Keynes: Open University Press.

David, M. (1993) *Parents, Gender and Education Reform*, Cambridge: Polity Press.

Davis, K. and Moore, W. E. (1967) 'Some Principles of Stratification' in Bendix and Lipset (1967) *Class, Status, and Power*, London: Routledge and Kegan Paul.

Dean, H. and Taylor-Gooby, P. (1992) *Dependency Culture*, Hemel Hempstead: Harvester Wheatsheaf.

Dearing, R. (1996) *Review of Qualifications for 16-19 Year Olds: Full Report* , London: Schools Curriculum and Assessment Authority.

Dennis N and Erdos G (1992) *Families Without Fatherhood*, London: IEA.

Derrida, J (1991*) A Derrida Reader: Between the Blinds*, Hemel Hempstead: Wheatsheaf.

Devine, F. and Heath, S. (1999) *Sociological Research Methods in Context*, London: Macmillan.

Devine, F. (1992) *Affluent Workers Revisited: Privatism and the Working Class*, Edinburgh: Edinburgh University Press.

Deway, J. (1916*) Democracy and Education*, New York: Free Press.

Dobash, R. E. and Dobash, R. (1979) *Violence Against Wives*, London: Open Books.

Dominick and Rauch (1972) 'The Image of Women in Network TV Commercials', *Journal of Broadcasting*, vol. 16.

Donzelot, J. (1980) *The Policing of Families*, London: Hutchinson.

Dore, R.P. (1965) *Education in Tokugawa, Japan*, Berkley, California: University of California Press.

Douglas, J.W.B. (1964) *The Home and the School*, London: Macgibbon and Kee.

Durkheim, E. (1938) *The Rules of Sociological Method*, New York: The Free Press.

Durkheim, E. (1912) (trans1961) *The Elementary Forms of Religious Life*, London: Colliers Books.

Durkheim, E. (1979) *Suicide: a Study in Sociology*, London: Routledge.

Dworkin, A. (1981) *Pornography: Men Possessing Women*, New York: Perigee.

Edwards, T. (1997) *Men in the Mirror*, London: Cassell.

Elias, N. (1992) *Time: an essay*, Oxford: Basil Blackwell.

Engles, F. (1972) *The Origin of the Family, Private Property and the State*, New York: Pathfinder Press.

Erikson, R. and Jonsson, J. (1996) *Can Education be Equalised?* Boulder: Westview Press.

Esping-Anderson, G. (1990*) The Three Worlds of Welfare Capitalism*, Cambridge: Polity.

Eversley, D. and Bonnerjea, L. (1982) 'Social Change and Indicators of Diversity' in R. N. Rapoport et al. (eds) *Families in Britain*, London: Rouledge and Kegan Paul.

Featherstone, M. and Hepworth, M. (1991) 'The Mask of Aging and the Postmodern Life Course' in M. Featherstone et al. (eds) *The Body: Social Process and Cultural Theory*, London: Sage.

Featherstone, M and Hepworth,M. (1995) 'Images of positive ageing', in Featherstone and Wernick, *Images of Ageing*, London: Routledge.

Ferguson, M. (1983) *Forever Feminine: Women's Magazines and the Cult of Femininity*, London: Heinemann.

Feyerabend, P. (1993) *Against Method* (3rd ed.), London: Verso.

Field, F. (1989) *Losing Out: the Emergence of Britain's Underclass*, Oxford: Blackwell.

Finch, J. (1989) *Family Obligations and Social Change*, Cambridge: Polity Press.

Finch, J. and Mason, J. (1993) *Negotiating Family Responsibilities*, London: Routledge.

Firestone, S. (1979*) The Dialectic of Sex: The Case for Feminist Revolution*, London: The Women's Press.

Fletcher, R. (1966) *The Family and Marriage in Britain*, Harmondsworth: Penguin.

Foucault, M. (1977) *Discipline and Punish: the birth of the prison*, Harmondsworth: Penguin.

Foucault, M. (1979) *The History of Sexuality*, vol. 1, London: Penguin.

Fullan, Michael G. (1991) *The New Meaning of Education Change*, London and NewYork: Cassell.

Galtung and Ruge (1981) 'Structuring and selecting news', in S. Cohen and J. Young (eds) *The Manufacture of News*, London: Constable.

Gans, H. (1974) *Popular Culture and High Culture*, New York: Basic Books.

Gardner, H. (1995) 'Cracking Open the IQ Box', in S. Fraser (ed.) *The Bell Curve Wars*, London: Basic Books.

Garfinkel, H. (1967) *Studies in Ethnomethodology*, Cambridge: Polity Press.

Gaskell, J. (1992) *Gender Matters: From School to Work*, Milton Keynes: Open University Press.

Gavron, H. (1966) *The Captive Wife: Conflicts of Housebound Mothers*, Harmondsworth: Penguin.

Giddens, A. (1984) *The Constitution of Society An Outline of the Theory of Structuration*, Cambridge: Polity Press.

Giddens, A. (1986) *Sociology: A Brief but Critical Introduction* (2nd ed), London: Macmillan.

Giddens, A. (1990) *The Consequences of Modernity*, Cambridge: Polity Press.

Giddens, A. (1991a) *The Consequences of Modernity*, Cambridge: Polity Press.

Giddens, A. (1991b) *Modernity and Self-Identity: Self and Society in the Late Modern Age*, Cambridge: Polity Press.

Giddens, A. (1992) *The Transformation of Intimacy: sexuality, love and eroticism in modern societies*, Cambridge: Polity Press.

Giddens, A. (1994) *Beyond Left and Right: The Future of Radical Politics*, Cambridge: Polity Press.

Giddens, A. (1997) *Sociology* (3rd ed), Cambridge: Polity Press.

Giddens, A. (1998) *The Third Way*, Oxford: Polity Press.

Gillborn and Gipps (1996) *Recent Research on the Achievements of Ethnic Minority Pupils*, London: HMSO.

Gillborn, D. (1990) *Race, Ethnicity and Education: Teaching and Learning in Multi-ethnic Schools*, London: Unwin Hyman.

Ginsburg, M. and Lindsay, B. (eds) (1995) *The Political Dimension in Teacher Education: Comparative Perspectives in Policy Formation, Socialisation and Society*, London: Falmer Press.

Giroux, H. and Mclaren, P. (eds) (1994) *Between Borders: Pedagogy and the Politics of Cultural Studies*, New York: Routledge.

Gittins, D. (1993) *The Family in Question: changing households and familiar ideologies* (2nd ed), Basingstoke: Macmillan.

Glaser, B. G. and Strauss, A. L. (1968) *The Discovery of Grounded Theory: Strategies for Qualitative Research*, Chicago: Aldine and Atherton.

Glasgow University Media Group (1982) *Really Bad News*, London: Writers and Readers.

Glasgow University Media Group (1976) *Bad News*, London: Routledge.

Glennon and Butsch, (1982) 'The Family as portrayed on television, 1946-1978', in D. Pearl et al. (eds) *Television and Behaviour*, Rockville, MD, National Institute of Mental Health.

Goffman, E. (1959) *Presentation of Self in Everyday Life*, Harmonsworth: Penguin.

Goffman, E. (1963) *Stigma: Notes on the Management on Spoiled Identity*, Harmonsworth: Penguin.

Golding, P. and Murdock, G. (1991) 'Cultural communication and political economy', in J. Curran and M. Gurevitch (eds) *The Mass Media and Society*, London: Arnold.

Goode, W. (1963) *World Revolution and Family Patterns*, New York: The Free Press.

Gould, A. (1993) *Capitalist Welfare Systems: A Comparison of Japan, Britain, and Sweden*, London: Longman.

Gouldner, A. (1975) *For Sociology*, Harmonsworth: Penguin.

Gouldner, A. (1971) *The Coming Crisis of Western Sociology*, London: Heinemann.

Gramsci, A. (1971) *Selections From the Prison Notebooks of Antonio Gramsci* (edited by Q. Hoare, G. Nowell-Smith), London: Lawrence & Wishart (orig. written 1929-35)

Green, A. (1997) *Education, Globalisation and the Nation State*, London: Macmillan.

Griggs, C. (1985) *Private Education in Britain*, London: The Falmer Press.

Habermas, J. (1989) *Jurgen Habermas on Society and Politics: a Reader* (edited by S. Seidman), Boston: Beacon Press.

Hagell, A. and Newburn, T. (1994) *Young Offenders and the Media: Viewing Habits and Preferences*, London: PSI.

Hall, S. with Critcher, C., Jefferson, T., Clarke, J., and Roberts, B. (1978) *Policing the Crisis: Mugging, the State and Law and Order*, Basingstoke: Macmillan.

Hall, S. (1982) *The State and Popular Culture*, Milton Keynes: Open University Press.

Hall, S. and Jacques, P. (eds)(1983) *The Politics of Thatcherism*, London: Lawrence and Wishart.

Hall, S. and du Gay, P. (eds) (1996) *Questions of Cultural Identity*, London: Sage.

Halsey, A., Health, A. and Ridge, J. (1980) *Origins and Destinations*, Oxford: Clarenden Press.

Halsey, A.H. (1995) *Decline of Donnish Dominion: The British Academic Professions in the Twentieth Century* (2nd ed), Oxford: Clarendon Press.

Hannaway, J. and Carnoy, M. (1993) *Decentralisation and School Improvement: Can We Fulfil the Promise?* San Francisco: Jossey- Bass.

Hargreaves, D. (1967) *Social Relations in a Secondary School*, London: Routledge.

Hartmann and Husband (1974) *Racism and the Mass Media*, London: Davis- Poynter.

Harvey, D. (1989) *The Condition of Postmodernity*, Oxford: Blackwell.

Heath, A. (1992) 'The Attitudes of the Underclass', in D.J. Smith (ed.) *Understanding the Underclass*, Policy Studies Institute.

Hebdige, D. (1979) *Subculture: The Meaning of Style*, London: Methuen.

Heidensohn, F. (1996) *Women and Crime* (2nd ed), Basingstoke: Macmillan.

Henig, J. (1994) *Rethinking School Choice: The Limits of the Market Metaphor*, Princeton: Princeton University Press.

Hey, V. (1997) *Company She Keeps: An Ethnography of Girls' Friendships*, Buckingham: Open University Press.

Hoggart, R. (1957) *The Uses of Literacy*, London: Chatto and Windus.

Humphreys, L. (1970) *Tearoom trade*, London:

Duckworth.

Illich, I. (1973) *Deschooling Society*, Harmonsworth: Penguin.

James, A. and Prout, A. (1990) *Constructing and Reconstructing Childhood*, Lewes: Falmer Books.

Jencks, C. (1972) *Inequality: A Reassessment of the Effects of Family Schooling in America*, New York: Basic Books.

Jessop, B. (1990) *State Theory: Putting the State in its Place*, Cambridge: Polity Press.

Jhally and Lewis (1992) *Enlightened Racism: The Cosby Show, Audiences and the Myth of the Dream*, Oxford: Westview Press.

Johnson, P. (1989) 'The structured dependency of the elderly: a critical note', in M. Jefferys (ed.) *Growing Old in the Twentieth Century*, London: Routledge.

Jones, K. (1989) *Right Turn: The Conservative Revolution in Education*, London: Hutchinson Radius.

Karabel, J. and Halsey, A .H. (eds) (1977) *Power and Ideology in Education*, New York: Oxford University Press.

Keddie, N. (ed.) (1973) *Tinker, Tailor: The Myth of Cultural Deprivation*, Harmonsworth: Penguin.

Kelly, A. (1985) 'The Construction of Masculine Science', *British Journal of Sociology of Education*, vol. 6, pp. 133-54.

Kenway, J. (ed.) (1994) *Economising Education: The Post Fordist Directions*, Geelong, Aus.: Deakin University.

Kimmel, A. (1988) *Ethics and Values in Applied Social Research*, London: Sage.

Kincaid, J.C. (1973) *Poverty and Equality in Britain: A Study of Social Security and Taxation*, Harmondsworth: Penguin.

Kohn, M. (1969) *Class and Confomity*, Homewood, Iilinois: Darsey Press.

Labor, W. (1972) *Language in the Inner City Philadelphia*, Pennsylvania: University of Pennsylvania Free Press.

Labov, W. (1973) 'The logic of non-standard English' in N. Keddie (ed) *Tinker, Tailor: The Myth of Cultural Deprivation*, Harmondsworth: Penguin.

Lacan, J. (1977) Ecrits: A Selection, London: Tavistock.

Lacey, C. (1970) *Hightown Grammar*, Manchester: Manchester University Press.

Laing, R. D. and Esterson, A. (1970) *Sanity, Madness and the Family*, Harmondsworth: Penguin.

Laing, R. D. (1976) *The Politics of the Family*, Harmondsworth: Penguin.

Lambert, J. et al. (1984) *The Image of the Elderly on TV*, Cambridge: University of the Third Age.

Land, H. (1995) 'Families and the Law' in J. Muncie et al. (eds) *Understanding the Family.*,London: Sage.

Laslett, P. (1965) *The World We Have Lost*, London: Methuen.

Laslett, P. (ed) (1972) *Household and Family in Past Time*, Cambridge: Cambridge University Press.

Layder, D. (1994*) Understanding Social Theory*, London: Sage.

Lazarsfeld, P., Berelson, B. and Gaudet, H. (1944) *The People's Choice*, New York: Columbia University Press.

Lewis, O. (1961) *The Children of Sanchez*, New York: Random House.

Longmore, F. (1987) 'Screening Stereotypes: Images of Disabled people in TV and Motion Pictures' in A. Gartner and T. Foe (eds) *Images of the Disabled, Disabling Images*, New York: Praeger.

Lurie, A. (1998) *Imaginary Friends*, New York: Henry Holt.

Lyotard F. (1993) 'Answering the Question: What is Postmodernism?' in T. Doherty *Postmodernism: A Reader*, Hemel Hempstead: Harvester Wheatsheaf.

Lyotard, J-F. (1984) *The Postmodern Condition*, Manchester: Manchester University Press.

Mac an Ghaill, M. (1988) *Young, Gifted and Black*, Milton Keynes: Open University Press.

Mac an Ghaill, M. (1994) *The Making of Men: Masculinities, Sexualities and Schooling*, Buckingham: OUP.

Mac an Ghaill, M. (1996) 'Sociology of Education, State Schooling and Social Class: Beyond Critiques of the New Right Hegemony', *British Journal of Sociology of Education*, vol. 17, no. 2, June 1996.

Mack, J. and Lansley, S. (1985) *Poor Britain*, London: Allen and Unwin.

Marcuse, H. (1964) *One-Dimensional Man*, London: Routledge & Kegan Paul.

Marginson, S. (1993) *Education and Public Policy in Australia*, Melbourne: Cambridge University Press.

Marsh, I. (1996) *Making Sense of Society*, London: Longman.

Marsh, I. (ed.) (1999) *Sociology: Dealing with Data*, Harlow: Longman.

Marsland, D. (1996) *Welfare or Welfare State? Contradictions and Dilemmas in Social Policy*, London: Macmillan.

Marx, K. and Engels, F. (1977) *The German Ideology* (edited by C.J. Arthur) London: Lawrence and Wishart (orig. written 1845).

Marx, K. and Engels, F. (1967) *The Communist Manifesto*, Harmondsworth: Penguin (orig. pub. 1848).

Masmoudi, M. (1979) 'The New World Information Order ', *Journal of Communication*, vol. 29, no. 2, pp.172-85.

May, T. (1993*) Social Research: Issues, Methods and Process*, Buckingham: OUP.

Mayo, E. (1933) *The Human Problems of an Industrial Civilisation*, New Basingstoke: Macmillan.

McCarthy, C. and Crichlow, W. (eds.) (1993) *Race Identity and Representation in Education*, New York: Routledge.

McCombs and Shaw (1973) 'The Evolution of Agenda-Setting Theory: 25 Years in the Market Place of Ideas', *Journal of Communication*, vol. 43, no. 2.

McLuhan, M. (1963) *The Medium is the Message*, Harmondsworth: Penguin.

McQuail (1972) *The Sociology of Mass Communications*, Harmondsworth: Penguin.

McRobbie, A. (1991) *Settling Accounts with Youth Subcultures* in A. McRobbie, *Feminism and Youth Cultures*, Basingstoke: Macmillan.

Mead, G. H. (1934, 1967) *Mind, Self and Society*, Chicago: University of Chicago Press.

Measer, I. and Woods, P. (1984) *Changing Schools: Pupils Perspectives on Transfer to a Comprehensive*, Buckingham: Open University Press.

Measer, I. and Sikes (1992) *Introduction to Education: Gender and Schools*, London and New York: Cassell.

Meehan, D.M. (1983) *Ladies of the Evening*, New York: Scarecrow Press.

Meikle, J. (1991) 'Asian Pupils Doing Better Than English Classmates', *The Guardian*, 16 February 1991.

Merton, R. K. (1957) *Social Theory and Social Structure*, New York: Free Press.

Meyrowitz, J. (1984) 'The Adult Child and the Childlike Adult', *Daedalus* 113(3).

Middleton, S. (1993) *Educating Feminists: Life History and Pedagogy*, NewYork: Teachers College Press.

Miles, R. (1989) *Racism*, London: Routledge.

Miller, D. and Swanson, D. (1958) *The Changing American Parent*, New York: Wiley.

Mills, C. W. (1959) *The Sociological Imagination*, New York: Oxford University Press.

Mishra, R. (1984) *The Welfare State in Crisis*, Brighton: Harvester Wheatsheaf.

Moon, B. and Mayes, A. (1994) *Teaching and Learning in the Secondary School*, London: Routledge in association with OUP.

Morgan, D. H. J. (1996) *Family Connections: An Introduction to Family Studies*, Cambridge: Polity Press.

Morley, D. (1980) *The Nationwide Audience*, London: British Film Institute.

Morris, L. (1994) *Dangerous Classes: The Underclass and Social Citizenship*, Routledge: London.

Muncie, J. and Watherell, M. (1995) 'Family Policy and political Discourse' in J. Muncie et al. (eds) *Understanding the Family*, London: Sage.

Murdock, G. P. (1949) *Social Structure*, New York: Macmillan.

Murray, C. (1989) *The Emerging British Underclass*, London: IEA.

National Union of Teachers, 'The Teacher', *Journal of NUT*.

Newsom Report (1963) *Half Our Future*, Central Advisory Council For Education, London, HMSO.

Newson, J. and E. (1965) *Patterns of Infant Care in an Urban Community*, Hamonsworth: Penguin.

Nixon, S. (1996) *Hard Looks*, London: UCL Press.

Oakley, A. (1974a) *The Sociology of Housewor,* Oxford: Martin Robertson.

Oakley, A. (1974b) *Housewife*, London: Allen Lane.

Oakley, A. (1981) *Subject Women*, Oxford: Martin Robertson.

Oakley, A. (1981) 'Interviewing Women: A Contradiction in Terms' in H. Roberts (ed.) *Doing Feminist Research*, London: Routledge.

Oakley, A. (1982) 'Cypriot Families' in R. N. Rapoport et al. (eds) *Families in Britain* London: Routledge and Kegan Paul.

Oliver, M. (1990) *The Politics of Disablement*, London: Macmillan.

Orbach. S. (1986) *Fat is a Feminist Issue*, London: Arrow Books.

Outhwaite, W (1987) *New Philosophies of Social Science*, Basingstoke: Macmillan.

Pahl, J. (1980) 'Patterns of Money Management Within Marriage', *Journal of Social policy*, vol. 9 (3).

Parsons, T. and Bales, R. F. (1955) *Family, Socialization and Interaction Process*, New York: The Free Press.

Parsons, T. (1973) *The American University*, Cambridge, Massachusetts: Harvard University Press.

Pawson, R. (1999) 'Methodology' in S. Taylor (ed) *Sociology: Issues and Debates*, London: Macmillan.

Peters, M., and Marshall, J. (1996) *Individualism and Community: Education and Social Policy in the Post Modern Condition*, London: Falmer Press.

Phillipson, C. (1982) *Capitalism and the Construction of Old Age*, London: Macmillan.

Popkewitz, T. (1991) 'A political Sociology of Educational Reform: Power Knowledge' in *Teaching, Teacher Education and Research*, New York : Teacher College Press.

Popper, K. (1959) *The Logic of Scientific Discovery*, London: Hutchinson.

Postman, N. (1985) *The Disappearance of Childhood: How TV is Changing Children's Lives*, W H Allen.

Potts, P., Armstrong, A., Maskerson, M. (eds) (1995) 'Equality and Diversity', in *Education 1. Learning, Teaching and Managing in Schools*. London: Routledge.

Pryce, K. (1979) *Endless Pressure*, Harmondsworth: Penguin.

Rapoport, R. N. et al. (eds) (1982) *Families in Britain*, London: Routledge and Kegan Paul.

Rapoport, R. (1989) 'Ideologies About Family Forms - Towards Diversity' in K. Boh et al. (eds) *Changing Patterns of European Family Life*, London: Routledge.

Roberstson, R. in Bromley, G. (ed.) (1991) *New Developments in Theory and Research*, Greenwich, CONN: JAI Press.

Robertson, R. (1992) *Globalisation*, London: Sage.

Rose, G. (1982) *Deciphering Sociological Research*, London: Macmillan.

Rosen, H. (1974) *Language and Class: a Critical Look at the Theories of Basil Bernstein*, London: Falling Wall Press.

Rosengren, K.E. and Windahl, S. (1972) in McQuail 1972 see also 1989 *Media matters: TV use in childhood and adolescence*, Norwood, New Jersey: Ablex publishers.

Rosenthal, E. and Jacobson, L. (1968) *Pygmalion in the Classroom*, London: Holt Rinehart and Winston.

Rowntree, B.S. and Lavers, G. R. (1951) *Poverty and the Welfare State*, London: Longman,.

Rutter, M., Maughan, B., Mortimore, P. and Ousten, J. (1979) *Fifteen Thousand Hours*, London: Open Books.

Salter, B. and Tapper, T. (1985) *Power and Policy in Education: The Case of Independent Schooling*, Lewes: Falmer.

Sarason, S. (1990) *The Predictable Failure of Educational Reform*, San Francisco: Jossey- Bass.

Saussure, F. de (1974) *Course in General Linguistics*, London: Fontana (orig. pub. 1915).

Scase, R. (1994) *Higher Education and Corporate Realities*, London: UCL Press.

Schlesinger, P. (1978) *Putting Reality Together – BBC News*, London: Constable.

Schlesinger, P. and Tumber, H. (1993) 'BBC Crimewatch', *Criminal Justice Matters*, No 11, Spring 1993, published by Centre for Criminal Justice Studies.

Scott, J. (1994) *Poverty and Wealth*, London: Longman.

Segal, L. (1990) *Slow Motion: Changing Masculinities, Changing Men*, London: Virago.

Shakespeare, T. (1994), 'Disabled People: Dustbins for Disavowal?', *Disability and Society*, vol 9, no 3, pp. 283-299.

Sharpe, S. (1976) *Just like a Girl*, Harmondsworth: Penguin.

Shavit, Y. and Blossfield, H-P. (1993) *Persistant Inequality: Changing Educational Attainment in Thirteen Countries*, Boulder: Westview Press.

Shilling, C. (1993) *The Body and Social Theory*, London: Sage.

Shor, I. (1986) *Culture Wars: School and Society in the Conservative Restoration 1969-1984*, New York : Methuen.

Signorelli (1989) 'Television and Conceptions about Sex Roles', *Sex Roles*, 21, 5/6, pp. 341-60.

Smart, C. (1976) *Women, Crime and Criminology*, London: Routledge and Kegan Paul.

Smith, J. (1997) *Different for Girls: How Culture Creates Women*, London: Chatto and Windus.

Smith, R., and Wexler, P. (1995) *After Postmodernism; Education, Politics and Identity*, London: Falmer Press.

Sparks, C. (1998) 'Is there a global public sphere?' in D. K. Thussu (ed.) *Electronic Empires: Global Media and Local Resistance*, London: Arnold.

Spender, D.(1983) *Invisible Women: The Schooling Scandal*, London: Women's Press.

Stacey, J. (1990) *Brave New Families*, New York: Basic Books.

Stanley L (1989) 'Changing Households? Changing Work?' in N. Abercrombie and A. Warde (eds) (1992) *Social Change in Contemporary Britain*, Cambridge: Polity Press.

Stanworth, M. (19830 *Gender and Schooling*, London: Hutchinson.

Stone, L. (ed.) (1994) *The Education Feminism Reader*, New York : Routledge.

Swan Report (1985) *Education for All: Report of a Committee into the Education of Children from Ethnic Minorities*, London: HMSO.

Thorne, B. (1982) *Feminist Rethinking of the Family: An Overview*, New York: Longman.

Thornton, S. (1995) *Club Cultures*, Cambridge: Polity.

Thornton, S. (1995) *Club Cultures, Music Media and Subcultural Capital*, Cambridge: Polity Press.

Tiger, L. and Fox, R. (1972) *The Imperial Animal*, London: Secher and Warburg.

Tischler, H. (1996) *Introduction to Sociology* (5th ed), Fort Worth: The Harcourt Press.

Tomlinson, S. (1980) *Educational Subnormality: A Study in Decision Making*, London: Routledge.

Tomlinson, S. (1983) *Ethnic Minorities in British Schools*, London: Heinemann.

Townsend, P. (1979) *Poverty in the United Kingdom*, Harmondsworth: Penguin.

Trenaman, J. and McQuail, D. (1961) *Television and the Political Image*, London: Methuen.

Troyna, B. (1993) *Racism and Education*, Milton Keynes: Open University Press.

Tuchman, G. (1978) *Hearth and Home: Images of Women in the Mass Media*, New York: Oxford University Press.

Turkle, S. (1996) *Life on the Screen: Identity in the Age of the Internet*, London: Weidenfeld and Nicolson.

Usher, R. and Edwards, R.(1994) *Postmodernism and Education*, London: Routledge.

Van Dijk, T. (1991) *Racism and the Press*, London: Routledge.

Varis, T. (1984)'The International flow of television programmes', *Journal of Communication*, vol. 34, no. 1, pp. 143-52.

Wagner, P. (1994) *A Sociology of Modernity: Liberty and Discipline*, London: Routledge.

Walby, S. (1990) *Theorising Patriarchy*, Oxford: Blackwell.

Walby, S. (1990) 'Theorizing Patriarchy', *Sociology*, vol. 23, no. 2.

Walford, G. (ed.) (1984) *British Public Schools: Policy and Practice*, London: Falmer.

Walford, G. (ed.) (1992) *Private Schooling: Tradition, Change and Diversity*, London: Paul Chapman Publishing.

Walker, A. (1990) 'Blaming the Victims' in C. Murray (1990) *The Emerging British Underclass*, London: IEA.

Warnock Report (1978) *Special Education Needs: Report of a Committee of Enquiry*, London: HMSO.

Warwick, D. (1982) 'Tearoom Trade: Means and Ends in Social Research', in M. Blumer (ed.) *Social Research Ethics*, London: Macmillan.

Weber, M. (1030) *The Protestant Ethic and the Spirit of Capitalism*, London: Allen and Unwin.

Wedge, P. and Prosser, H. (1973) *Born to Fail*, London: Arrow Books.

Westergaard, J. and Resler, H. (1976) *Class in a Capitalist Society: A Study of Contemporary Britain*, Harmondsworth: Penguin.

Westergaard, J. and Resler, H. (1976) *Class in Capitalist Society*, Harmondsworth: Penguin.

Westergaard, J. (1995) *Who Gets What? The Hardening of Class Inequality in the Late Twentieth Century*, Cambridge: Polity.

Wexler, P. (1987) *Social Analysis of Education: After the New Sociology*, New York: Routledge.

Whale, J. (1997) *The Politics of the Media*, London: Fontana.

Williams, F. (1993) 'Gender, "Race" and Class in British Welfare Policy' in A. Cochrane and J. Clark (eds) *Comparing Welfare States*, London: Sage.

Williams, P. and Dickinson, J. (1993) 'Fear of Crime: Read all about it? The Relationship between Newspaper Crime Reporting and Fear of Crime', *British Journal of Criminology*, no. 33, pp. 33-56.

Williams, R. (1990) *Television, Technology and Cultural Form* (2nd ed), London, Routledge.

Willis, P. (1977) *Learning to Labour*, Farnborough: Saxon House.

Willis, P. (1990) *Common Culture: Symbolic Work at Play in the Everyday Lives of the Young*, Milton Keynes: Open University Press.

Willmott, P. (1986) *Social Networks, Informal Care and Public Policy*, London: Policy Studies Institute.

Wilson, W. J. (1987) *The Truly Disadvantaged*, Chicago: University of Chicago Press.

Wright Mills, C. (1954) *Mass Society and Liberal Education*, Chicago: Centre for the Study of Liberal Adults.

Wright Mills, C. (1959) *The Power Elite*, New York: OUP.

Young, M. (1958) *The Rise of the Meritocracy*, Harmondsworth: Penguin.

Young, M. and Willmott, P. (1962) *Family and Kinship in East London*, Harmondsworth: Penguin.

Young, M. and Willmott, P. (1975) *The Symmetrical Family*, Harmondsworth: Penguin.

Young, M. F. D. (ed.) (1971) *Knowledge and Control: New Directions for the Sociology of Education*, London: Collier Macmillan.

Zaretsky, E. (1976) *Capitalism, the Family and Personal Life*, London: Pluto Press.

Zweig, F. (1961) *The Worker in an Affluent Society: Family Life and Industry*, London: Heinemann.

Index